Facilitating Change in Higher Education:

The Departmental Action Team Model

Facilitating Change in Higher Education:

The Departmental Action Team Model

Courtney Ngai

Joel C. Corbo, Karen L. Falkenberg, Chris Geanious, Alanna Pawlak, Mary E. Pilgrim, Gina M. Quan, Daniel L. Reinholz, Clara Smith, Sarah B. Wise

Glitter Cannon Press
Boulder, CO

ISBN: 978-1-7359010-1-5 (Paperback)
ISBN: 978-1-7359010-0-8 (Hardcover)
ISBN: 978-1-7359010-2-2 (eBook)

Library of Congress Control Number: 2020919313

Front cover image and book design by Oath Agency.
Book editing by Kevin Commins.

Printed by IngramSpark, in the United States of America.

First printing edition 2020.

Glitter Cannon Press
Boulder, CO

www.dat-project.org

Table of Contents

Acknowledgements

This book would not exist without the support of a host of people who contributed to the success of the DAT Project: Noah Finkelstein, Mark Gammon, Gwen Gorzelsky, Mark Werner, our project's external evaluators (Andrea Beach and Jaclyn Rivard), and our project's advisory board (Charles Henderson, Anne-Barrie Hunter, Emily Miller, Kathryn Miller, and Edward Prather).

We also extend a huge thank you to the folks who kindly reviewed our manuscript before publication: Tessa Andrews, Brandon Campitelli, Stephanie Chasteen, Keely Finkelstein, Hannah Jardine, Cynthia Labrake, Paula Lemons, Erika Offerdahl, Kristin Patterson, Allen Rabinovich, and Blair Young. Their thorough, insightful, and critical feedback was instrumental in helping us write the best book possible.

We'd also like to thank our editor, Kevin Commins, and our designers, Becca Kaiser and Allyson Arrogante of Oath Agency (www.oathagency.com), for helping this book sound and look much better than it would have otherwise.

Finally, we'd like to thank the organizations whose money and resources made this work possible: the Center for STEM Learning, Academic Technology Design Team, Office of Information Technology, College of Arts and Science, and College of Engineering and Applied Sciences at the University of Colorado Boulder; The Institute for Learning and Teaching at Colorado State University; the Association of American Universities; and the National Science Foundation[1].

[1] This material is based upon work supported by the National Science Foundation under Grant No. 1626565. Any opinions, findings, and conclusions or recommendations expressed in this material are those of the authors and do not necessarily reflect the views of the National Science Foundation.

Preface

This book is the result of a multi-year process that started with the development of the first Departmental Action Teams (DATs) at the University of Colorado Boulder in 2014. DATs are facilitated teams of faculty, students, and staff who work together to create positive change in education in their departments and to learn skills that will make them better at creating change in the future. We were motivated to create DATs to support critically needed educational reforms and to support people at other institutions in facilitating such change themselves.

Today, we know more than ever about high-quality teaching practices and supportive environments that help students thrive. Education research consistently demonstrates that techniques that actively involve students in the learning process are more effective than traditional lectures (Freeman et al., 2014). There are numerous well-documented educational practices that have a significant impact on student success (Kuh, 2008). However, these practices have spread very slowly (cf. Egan et al., 2014) and are not standard practice in most academic institutions (President's Council of Advisors on Science and Technology, 2012). Low-quality learning environments impact students in myriad ways, preventing many from pursuing STEM (science, technology, engineering, and mathematics) careers (Seymour & Hewitt, 1997; Seymour & Hunter, 2019) and discouraging underrepresented and minority students, who experience negative impacts more strongly than their peers from dominant groups (Quaye & Harper, 2014).

Beyond teaching, numerous economic, political, and social factors impact higher education. Student bodies are becoming more diverse as a result of changing national demographics. Higher education is becoming increasingly corporatized and privatized as many states reduce their support for education. Technology is transforming society at every level, forcing institutions to quickly adapt or fall behind their competitors. Because universities are complex, multi-faceted systems, they have not been able to evolve in a way that keeps up with these many changing factors. Clearly, universities must change in a focused and intentional manner. If universities passively respond to our changing world rather than actively embracing it, they are likely to fall behind and fail to support their students in achieving their potential.

That said, change within higher education is not easy. Many higher education change efforts fail because leaders use overly simplistic models that assume data demonstrating the value of the change and/or the dissemination of best change practices in papers and conferences will drive the desired change. These models fail to take into account culture and context, leverage the expertise of all members of a university community, and build grassroots support (Austin, 2011; Borrego & Henderson, 2014; Fairweather, 2008; Henderson et al., 2011; Kezar, 2011). Moreover, creating change in academia is not the same as creating change in businesses and nonprofits (the traditional focus of the vibrant field of organizational change research). The strategies that work well in a corporation are unlikely to succeed at a university without significant adaptation and the development of new models that attend holistically to the complex structures of a university (Kezar, 2014).

To address these considerable challenges, we've spent the last six years developing, studying, and implementing Departmental Action Teams at our universities. Through tens of thousands of person-hours, we collectively created the DAT model, facilitated DATs in 17 departments, and demonstrated how to create change in universities. This work has both challenged and energized us. We have deeply enjoyed witnessing the accomplishments of our DATs. We hope that this distillation of our work will be useful as you enact change in your own institutions.

The Authors

When we use the term "DAT Project," we are referring to the collaborative work that led to the development of the DAT model, which we began in 2014. All the authors of this book have been members of the DAT Project team and almost all of them have facilitated DATs. You are probably not accustomed to a book with this many authors (we aren't either). As with most aspects of the DAT Project, the process of writing this book was highly collaborative, to the point that it's not possible to assign credit for sections to particular authors. Instead, we take collective ownership of this text.

That said, Courtney Ngai took on the lion's share of the organizational work required to successfully complete the project. She did a masterful job of keeping track of the status of the writing, assigning tasks, coordinating communication, facilitating discussions, and generally ensuring that we finished this book in a reasonable length of time (all while writing a significant amount herself).

In recognition of these author roles, we list Courtney first, with the rest of us following alphabetically.

Who Should Read This Book?

This book is a how-to guide for anyone who wants to facilitate DATs in departments at their own institution of higher education. As such, our target audience is future DAT facilitators. Our aim is to provide a complete roadmap to guide future facilitators to successfully implement the DAT model.

That said, other audiences may find value in reading what we have written. While our team has developed this material primarily in the context of DATs, much of it could be translated into other contexts for people facilitating other kinds of groups (e.g., faculty-only groups or cross-departmental groups). Additionally, DAT participants may find that the ideas and practices put forward in this book may help them to lead change in their departments after their DAT has formally ended. Finally, university administrators who could play a role in supporting DATs at their institution may use the book to better understand the value of DATs. Each chapter begins with a "Key Messages" box that can guide the reader to the content that they find most relevant.

How to Read This Book

This book will support you in learning about all stages of running a DAT. For example, you will learn how to:

- Encourage departmental members to engage in high-quality change work
- Facilitate conversations about diversity and student success
- Develop a shared departmental vision for undergraduate education
- Engage in continuous improvement

- Focus on successes and celebrate achievements

- Recruit department members into new DATs

- Create an environment in which students, faculty, and staff form genuine partnerships

We start with introductory material that will provide the background necessary to understand the DAT model at a high level (Chapter 1). The next two chapters focus on the work required to form a DAT: creating relationships with departments (Chapter 2) and building capacity as a facilitator (Chapter 3). We then discuss how to build a high-functioning DAT (Chapter 4), how to develop DAT members' change agency (Chapter 5), and how to implement change through a DAT structure (Chapter 6). From there, we focus on the crucial relationship between the DAT and the department in which it is embedded (Chapter 7). We conclude with options for transitioning a DAT after its initial work is done (Chapter 8) and some final thoughts (Chapter 9). A Glossary of key terms used throughout the book and a Bibliography of all the works cited are included at the end of the text.

In order to facilitate change, it's valuable to understand both practice and theory. By practice, we refer to the practical implementation of a change effort; in other words, the *how*. By theory, we refer to the reasons that an effort is likely to be effective; or, the *why*. Our stance is that it is not possible to implement certain practices, especially when one is trying to adapt them to one's context, without knowing the reasons why they are the way they are. At the same time, describing theory disconnected from practical implementation is too abstract to be of use to the novice DAT facilitator. Therefore, we integrate both components, the how and the why, throughout this book, by articulating the theoretical justification for each strategy we recommend. Understanding both pieces will support you in adapting these skills and strategies to new contexts and utilizing them creatively in your own work.

Finally, when we use a first-person pronoun (us, we, our, etc.), we are referring to the book's authors.

CHAPTER STRUCTURE

We've included a consistent structure to support you in navigating the text. Each chapter includes the following sections:

- **Key Messages:** A concise statement of the key ideas that are discussed in more detail in the chapter.

- **Theory of Change Context:** The DAT Theory of Change (DAT TOC) describes the outcomes that DAT facilitators are trying to achieve in a department that has a DAT and the logical relationships among those outcomes. We introduce the DAT TOC in Chapter 1. Starting in Chapter 2, we include a brief overview of the components of the DAT TOC that are relevant to that particular chapter.

- **Indicators of Success:** From Chapter 2 onwards, we include a section that describes the kinds of evidence that new DAT facilitators can look for to help them determine if their DATs are achieving success. When relevant, these sections include the DAT Innovation Configuration (IC) Maps. The DAT IC Maps describe the key features of the DAT model and a range of ideal, acceptable, and unacceptable variations within each feature. They are introduced in Chapter 1.

- **Recommended Reading:** Each chapter ends with suggested readings related to the chapter topics.

Interspersed throughout each chapter are a few other elements to enhance the material:

- **DATs in Real Life:** To show how we reason through complex facilitation situations, we include detailed vignettes of challenges that we encountered in real DATs. We present these vignettes in line with the text that they relate to in order to help the reader connect theory and practice. For each vignette, we describe the situation, our assessment, our course of action, and the outcome. We provide a list of these examples in the Index of DATs in Real Life Examples on page 160.

- **Core Principle Callouts:** In Chapter 1, we introduce the DAT Core Principles, which serve both as a statement of the values that underlie the DAT model and as a description of the kind of culture that we hope to foster in departments. Throughout the text, we call out examples of the use of Core Principles in practice by placing icons in the margins next to a section where a principle is relevant. We do not identify every example of principle use in this text, but instead have called out a selection of examples throughout the book. The icons associated with each principle are in Chapter 1, and we provide a list of these examples in the Index of Core Principles Examples on page 156.

- **DAT Digital Toolkit:** To help new DAT facilitators, we have compiled an extensive set of editable digital resources, including detailed how-to guides, handouts, and slides. You can find them at www.dat-project.org. We mark where a particular resource is relevant to the text using an icon for the DAT Digital Toolkit along with the type of resource and its corresponding number in the margins of the book.

A NOTE ON INCLUSION

We felt it important to incorporate language and terms that we hope are respectful and inclusive of all communities. We also asked reviewers to check our work so that we do not inadvertently exclude certain groups; that our language is free from sexist, racist, and discriminatory undertones; and that we avoid stereotypes and patronizing descriptors. In addition, we use the singular "they" as a gender-neutral third-person pronoun. This follows the guidance of the seventh edition of the Publication Manual of the American Psychological Association as a best practice, and it is aligned with one of the DAT Core Principles that we use as a beacon to guide our work (namely, Principle 6: Work is grounded in a commitment to equity, inclusion and social justice).

CHAPTER 1

Introduction

To promote effective change in higher education, all department members need to work together to make intentional, sustainable change at the local level. In this book, we describe a concrete, tested process for accomplishing this type of change through Departmental Action Teams (DATs). We rely on theory and empirical knowledge to construct a model for how positive, lasting change can occur in a department. Anybody working with university departments and faculty to produce improvements in educational outcomes will find the work described here valuable. Our goal with this book is to support future DAT facilitators in successfully adapting and implementing the model.

This chapter provides the necessary background to contextualize the rest of the guide. We describe the basics of what a DAT is (and isn't) and include a deep discussion of our focus on departments and the importance of developing change agents. We also introduce three components of the DAT model that form its conceptual backbone: the Core Principles, Theory of Change, and Innovation Configuration Maps.

KEY MESSAGES

- DATs have two main goals: supporting departmental change and supporting DAT members in becoming better change agents. DATs are carefully structured to achieve these goals.

- Anyone can be a change agent and "change agency" is a skill that can be developed.

- The DAT Core Principles describe the values that underpin the DAT model and the culture that we try to foster in departments.

- The DAT Theory of Change describes the step-by-step outcomes that a DAT must achieve on its way to supporting its department in creating sustainable, positive, iterative change.

- The DAT Innovation Configuration Maps describe variations in the implementation of a DAT. Alignment with ideal variations will best prepare a DAT for success.

What is a Departmental Action Team?

A Departmental Action Team (DAT) is a group of roughly four to eight faculty members, students, and staff within a single department. As facilitators, we have two overarching goals for each DAT: to support DAT members in creating sustainable improvement to education in their department and to support them in becoming more adept at creating change in the future. The decisions that DAT facilitators make in how to structure DATs are aimed at achieving these goals.

Basic Characteristics: At its most basic level, a DAT is a group of department members from a diversity of backgrounds (including their roles in the department) that meets regularly over an extended time (typically, for an hour every other week over the course of two to four semesters). It is facilitated by people from outside the department, but it is driven by the needs and interests of its members. These members are volunteers who share a commitment to improve education in their department. While we initially ran DATs in STEM (science, technology, engineering, and math) departments, we have since branched out to social science and humanities departments with great success. Thus, we see the DAT model as applicable to any academic department, regardless of discipline.

DATs explicitly focus on creating broad-scale, sustainable change in their department, often through the creation of new departmental structures (e.g., activities, policies, courses, assessment tools) and cultural features (e.g., communication norms, sense of belonging, decision-making practices). Each DAT chooses its own education-related focus and goals based on departmental needs and the DAT members' vision for their ideal department. DATs maintain active communication with their department leadership and other department members (faculty, students, and staff). This allows them to respond to the perspectives of colleagues outside of the DAT, to share progress, and to work with key department members to ensure that their work takes hold in the department.

DAT facilitators are typically external to the department[2]. These facilitators provide the DAT with expertise in educational research and institutional change, help coordinate logistics, connect with campus resources and provide an outside perspective to DAT members. The facilitators teach DAT members, both implicitly and explicitly, how to successfully create change in their department so that they can continue to do so once external facilitation of the DAT ends.

They also focus on the process that the DAT uses to carry out its work—for example, how members communicate, make decisions, distribute tasks, and so on—by introducing important " " and modeling productive behaviors. Facilitators incorporate this "change education" during meetings by dedicating a small amount of time to different process skills.

We discuss all these characteristics in more detail throughout this book (and they are summarized in Table 1.1). It's important to note, though, that we intend the DAT model to be

---

[2] *It may be that departmental insiders can facilitate a DAT just as well as outsiders. However, thus far, all of our DATs have been facilitated by outside facilitators, so we can't say for sure what would change with an insider.*

flexible, so that future DAT facilitators can adapt the DAT model to their local context. While we implement DATs in our preferred manner, new facilitators can experiment with what works best for them. That said, it is possible to deviate so far from the model that a group would not be considered a DAT. Examples of deviations that would compromise the integrity of the DAT model include:

- Having an externally imposed focus that DAT members have no agency to shape
- Meeting too infrequently or for too short a time to create meaningful change
- Lacking a diversity of membership (e.g., not having student members)
- Working in isolation from the rest of the department
- Eliminating a focus on process

We developed the DAT Core Principles, Theory of Change, and Innovation Configuration Maps as tools that facilitators can use to guide local adaptations to the DAT model. Thus, we strongly encourage new facilitators to familiarize themselves with these components of the model

	DAT Characteristics	DAT Anti-characteristics
Membership	4–8 members from a single department, acting in a volunteer capacity Diversity in roles (tenure-track and non-tenure-track faculty, undergraduate and graduate students, staff) Diversity in demographics, perspectives, and experience	Members chosen by department leaders, "volun-told" to participate Members represent narrow slice of department (e.g., only tenured faculty)
Timing & Duration	Meet once every other week for 60–90 minutes 2–4 semesters of facilitated work	Meetings too limited in duration and/or too infrequent for meaningful change to happen
Area of Focus	Broad-scale issue related to education Chosen/refined by participants through visioning process Work results in new, sustainable structures	Externally mandated Work consists of isolated activities with no sustainability plan
Relationship to Department	Supportive chair Regular communication to cultivate allies and support, gather information, etc	Isolated from/marginalized by the chair and the rest of the department
Explicit focus on Process	Facilitators explicitly support the development of the DAT into an effective team Time spent in meetings on process skills	No attempt to develop DAT members as change agents Lack of emphasis on process or active opposition to it

Table 1.1: Basic characteristics (and anti-characteristics) of a DAT

(introduced later in this chapter) to help them make informed choices about implementing their own DATs.

Life Cycle. A typical DAT goes through a set of stages as it progresses, as depicted in Figure 1.1. Once the facilitators have helped the department assemble a diverse team of DAT members, the DAT engages in a series of activities that allow it to determine its vision and focus. After they choose the focus, the DAT works collaboratively to address it. They start by coming to consensus on goals to pursue and specific projects to achieve those goals. They then implement the projects, assess the results, and reflect on what they have achieved. Throughout this process, the DAT collects, analyzes, and interprets data relevant to their focal issue. At the outset, the DAT strives to thoroughly understand the state of the department. They use this understanding to set goals and implement projects that are achievable given the different

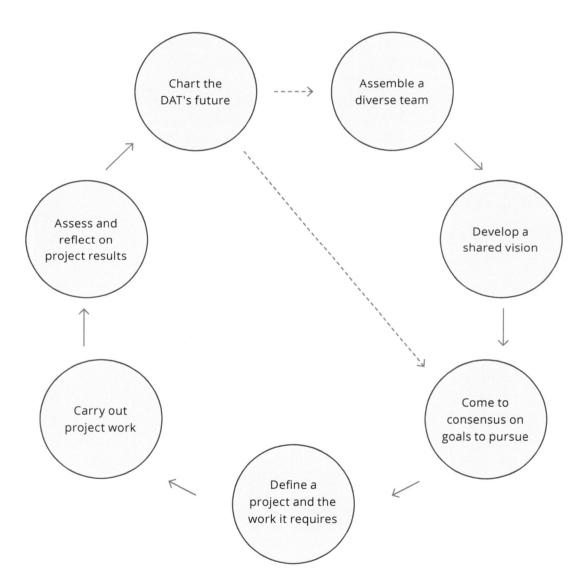

Figure 1.1. The life cycle of a typical DAT. Solid arrows indicate the DAT's trajectory, from "Assemble a diverse team" to "Chart the DAT's future." Dotted arrows indicate possible outcomes of charting the DAT's future (assuming that it continues): either modifying the team or reconsidering goals.

people involved and that address needed change. As the DAT progresses in its work, DAT members evaluate whether they have made actual improvements and describe successes to the rest of the department and other external stakeholders (e.g., deans).

After reflecting on its results, the DAT can then plan its future. This may include altering its membership, coming to consensus on a modified vision, or reassessing its goals and projects. Eventually, external facilitation of the DAT will end. At that point, the DAT members must decide whether and how they will continue to work together on their own. DATs often opt to continue working together after external facilitation ends; in so doing, they effectively become a new structure in their department.

Foci and Outcomes. DATs focus on addressing issues that cannot be easily solved by a single person and on creating sustainable changes that cut across the department and alter departmental structures and culture. Because of our commitment to education, the DATs

Focus	Outcomes
Underrepresented students in the major	Issued two reports on diversity and inclusion in the department; increased access to honors intro course; set up gender neutral bathrooms; organized monthly seminar on equity and inclusion and welcome event for admitted students from underrepresented groups
Curriculum coordination	Received departmental approval to provide course releases and title changes for three instructors, and to support ongoing faculty teaching development and curricular reform across the department
Establish a new major	Created foundation and structure for a new major
Engage undergraduates in departmental community	Held welcome events for new and prospective majors; established departmental Facebook and LinkedIn presence; created annual Industry Night; improved ways to involve undergraduates in departmental committees
Use data to inform teaching	Developed long-term plan to assess disciplinary skills across the major; developed and piloted skills assessment
Undergraduate employability	Structured interdisciplinary options to increase participation and employability of majors
Departmental communication	Hosted interactive Department Forum and Welcome Events; published report making departmental structure transparent; coordinated major website improvements
Develop and implement a peer mentoring program	Designed and implemented a peer mentoring program for freshmen students from underrepresented groups (students of color, first generation, PELL eligible); developed two courses in the department for peer mentors and mentees
Develop departmental learning outcomes	Created departmental learning outcomes and began aligning these with course level outcomes for the major

Table 1.2: Examples of DAT foci and outcomes

that we facilitated focused on improving education. That said, we take a broad view of what constitutes education—we include not only curricular issues, but also issues connected to extracurricular activities, departmental climate, and so on. Basically, anything that involves the student experience can be a good focus for a DAT. To illustrate the breadth and scope of DAT work, Table 1.2 lists foci and outcomes from DATs that we have facilitated.

Focusing on departments

Historically, educational reform initiatives typically attempted to create change either through top-down mandates from administrators or through developing the teaching knowledge and skills of individual instructors. While these approaches are valuable, they are not likely to lead to broad-scale, sustainable improvements in education for the following reasons:

- Top-down mandates, like other one-size-fits-all approaches, typically fail to account for the individual and highly variable cultures of different departments. This leads to resistance and poor implementation of the reform.

- Approaches that focus on individual instructors and one-off course reforms are not appropriate to address cross-cutting issues (e.g., curricular alignment, assessment practices, equity and inclusion) and thus cannot create change on a broad scale.

Therefore, we find ourselves in a situation where our knowledge of how to create ideal learning environments is far ahead of actual practice.

Experts in educational change are increasingly pointing to academic departments as key sites for educational improvement (e.g., American Association for the Advancement of Science, 2011; Association of American Colleges and Universities, 2014). As mentioned earlier, many of the changes that need to be made in academia to better support students are simply beyond the reach of efforts that focus on isolated individuals—those changes must be addressed by efforts that engage entire departments. By working with the department as a whole, those supporting change will likely impact the majority of department members and create a series of sustainable changes that mutually reinforce each other.

Individual departments have relatively coherent cultures that remain stable over time (Lee et al., 2007). While aspects of these cultures—like policies, disciplinary norms, and faculty interactions—may be relatively consistent within a single department, they can vary widely between departments. While one department may have a culture that is amenable to a particular reform, change efforts that mandate the same change across many departments are almost certain to fail. Instead, change efforts that adapt to the unique context of each department are more likely to succeed and to be sustainable over time.

All of this explains why we chose to implement DATs at the department level. We designed the model to target a component of a university that we believe has the greatest potential for change. We also aligned the DAT model with the overarching culture of academia in key ways (e.g., the DAT model's focus on distributed leadership echoes academia's espoused value of shared governance). The DAT model may work well in other campus contexts, such as an interdisciplinary DAT that spans multiple departments, or a DAT in an administrative unit like academic advising. Just because we haven't implemented the model in those contexts doesn't mean that others shouldn't—in fact, we're excited to see the model taken in new directions.

Developing change agents

Complex departmental change is a process, not an event. Since the world outside of a department is constantly evolving, its student population and its institutional environment will constantly change as well. Because of this, today's solutions will become increasingly ineffective over time due to changing student needs or shifts in institutional structure; in fact, they may become tomorrow's problems. Thus, one of the key goals of the DAT model is not just to create change in a department, but also to develop change agents. These change agents will then be able to design and implement successful change efforts in the future, and ideally, support the development of a culture of change in their department that will transcend them as individuals.

But what is a change agent? Simply put, a change agent is someone who is dissatisfied with the status quo and is therefore seeking to spur change (Dunne & Zandstra, 2011). A change agent may hold a traditional leadership position in their organization, such as that of a president or a CEO, but they may also be someone who holds little institutional authority or status. We refer to authority that someone in an organization wields by virtue of their position in the organization's structure and hierarchy as positional power. Change agents can be effective whether they have high or low positional power; they just have to know how to enact change given their position (Hyde, 2018).

In the context of academia, change agents with high positional power generally include senior administrators, department chairs, and faculty members that are perceived as high status (e.g., because of their research output or experience in the department). These change agents often use a top-down, directive approach to change. They will engage in activities that only those with authority can initiate, that take advantage of the university's hierarchy, and that result in new or altered formal structures to support the change effort. On the other hand, change agents with low positional power include students, staff members, and faculty members who are perceived as low status (e.g., non-tenure track faculty). Because they don't hold much individual authority, these change agents will use grassroots, collaborative approaches to change. They will rely on persuading and mobilizing others in the university and leveraging existing structures and cultural features to enact change. See Table 1.3 for further details.

The DAT model is grounded in the idea that anyone in a department can be a change agent and that change agency is a skill that can be developed. We deliberately bring together people with many different roles within a department so that the group can benefit from the different positions of power held by its varied members. We also encourage the group to adopt behaviors of horizontal leadership, in which traditional leadership roles and responsibilities are distributed among many people rather than placed on a single individual (Binkhorst et al., 2018). This distributed power structure supports DATs in being more inclusive of the multiple perspectives of its members. As DAT members carry out their work, the facilitators continuously support them in building their capacity as change agents through engaging in and reflecting on specific facets of the change effort. Through these features of a DAT, members grow their personal power and their ability to influence people and events to create change regardless of their formal authority. Ideally, they will use this new power to act as change agents beyond the project they are working on as part of the DAT.

Since developing change agents is integral to the DAT model, we will refer to this concept repeatedly throughout the book. While focusing on the desired change is obviously necessary, DAT facilitators should always strive to develop change agents as they make choices about how to work with DATs. DAT facilitators should also remember that they themselves are change agents and must take that responsibility seriously while supporting DAT members.

Table 1.3.
Characteristics of
change agents
with different
positional power
within a university

	High positional power	**Low positional power**
Roles	Senior administrators Department chairs Senior or tenured faculty members	Junior or untenured faculty members Non-tenure track faculty members Staff members Undergraduate and graduate students
Approach to change	Top-down, directive, hierarchical	Grassroots, collaborative, distributed
Activities to enact change	Creating a vision or mission statement Developing an action plan with assigned responsibilities Changing reward structures to incentivize desired behavior Allocating resources to support the change effort Altering hiring or training processes	Creating opportunities to talk about issues and raise awareness Providing professional development to nurture skills and connect people with similar interests Gathering resources and data that already exist on campus

What are the components of the DAT Model?

All departments are different, so a DAT in one department will not necessarily look the same as a DAT in another department. This leaves the potential facilitator with choices about how to adapt the DAT model to fit different contexts. To support that decision-making process, we provide the rationale behind the step-by-step processes involved in running a DAT, so that a facilitator can better understand how to adapt a DAT to different contexts.

This section lays out three components that underpin the DAT model: the Core Principles, the Theory of Change, and the Innovation Configuration Maps. We developed these components to clarify for ourselves what DATs are, how they operate, and what they are trying to achieve—but in an abstract sense, removed from any given department's context. Distilling this "DAT essence" provided us with touchstones that we could return to any time when we had to make tough choices about how to enact a DAT in practice. We include these components in the hope that new DAT facilitators will be able to use them in a similar way. Throughout the book, we return to these components, making connections between the details in each chapter and the "DAT essence" presented here.

Setting guideposts: The DAT Core Principles

Principles are statements which identify the core values, philosophy, and operating assumptions of a project or intervention. Principles are especially useful in complex systems that have many ways to solve challenging problems. Rather than identifying specific actions, goals, or rules that everybody involved in the project should adhere to, principles allow flexible solutions that can be interpreted contextually. For example, "Limit TV to one hour daily" is a rule; "Children should watch no more than one hour of TV a day" is a goal; and "Set limits on TV watching so children are involved in a range of daily activities" is a principle. Thus, principles allow a project to make its implicit values explicit, externalize all of its values, and create accountability for enacting them. A well-written principle also allows project participants to better define their interventions by providing guidance and informing choices (Patton, 2017).

For the DAT model, we developed a set of six Core Principles. They serve both as a statement of the values that underlie our work and as a description of the kind of culture that we hope to foster in departments. The principles are grounded in the literature on best practices for creating and sustaining change, particularly in educational contexts. They reflect some of the best practices in organizing teams to make lasting changes and best practices for DAT designers in partnering with students and promoting equity. These principles are infused throughout the DAT model and are brought to life through examples later in the book. We hope that new DAT facilitators will be able to incorporate the principles underlying these examples in their own change projects.

Statements and brief descriptions of each Core Principle are on page 10. Although we numbered the Core Principles, this numbering does not indicate their relative importance; they are just handy labels. We view all of them as equally important and mutually reinforcing. The Digital Toolkit contains slides that can be used to introduce the Core Principles to DAT members.

Digital Toolkit
Slides 1.0–1.6: DAT Core Principles, Handout 1: DAT Core Principles

---

HOW CAN A FACILITATOR USE THE CORE PRINCIPLES?

- Share them with a department that is interested in forming a DAT to help department members understand what the DAT model is trying to achieve

- Discuss them with DAT members and support members in incorporating them into their work

- Use them as criteria for assessing applications from departments for forming DATs

- Use them to assess the progress of the DAT or the level of change in a department

- Make decisions about how to facilitate a DAT so that Core Principles are reflected in the DAT's operation

---

Mapping outcomes: The DAT Theory of Change

At its most basic, a theory of change (TOC) is a diagram and accompanying text that describe the early and intermediate outcomes that must be achieved in order to produce the long-term outcome that is the goal of a change effort. A TOC explains the relationships among the outcomes (for example, which outcomes must be achieved before others can be achieved), articulates the mechanisms through which outcomes will be achieved, identifies any assumptions that these mechanisms rely on, and specifies indicators to determine if an outcome has been achieved. Many change experts advocate that people undertaking a change effort develop a theory of change so that they can fully articulate how they expect their change effort will work (Anderson, 2006; Connolly & Seymour, 2015; Kezar et al., 2015; Reinholz & Andrews, 2020; Weiss, 1995).

As such, the DAT TOC describes the various outcomes and the logical relationships between them that we are trying to achieve. The TOC is department-independent—it provides an abstract, idealized view of the outcomes that must be met for a DAT to succeed. In the rest of this book, we describe what those outcomes look like in practice and how they can be achieved.

DAT PROJECT CORE PRINCIPLES

Principle 1: Students are partners in the educational process.
Students are empowered to make meaningful decisions about their education and to impact departmental decision-making around undergraduate education. Faculty and staff actively seek out student input on the group's activities and structure on an ongoing basis. Students see themselves as having a say in how the group's decisions are made. There is continuous student involvement to meet the needs of the current student population.

Principle 2: Work focuses on achieving collective positive outcomes.
Group members use a shared vision to guide work aimed at achieving change. The process of developing the group's vision includes a diversity of relevant stakeholders. Focusing work around outcomes of the long-term vision, rather than immediate problems, allows the group to be more creative, cooperative, and flexible.

Principle 3: Data collection, analysis, and interpretation inform decision-making.
The group collects multiple forms of evidence about undergraduate education (e.g., institutional data, research literature) on an ongoing basis. Group members actively identify and avoid bias in interpreting data by distinguishing observation from inference, developing multiple interpretations of the same data set, considering both systemic and individual factors, and working toward individuals' cultural proficiency and understanding of others' perspectives. These interpretations, rather than personal preferences or idiosyncratic anecdotes, are what drive decision-making.

Principle 4: Collaboration among group members is enjoyable, productive, and rewarding.
All members of the group are collaborators with equal access to contributing to decision-making. The group develops community through activities such as eating together and having celebrations. Members of the group interact with one another in functional and productive ways.

Principle 5: Continuous improvement is an upheld practice.
Group members view change as an ongoing process rather than an event (e.g., they recognize that complex problems do not simply stay solved on their own). Group members regularly reflect on how the department can be improved and explicitly attend to long-term sustainability when making changes to the department. Incremental accomplishments are incorporated into the change process to support internal momentum and communicate success to maintain external support.

Principle 6: Work is grounded in a commitment to equity, inclusion, and social justice.
Group members recognize the existence of systemic oppressive power structures, so they actively mitigate power imbalances and work to create anti-oppressive structures. Group members consider the impact of their decisions on underrepresented populations. Group members feel a sense of individual responsibility toward improving inclusion in the department. The group intentionally recruits a diverse membership.

Each chapter covers a different set of outcomes:

- Chapter 2: Outcomes 1, 2, 3A–C, and 4
- Chapter 3: Outcomes 3D and 5
- Chapter 4: Outcome 6B
- Chapter 5: Outcome 6A
- Chapter 6: Outcomes 5 and 6C
- Chapter 7: Outcomes 6D and 6E
- Chapter 8: Outcomes 7–10

By articulating the logic behind the DAT model, we hope that readers will be able to make decisions that are guided by both the TOC and their local context.

Our desired long-term outcome with a DAT is building a structure and capability whereby "[t]he department is supported by its members in making sustainable, positive, iterative changes that are aligned with the DAT Core Principles" (Figure 1.2). To get there, a department goes through three stages: Before the DAT (Stage 1), During the DAT (Stage 2), and After the DAT (Stage 3). Stages 1 and 2 are the primary subject of this book, with Stage 3 briefly discussed in Chapter 8. See Figure 1.2 for the "overview" version of the DAT TOC, which illustrates the main outcomes in all three stages.

Stage 1 (Before the DAT) consists of foundational work that is necessary before a DAT can launch. It focuses on getting all the relevant stakeholders—department members, department leadership, the department as a whole, and the facilitators—ready to have a DAT. Successful readiness is largely driven by facilitators setting expectations about what a DAT might look like and what it might accomplish in a department through communication with department members and department leadership. At the same time, external support (e.g., from relevant administrators) is often helpful in supporting the readiness of these stakeholders. All of this leads to the Stage 1 outcome "A DAT forms in the department." See Figure 1.3 for a detailed version of DAT TOC Stage 1.

Stage 2 (During the DAT) focuses on the work of the DAT. DAT members engage in a change effort to improve undergraduate education and to build a positive relationship with their department and external stakeholders. Simultaneously, DAT members grow as change agents and develop their own norms and practices (components of the DAT's culture). The facilitators are instrumental in supporting this work, all of which leads to four Stage 2 outcomes:

- The department values the work of the DAT
- The DAT has affected change related to undergraduate education
- DAT members are change agents
- DAT members enact DAT culture without help

These Stage 2 outcomes are important stepping stones toward developing a broader departmental culture that supports continuous, sustained improvement to undergraduate education. See Figure 1.4 for a detailed version of DAT TOC Stage 2.

---

[3] *We have received some feedback that "theory of change" is not the best name for the concept described in this section. However, there is a body of literature that names these kinds of diagrams as "theories of change." Since we drew on them to develop the DAT TOC, we want to honor the name applied to them by the scholars who created the concept (Weiss, 1995).*

HOW TO READ THE THEORY OF CHANGE

The DAT Theory of Change may look complex, but a few simple rules help to unlock its meaning.

To begin, TOCs are usually read from the bottom of the page to the top. However, we decided to present our TOC top-to-bottom, since that is a more natural way for English speakers to parse information.

Each box in the TOC, whether standalone or embedded in another box, is an *outcome* that we are hoping to achieve. The ultimate outcome is called the *Long-Term Outcome*. Outcomes can have a variety of relationships to each other:

- *Sub-outcome*: Some outcomes are sufficiently complex that it's helpful to divide them into components, which we call *sub-outcomes*. The sub-outcomes that comprise an outcome are equivalent to the outcome in the sense that achieving all the sub-outcomes is equivalent to achieving the outcome. In the diagram, this relationship is represented by outcome boxes inside of another outcome box. For example, in our TOC, Outcomes 3A–3D are sub-outcomes of Outcome 3.

- *Precondition*: If Outcome A is a precondition of Outcome B, that means that Outcome B can only be achieved once Outcome A is achieved. In the diagram, this relationship is represented by an arrow pointing from Outcome A to Outcome B. For example, in our TOC, Outcome 3 is a precondition for Outcome 4.

- *Co-condition*: If two outcomes are co-conditions of each other, then their achievement is mutually dependent: one can only be achieved if the other is achieved, and vice versa. In the diagram, this relationship is represented by sub-outcomes that are part of the same outcome, but don't have any arrows drawn between them. For example, Outcomes 3A–3D are all co-conditions of each other.

- *Independent*: Two outcomes are independent of each other if achieving one is not required for achieving the other, and vice versa. In the diagram, independent outcomes are represented as entries on a list. For example, the sub-outcomes of Outcome 3C are independent of each other.

Each outcome also has one or more *stakeholders* associated with it (e.g., the DAT facilitators, the DAT members, the department, etc.). Stakeholders are represented in the TOC diagram by the colored bars at the top of the outcome boxes, where:

- ▬ Navy = Individual department members (in stage 1) or DAT members (in stage 2)
- ▬ Teal = The department where the DAT resides or its leadership
- ▬ Light blue = The DAT as a unit
- ▬ Orange = Facilitators
- ▭ Beige = External stakeholders, such as administrators

Most of the outcomes in the DAT TOC do not describe discrete events, but rather ongoing processes (i.e., they are more like progress bars than ready lights). Therefore, any given outcome may never be "fully" achieved. Instead, we think of outcomes as being *sufficiently* or *insufficiently* achieved for progress to be made on subsequent outcomes. Moreover, progress on an earlier outcome does not need to stop just because progress on a later outcome has been made. It is possible (and indeed often necessary) to continue making progress on an outcome beyond mere "sufficiency."

Figure 1.2. DAT Theory of Change Overview

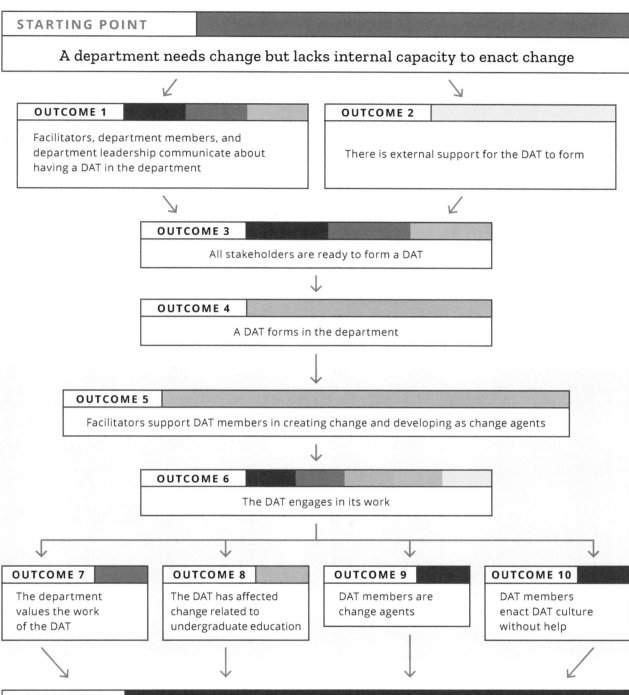

Legend: Individual DAT members · DAT's department or its leadership · The DAT as a unit · Facilitators · External Stakeholders

STARTING POINT

A department needs change but lacks internal capacity to enact change

OUTCOME 1

Facilitators, department members, and department leadership communicate about having a DAT in the department

OUTCOME 2

There is external support for the DAT to form

OUTCOME 3

All stakeholders are ready to form a DAT

OUTCOME 4

A DAT forms in the department

OUTCOME 5

Facilitators support DAT members in creating change and developing as change agents

OUTCOME 6

The DAT engages in its work

OUTCOME 7

The department values the work of the DAT

OUTCOME 8

The DAT has affected change related to undergraduate education

OUTCOME 9

DAT members are change agents

OUTCOME 10

DAT members enact DAT culture without help

OUTCOME 11

DAT members share DAT culture with other department members and work with them on more change efforts

LONG TERM OUTCOME

The department is supported by its members in making sustainable, positive, iterative changes that are aligned with the Core Principles

STAGE 1: BEFORE A DAT

STAGE 2: RUNNING A DAT

STAGE 3: AFTER A DAT

Figure 1.3. DAT Theory of Change Stage 1: Before the DAT

■ Individual DAT members   ■ DAT's department or its leadership
□ The DAT as a unit   ▨ Facilitators   □ External Stakeholders

STARTING POINT

A department needs change but lacks internal capacity to enact change

OUTCOME 1

Facilitators, department members, and department leadership communicate about having a DAT in the department

OUTCOME 2

There is external support for the DAT to form

OUTCOME 3

All Stakeholders are Ready to Form a DAT

OUTCOME 3A

Some department members are ready to participate in a DAT

Some department members have an understanding of DATs

Some department members recognize a need for change that is aligned with the DAT model

Some department members have a desire to develop as change agents

OUTCOME 3B

The departmental leadership is ready for a DAT

Departmental leadership has an understanding of DATs

Departmental leadership recognizes a need for change that is aligned with the DAT model

OUTCOME 3D

Facilitators are ready to run a DAT

Facilitators understand departmental needs and context

Facilitators have the capacity to support a DAT in the department

Facilitators have legitimacy in the eyes of potential DAT members and department leadership

OUTCOME 3C

The department is ready to have a DAT

The department has:

1. The potential to align with the Core Principles
2. The capacity and structures to support a DAT

OUTCOME 4

A DAT forms in the department

Figure 1.4. DAT Theory of Change Stage 2: During the DAT

■ Individual DAT members ■ DAT's department or its leadership
■ The DAT as a unit ■ Facilitators □ External Stakeholders

OUTCOME 5

Facilitators support DAT members in creating change and developing as change agents

| Help manage DAT logistics | Supports the development of a high functioning team | Provide support that is customized to the DAT's goals and needs | Cultivate an environment external to the DAT that is conducive to the DAT's success |

OUTCOME 6

The DAT Engages in its Work

OUTCOME 6A

DAT members and facilitators co-create the DAT's culture

DAT members and facilitators co-create the DAT's

1. Observable behaviors
2. Underlying values

OUTCOME 6B

DAT members grow as change agents

DAT members increase their capacity around
1. Collaboration
2. The local context
3. The DAT's focus
4. Change

DAT members increase their sense of
1. Capability to create change
2. Opportunity to create change
3. Motivation to create change
4. Identity as a change agent

OUTCOME 6C

The DAT has a shared vision for undergraduate education

↓

The DAT engages in change cycles for outcomes at multiple scales

↓

The DAT achieves outcome(s) of appropriate scale

OUTCOME 6D

The DAT builds a positive relationship with the department

The DAT regularly communicates progress, outcomes, and successes to the department

| The DAT cultivates department allies for its work | The DAT seeks department input for its work |

OUTCOME 6E

The DAT builds a positive relationship with relevant external stakeholders

OUTCOME 7

The department values the work of the DAT

OUTCOME 8

The DAT has affected change related to undergraduate education

OUTCOME 9

DAT members are change agents

OUTCOME 10

DAT members enact DAT culture without help

DAT TOC Stage 3: After a DAT (Under Development)

Figure 1.5. DAT Change Cycle

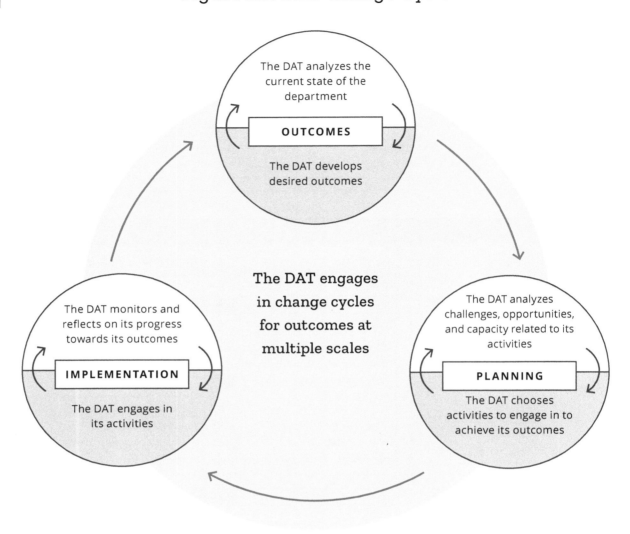

Assessing Variations: The DAT Innovation Configuration Maps

An innovation configuration (IC) map[4] is a tool that describes the constellation of features that define an innovation (e.g., a new teaching strategy or curriculum) and the acceptable (and unacceptable) ways in which those features can vary from one implementation of the innovation to another. Rather than forcing a one-size-fits-all approach, IC Maps recognize that context will impact how an innovation is implemented and that there will be acceptable variations and features in different situations. On the other hand, some variations are fatal to the innovation and will cause the innovation to be ineffective, or worse, to do harm (Hall & Hord, 2015).

---

[4] Similar to our decision to stick with "theory of change" as a name, we are using the term "innovation configuration maps" rather than something more familiar, like "rubrics," to honor and recognize the prior work that we drew upon to design our IC Maps (Hord et al., 2013).

We created six DAT IC Maps that outline the key features of the DAT model and describe the ideal, acceptable, and unacceptable variations within each feature. We designed them so that the features align with the DAT TOC, and the variations are all drawn from our facilitation experience. The six DAT IC Maps are included in the chapter where they are most relevant, as follows:

- Chapter 1: Core Principles

- Chapter 2: Structural Characteristics of a DAT

- Chapter 3: DAT Facilitator Behaviors

- Chapter 4: DAT Member Participation

- Chapter 6: DAT Project Work

- Chapter 7: Relationship Between the DAT and the Department

HOW CAN A FACILITATOR USE THE INNOVATION CONFIGURATION MAPS?

- *To assess fidelity with the DAT model*: If facilitators find that the groups they are working with have unacceptable variations on some IC Maps, then they should try to shift the group into the acceptable region (or else they shouldn't call what they are doing a DAT).

- *To prompt reflection with DAT members*: By introducing the IC Maps to DAT members, facilitators can prompt them to reflect on where on the Maps their DAT falls and whether it should land somewhere else.

- *To assess a DAT's progress over time*: By monitoring a DAT's alignment with the ideal and acceptable IC Map variations, facilitators can predict how successful the group is likely to be at achieving their goals. The more aligned they are, the more likely the group will succeed.

- *To demonstrate progress to administrators*: A DAT's work can take years to shift traditional measures of student success (e.g., graduation rates, time to degree). The IC Maps provide a way to show progress on shorter timescales.

- *To support new facilitators in learning about DATs*: Studying the IC Maps can help new facilitators understand what a DAT is, and what it isn't.

Digital Toolkit
How-To Guide 1:
Using Innovation
Configuration
Maps

┌─ HOW TO READ AN INNOVATION CONFIGURATION MAP ─┐

IC Maps are structured like rubrics, except that instead of the strict hierarchy of better to worse that one would expect with a rubric, each row of an IC Map has only two or three levels of "goodness." Variations to the right of the bold, solid vertical line are unacceptable, while variations to the left are acceptable. A dotted vertical line separates ideal variations (to the left of the dotted line) from acceptable variations (between the dotted and bold solid line).

IC Map: Core Principles

The Core Principles IC Map describes how variations of a DAT can be aligned with the Core Principles. Since these principles are central to the DAT model, alignment with ideal or acceptable variations of this IC Map is critical to a DAT's success and to achieving long-term outcomes.

Students are partners in the educational process.

The DAT has student members. Student members participate meaningfully and see themselves as partners.	The DAT has student members that contribute to decision-making to an extent and see themselves as partners in the DAT some of the time.	The DAT seeks input from students to inform its work, but does not have student members.	The DAT has student members, but they do not see themselves as partners in the DAT.	The DAT does not have student members, and the DAT does not seek input from students to inform its work.

Work focuses on achieving collective positive outcomes.

The DAT engages in consensus-based decision-making in DAT meetings. Input from all department stakeholders informs DAT decisions.	The DAT engages in consensus-based decision-making in DAT meetings and provides opportunities for some departmental stakeholders to provide input.	The DAT engages in consensus-based decision-making in DAT meetings, but does not provide opportunities for departmental input.	The DAT arrives at consensus for decisions, but the process is strongly driven by one or a few individuals.	The DAT work is not consensus-based. It represents the interests and ideas of only one or a few individuals.

The DAT is on track to make positive change for all undergraduates in the department.	The DAT is on track to make positive change for a subset of undergraduates.	The DAT is on track to make positive change for the department, but it does not significantly impact undergraduates.	DAT work has no meaningful positive outcome for any department stakeholders.	DAT work negatively impacts undergraduates.

Data collection, analysis, and interpretation inform decision-making.

The DAT frequently looks at diverse sources of data, seeks to collect more data when necessary, and has processes to uncover and guard against biases in decision-making.	The DAT looks at diverse sources of data to make decisions, but does not try to collect additional data, review data periodically, and/or examine possible bias in their interpretation	The DAT looks at one source of data, but does not try to collect additional data, review data periodically, and/or examine possible bias in their interpretation.	The DAT primarily relies on anecdotal data to make decisions.	The DAT makes decisions without considering data or other forms of evidence.

Collaboration among group members is enjoyable, productive, and rewarding.

DAT members make attendance a priority, show appreciation for each other's contributions, work to maintain a positive atmosphere, and accomplish their goals.	DAT members enjoy attending meetings and maintain a positive atmosphere, they but have difficulty accomplishing their goals.	DAT members have variable attendance and/or some members routinely engage in negative behaviors.	There is a hostile atmosphere in DAT meetings, and DAT members are very unsatisfied with their experience.

Continuous improvement is an upheld practice.

DAT members expect that their plans will change over time. They develop assessments to guide that change and plan for sustainability.	DAT members expect that their plans will change over time and develop assessments to guide the change, but they do not plan for sustainability.	DAT members expect changes to their plans over time, but they do not assess their work or plan for sustainability.	DAT members design projects with the intent to "fix" a problem with a single effort, but they also plan to continue working together.	DAT members intend to fix one problem and then stop working together.

Work is grounded in a commitment to equity, inclusion, and social justice.

The DAT has a diverse membership along a number of demographic categories.	The DAT lacks a diverse membership.

The DAT seeks out and includes unique perspectives, and an expressed commitment to equity is foundational to the DAT's work.	The DAT routinely considers equity in its work but does not seek out diverse perspectives outside the group.	The DAT considers how its work impacts diverse populations only when prompted.	Diversity, equity, and inclusion are not factors in the DAT's work.

Recommended Reading

Reinholz, D. L., Pilgrim, M. E., Corbo, J. C., & Finkelstein, N. (2019, September 24). Transforming undergraduate education from the middle out with Departmental Action Teams. *Change: The Magazine of Higher Learning, 51*(5), 64–70. https://doi.org/10.1080/00091383.2019.1652078

> This a short article summarizing DATs and providing a few vignettes of DATs in action, suitable for administrators, department members and leaders, and other stakeholders.

Quan, G. M., Corbo, J. C., Finkelstein, N. D., Pawlak, A., Falkenberg, K., Geanious, C., Ngai, C., Smith, C., Wise, S., Pilgrim, M.E., & Reinholz, D. L. (2019). Designing for institutional transformation: Six principles for department-level interventions. *Physical Review Physics Education Research, 15*(1), 010141. https://doi.org/10.1103/PhysRevPhysEducRes.15.010141

> This article is a deeper dive into the Core Principles, including the research underpinning them and illustrative examples from real DATs.

Anderson, A. A. (2006). *The Community Builder's Approach to Theory of Change: A Practical Guide to Theory Development.* The Aspen Institute Roundtable on Community Change. http://www.theoryofchange.org/pdf/TOC_fac_guide.pdf

> Anderson's guide provides a practical approach to understanding and developing a theory of change.

Hord, S. M., Stiegelbauer, S. M., Hall, G. E., George, A. A. (2013). *Measuring Implementation in Schools: Innovation Configurations.* Southwest Educational Development Laboratory.

> This SEDL resource is a practical guide to understanding and developing an innovation configuration map.

CHAPTER 2

Preparing for the Formation of a DAT

The Departmental Action Team (DAT) model is designed to create the capacity for sustainable department-wide change. Besides providing a mechanism for enacting change, the DAT model helps participants develop change agent skills which can be applied to other projects and in other work settings. The process of forming a DAT should be adapted to the needs and culture of the department and should not be rushed. The success of a DAT in a department requires support from many stakeholders, especially departmental leaders.

This chapter outlines the steps that DAT facilitators should take to form a DAT in a department. We cover how to present the DAT model to the department and why it is crucial to establish frequent and transparent communication. There are many ways to initiate a DAT, and we outline several different starting points. An essential part of the DAT model is a consideration of diversity and equity, so we include methods for ensuring your messaging and recruitment process are equitable and reach many groups in the department. We conclude this chapter with a discussion of how to assess whether a department is ready to host a DAT.

KEY MESSAGES

- DAT facilitators must effectively communicate the structure of the DAT model, how it will benefit the department, and the role that departmental members who join the DAT will be expected to perform.

- A department is ready to form a DAT when there is sufficient interest in and understanding of the DAT model among department members and leaders.

- The DAT should be diverse along multiple dimensions (e.g., gender identity, race, ethnicity, sexuality, ability), including positions within the department (e.g., tenure-track faculty, non-tenure track faculty, undergraduate and graduate students, staff).

Theory of Change Context

This chapter covers steps found in Stage 1 of the Theory of Change, which is focused on preparing for the formation of a DAT. At the beginning of this stage, a department (or members of the department) recognizes a need for change in the undergraduate program. This sets the foundation for future change through the DAT model, and leads to communication about the DAT model and external support for the DAT to form in the department. External support includes support from the facilitator's supervisor for the facilitator to spend time implementing the DAT model, along with other stakeholders outside of the department who may support the formation of a DAT.

STARTING POINT

A department needs change but lacks internal capacity to enact change

OUTCOME 1

Facilitators, department members, and department leadership communicate about having a DAT in the department

OUTCOME 2

There is external support for the DATs to form

Communication about the DAT model and support from external stakeholders (outcomes 1 and 2) leads to several outcomes. This chapter includes the outcomes (3A, 3B, 3C) that are related to departmental stakeholders. Communication with stakeholders about the DAT model results in readiness to participate in and support a DAT. Cultivating and assessing this readiness is an important task for facilitators, and this chapter covers strategies for setting the foundation with different stakeholders for a successful DAT.

OUTCOME 3A

Some department members are ready to participate in a DAT

Some department members have an understanding of DATs

Some department members recognize a need for change that is aligned with the DAT model

Some department members have a desire to develop as change agents

OUTCOME 3B

The departmental leadership is ready for a DAT

Departmental leadership has an understanding of DATs

Departmental leadership recognizes a need for change that is aligned with the DAT model

> **OUTCOME 3C**
>
> **The department is ready to have a DAT**
>
> > **The department has:**
> >
> > 1. The potential to align with the Core Principles
> > 2. The capacity and structures to support a DAT

Stage 1 of the TOC concludes with intermediate Outcome 4: A DAT forms in the department. This chapter, along with Chapter 3, covers the steps necessary to prepare for a DAT to form.

> **OUTCOME 4**
>
> A DAT forms in the department

How Do Department Members View Departmental Change?

Before developing motivation to join a DAT, some department members must recognize that there is a need for change and that this need is not being adequately addressed by the department. It is important to have support and enthusiasm for a DAT among department members, as a bottom-up approach to change will likely produce more sustainable results than mandated improvement in higher education settings. There are many ways in which department members may develop an awareness of the need for change: the DAT project team's recruiting process, information propagated by higher authorities, conversations with colleagues, or their own dissatisfaction with the current state of undergraduate education. In some cases, department members simply do not realize that an alternate state is possible, they believe the barrier for change is too high, or they do not feel empowered to make changes.

Department members must also consider the scope of the change that may be necessary. Traditionally, many education change initiatives addressed single courses or individual faculty within a department. The changes enacted by these initiatives have proven particularly hard to sustain (Henderson et al., 2011). Generally, the types of changes DATs promote influence the entire department. Thinking about enacting department-wide change may be a new concept for many department members. In early conversations, DAT facilitators must make clear that the scale of DAT projects differ from typical education reform efforts. Work that affects only one or a few faculty, or one course, is not part of the DAT model.

Sometimes department members have very specific ideas, but those ideas often can be used as a platform to reach a larger department-wide goal. In these cases, DAT staff can describe how the DAT visioning process (see Chapter 6) will accommodate those ideas while providing room for the ideas of others. As department members come to understand the scale of DAT projects, they start to recognize that this type of change takes place over long periods of time, and thus the change efforts are a long-term investment. In recognition of the time needed for a change effort to take place, the DAT model recommends external facilitation for about 1 to 2 years.

Although it is not necessary for all department members to recognize a need for change, the support of the department chair is vital in the process of DAT formation and greatly increases the likelihood that the DAT will impact the department. If a chair does not believe that changes are necessary to improve undergraduate education within the department, it is unlikely they will be open to supporting a DAT.

University administrators who recognize that departments need support in making change can greatly aid the success of DATs. Administrators, such as associate deans, deans, and provosts, have the potential to grant support for DATs that DAT staff and department chairs may not have access to. Examples of such support might be publicity for the DAT model, financial support, support from other resources on campus (e.g., institutional data), and high-profile recognition of individuals and departments participating in DATs. Support from administrators is not essential for a DAT's success in a department, but it is important for the long-term success of a DAT program across an institution. However, when administrator support is highly visible, steps must be taken to ensure that the formation of a DAT is not perceived as a command coming from the top (Kezar, 2014).

Framing the DAT Model as a mechanism for departmental change

Most departments are used to change occurring through departmental committees, faculty committees across the university, or via upper administration directives. During interactions with department members, the DAT model should be presented as an alternative way to enact change in a department. Communication among facilitators, department members, and department leadership helps the department understand crucial aspects of the DAT model and helps all parties understand what a DAT could look like in that department. This conversation can be used to explain how the DAT model supports sustainable change and might help department members gain insight into why previous change initiatives may have failed. Conversations with department members may reveal efforts that are already underway that could lend themselves to a future DAT. Aligning with existing efforts can help position the DAT model to propel these other efforts forward. Introducing the DAT model as a method for making sustainable changes over time will help department members to see the DAT model as a process that they can incorporate into the department structure to continue to make changes after the initial change goals have been achieved.

DAT staff can also voice how participation on a DAT can impact individual department members, who in turn can further impact their departments. Participation on a DAT provides an opportunity for departmental members to engage in effective service and develop skills as change agents. The DAT model promotes explicit attention to thinking about and planning for change. DAT members will develop knowledge about departmental change and learn skills that can be used in future settings. For example, DAT members learn how to infuse the DAT project's Core Principle of continuous improvement in their work, and then bring that concept into the work of other committees. As DAT members move into other departmental committees and behave as change agents, other non-DAT members can also recognize and develop these skills.

DATS IN REAL LIFE

What if department members misperceive the DAT model to be similar to other change efforts?

When working with one department, we found that their prior experiences with change efforts led them to have misperceptions of what the DAT model would provide. We engaged in many small group meetings with department members and participated in two whole-faculty visioning retreats. The faculty involved in the small group meetings stated that their greatest need was hands-on support for course alignment and transformation, not facilitation. Previously, the department had been involved in a long-term grant-funded project, the Science Education Initiative, where postdoctoral fellows were provided to assist in the initiative. A number of faculty had projects that they were seeking help in implementing. They wanted the DAT Project to provide funds to hire postdocs or graduate students to work on their projects, beyond the honoraria provided to DAT student members. When it became clear that the DAT Project wouldn't be able to provide support in that way, faculty complained that we had wasted their time with too many meetings and decided to part ways with the DAT model.

This partnership was brokered in the very early stages of developing the DAT model. At that time, the one-page description of the DAT model did not exist and the roles of facilitators were not yet fully articulated. Therefore, it may have appeared to these faculty that the facilitators were offering little support beyond convening meetings and taking notes.

Repeated and transparent communication about the DAT model is important to avoid misperceptions. We recommend using introductory materials that clearly articulate the DAT model, the Core Principles, and potential outcomes of engaging in the DAT model. Provide clear descriptions of the functions and values of external facilitators. If you know a department has engaged in previous change efforts, clarify the difference between the DAT model and these other initiatives.

Digital Toolkit
How-To Guide 4:
Building Awareness
of DATs, DT Slides
2.0-2.10: DAT
Model Overview

How Do Facilitators Know if a Department Is Ready for a DAT?

Before recruitment for a DAT can begin, it is useful to consider whether the DAT model wil be a good fit for the department based on the information available to you. This is often accomplished by meeting with the department chair or your point of contact for the department to discuss whether the DAT model will match the needs of the department. Take time to ask about the types of change the department has previously pursued and the current direction of the department. Be open about the types of change that can be expected through the DAT model, in addition to the process and timeline for change. While this is not the only time you should assess the fit of the DAT model and the department, this initial meeting will set the stage for later assessment. This will also help to ensure that any people promoting DATs in the department set clear expectations for the rest of the department. Additionally, this checkpoint is an opportunity to pause the formation of a DAT if either party determines the department and the DAT model are not a good match.

Not all departments will be interested in a DAT, and of those that are interested, not all departments will be sufficiently prepared to start a DAT. Being able to thoughtfully assess departmental readiness is an important facilitator skill. If departments are not ready to move forward with the DAT model, it is unlikely that their expectations will match the reality of hosting a DAT. This can create tension between the facilitators and the stakeholders, and dissatisfaction with the DAT model. A negative first encounter with the DAT model may prevent departments from wanting to engage in the DAT model as a mechanism for change in the future, even when they are ready.

As a facilitator, you should look for evidence that a DAT is likely to be successful in a department. Although a department may not exhibit all of the signs below, look for evidence of as many as you can. Our DAT model employs a notion of sufficiency when engaging in change; there will be a level of progress for these indicators that is sufficient for that department to move forward. Continued growth in these areas is encouraged even after a DAT has formed. Here are some signs of DAT readiness:

There is a sufficient number of potential DAT members. To set the stage for a successful DAT, there needs to be a sufficient number of department members who are ready to participate in a DAT. Following the introductory faculty meeting or other recruitment events, at least some potential DAT members should recognize that (1) the goal of the DAT is to improve undergraduate education by making changes that are supported and sustained by the department and (2) during this process they will increase their capacity as change agents, which includes developing knowledge, skills, and behaviors to cultivate high functioning groups and enacting change. Accordingly, at least some potential DAT members should have an interest in increasing their capacity as change agents.

There is sufficient support from the department leadership. The departmental leadership must exhibit some support for the formation of a DAT. "Leadership" refers to the individuals who play a central role in department decision-making, and typically involves a department chair, an executive committee, and/or assistant chairs. For a department to be ready, department leadership must have a sufficient understanding of the DAT model, recognize a need for the type of change aligned with the DAT model, and support the formation of the DAT in the department. If this does not happen, they may (intentionally or unintentionally) derail the DAT's progress. Typical power dynamics within a department suggest that the support of leadership can greatly enhance the efficacy and motivation of a DAT. Practically, the leadership is also able to award service credit to DAT members, which can increase motivation and the perception that the DAT provides value. Additionally, early involvement of department leadership ensures maximal transparency of the DAT's motivations and intentions.

The department has the capacity for a DAT. Since DATs aim to foster a culture aligned with the Core Principles, the overall department must have opportunities to align with these principles. If a department has a culture that is in opposition to one or more of the principles, then a DAT is very unlikely to succeed in that department. Additionally, the department must have the capacity and structures to support a DAT. Without the means for a DAT to form (e.g., communication structures) and the resources for a DAT to function (e.g., time), running a DAT will be logistically impossible.

There may be other departmental aspects that must be addressed before a DAT can officially be formed. For example, it is possible that the department may typically vote on the formation of new groups. It is important to adhere to the culture and processes that already exist in the department when forming a DAT so it is not perceived negatively from the start.

DATs in Real Life

What if the department is overwhelmed with ongoing change?

DAT project staff held several meetings and phone conversations with members of a department that had numerous "pain points" related to massive growth in their undergraduate majors, introductory service courses, and master's programs. There was a great deal of change occurring with faculty hires and new course development. The faculty interested in convening a DAT had several promising foci in mind, any of which would be fruitful for the department and which aligned with the department's strategic objectives. However, the partnership stalled when we indicated that the next step would be to meet with the department chair. The junior faculty taking the lead seemed uncomfortable approaching the chair and, once they did, they reported that the chair did not respond to their request.

Several months passed and we issued the first official call for new DAT proposals. DAT staff continued to encourage the interested faculty to apply through the proposal period, but a meeting with the chair never occurred and this group never submitted a proposal.

We interpreted this to be a situation in which there were too many "pain points" across the department. The faculty and chair were not able to focus on a long-term change project when they were in the midst of managing so much other change. We recognized that the DAT model was not a good match for the department's needs at that time, and that they might be willing to engage in the model at a later time. In the end, they formed a DAT the following year.

There is external support for DATs to exist. External support for DATs must exist to some extent. External support for DATs to form can involve advocacy, financial support, and allocation of resources from outside stakeholders such as administrators and funding agencies. External support typically starts with the support that is provided for facilitators to work with DATs. This support may originate from a grant or from internal departmental resources. The time and other resources you might need as a facilitator are covered in more detail in Chapter 3. Additional sources of external support might be other departments or campus groups. This support might take the form of stipends for student DAT members or even snacks for group meetings.

Assessing a department's readiness for a DAT

Principle 3:

Data collection, analysis, and interpretation inform decision-making.

Conversations with those interested in starting a DAT are valuable for learning about current departmental practices and perspectives. A conversation with the department chair can also provide context on existing or upcoming department initiatives, in addition to gaining information on the identity of influential department members. If a teaching and learning center (TLC) exists at your institution and you are not a member of the center, contact them to learn about other educational projects the department has pursued and to gain insight on what it was like to collaborate with department members.

The recruitment process also serves as a valuable information-gathering exercise for facilitators. How department members judge and respond to various recruitment methods can reveal aspects of departmental culture. For example, if department members wish to vote on whether to proceed with a DAT, it suggests that the department often makes decisions by consensus. In another case, if a department offers little critique or concern about the DAT, it may suggest the department values autonomy of faculty decision-making—or may suggest a lack of support for the DAT among faculty members. These initial interactions can also be used to identify which issues around undergraduate education are of particular concern for department members.

Digital Toolkit

How-To Guide 2: Conducting a Listening Tour

In some cases, you may wish to collect more specific information about a department in order to assess whether it would support a DAT. One way you can accomplish this is by conducting a Listening Tour. The Listening Tour consists of interviewing different department members to learn about their prior experiences with change initiatives at the institution, the ways in which the department typically undergoes change, and departmental interest in improving undergraduate education. You can tailor the Listening Tour to explore other aspects of the department that you think may prevent a department from supporting a successful DAT.

If you find that a department is not ready for a DAT, speak with the DAT champion about how the department can become better prepared to host a DAT. Steps that can be taken to prepare for a future DAT include:

Principle 2:

Work focuses on achieving collective positive outcomes.

- Starting a learning community in the department related to undergraduate education
- Introducing DAT Core Principles to the department
- Completing other initiatives that are taking up department members' time
- Applying for funding opportunities that can support the work of a future DAT

DATS IN REAL LIFE

What if features of the department hinder a DAT's progress?

Departmental structure hindered the progress of one DAT we worked with. Before beginning the DAT, we had not conducted any interviews to learn about the department, so these issues were revealed as the DAT progressed. One departmental feature that interviews likely would have revealed was the fragmentation of the faculty into groups according to research subdiscipline. This led to a lack of communication and lack of trust between individuals in these subgroups. This also meant that the department did not have a coherent set of values or a group identity, because each subgroup had its own.

The disconnect among groups became especially relevant when the department changed chairs. Because the department did not have a core set of values or norms, the new chair imposed their own. As someone who valued research recognition, they aimed to cut departmental service, because they saw it as getting in the way of research. One of their early proposals was to disband the DAT.

Digital Toolkit
Slides 7.0-7.13:
Models of
Organizational
Change

This created an unexpected challenge for the DAT; they had to organize to defend their existence to a leader who had not bought into the DAT process. As facilitators, we drew from the political, social, and cultural models of change (Kezar, 2014) to help the DAT strategize around how to engage their chair. We discussed several strategies, including drumming up support from other department members (such as the past chair). Ultimately, the group decided not to pursue that strategy because they had not built many committed allies. Other DAT members considered continuing to meet, in violation of the chair's request to disband. We discouraged this option because it could hinder future progress. After analysis of the chair's position, the group noticed that some of chair's objection to the DAT stemmed from differences in how they believed change happened. They noticed that the chair used simplistic change models (seeing change as "one-and-done") and that the chair thought their work was complete. The group decided to propose an alternative change model using the analogy of a doctor monitoring a chronic condition, in which complex change requires ongoing effort. This new change model resonated with the chair, and they then agreed that the DAT should become a standing committee within the department.

Several steps could have been taken early on to reveal and address existing departmental features that inhibited progress on a DAT. Interviews with DAT members could have shown facilitators where the DAT would likely face resistance and challenges. Because it contained members from different subdisciplines, the DAT would have benefited from reflecting on the different departmental groups and their different values, and from frequent strategic engagement with the rest of the department about their shared goals. Early and frequent communication with the department chair might have prevented challenges when the chair changed.

Taking these types of steps can help facilitators anticipate and proactively handle roadblocks.

How Do Facilitators Form a DAT?

There are many different approaches to forming a DAT. As a facilitator, tailor your approach to the culture and needs of the department. As you begin setting the foundation for a DAT, you will learn more about the department and be able to adjust your approach as needed. The following list contains the general steps to take when setting up for a DAT:

1. Advertise the opportunity for a department to have a DAT

2. Establish transparent communication with a point of contact in a department

3. Recruit a diverse DAT membership

In pursuing these steps, communications should include the information from the previous sections about awareness about change and the DAT model as a mechanism for change. It is up to you when and how much information to include. We outline the general steps for forming a DAT in the following sections.

Communicating about the opportunity for a DAT

Effective organizational change begins with stakeholders understanding the change that is proposed. Such understanding is straightforward when there is transparent sharing of information. Being transparent about the formation and subsequent work of the DAT can have big impacts on the sustainability of the DAT's work. Because DATs aim for department-wide change, all stakeholders in the department—including students, staff, instructors, and faculty— should feel like they understand the DAT's work and their role, if any, in that work. Furthermore, the development of positive and productive conversation norms among a diverse group of stakeholders can establish and nurture inclusive practices and perspectives which, in turn, can support departmental change.

When deciding which departments might be candidates to host a DAT, identify departments that are about to make changes to their undergraduate education or that have reached out for help with making changes to education. These departments may already be considering methods for effecting change and may be more prepared to hear about the DAT model. Do not limit yourself to these departments, however, as it is likely there are department members in other departments who are interested in effecting change in undergraduate education but do not know how to move forward with this work.

Digital Toolkit
How-To Guide 3:
Recruiting DAT
Departments

To provide equitable opportunities for departments to establish DATs, facilitators can make a call for DAT applications and publicize the idea widely via one or more of the following strategies:

- Emails to departments that can be distributed to department members

- Postcards that can be placed in mailboxes

- Flyers that can be hung in departmental common areas

- Presentation(s) at a department meeting or to groups with interests in undergraduate education

Publicizing the opportunity to have a DAT in the department generates awareness and interest. At the inception of a DAT program at an institution, DATs may naturally emerge out of informal conversations with department members who facilitators already know. Time the deadline for DAT applications carefully, so new DATs can be scheduled to launch early during a semester.

DATS IN REAL LIFE

What if a department does not believe they have the time to engage in a slow change process?

We worked with one department that did not believe they had time to engage in a slow change process. This department was interested in a DAT due to their large enrollment of students in the undergraduate program. The chair and a tenure-track faculty member met with facilitators several times over the course of the semester to determine if a DAT would be a good fit for the department's needs. The chair and faculty member were very interested in the request for proposals that was being offered at the institution. Interested departments could submit a proposal for the work their DAT planned to do, and if accepted, the DAT would receive funding to carry out their proposal.

From the first meeting, both the chair and the faculty member brought up the department's need for more staffing in order to improve undergraduate education. The facilitators made it clear that DATs address challenges regarding undergraduate education as a team, and that the funding would not be sufficient to buy out faculty time. Moreover, they stressed that the DAT model focuses on developing sustainable solutions for issues in undergraduate education, and that another faculty line would not necessarily promote long-term change in the department.

Ultimately, when the possibility of hiring more staff or buying out faculty time was taken off the table, the chair and department member were not interested in participating in the DAT model. As they explained, few department members had the time to engage in the slow process of creating change using the DAT model.

Since most departments are short on time and other resources, as a facilitator you can emphasize the unique perspective the DAT model adopts for change. The slow process can be framed as a more sustainable approach for many of the challenges departments are facing. For example, if a DAT had been formed to improve the undergraduate program in this department, it likely could have made concrete sustainable changes (e.g., the creation of a student learning community) and identified specific ways that additional faculty or staff time could help the undergraduate program. Rather than just assuming that more time was what they needed, departmental leaders would then have had a more compelling argument for requesting additional resources from the campus.

As a facilitator, it's important to help department members recognize the value in taking an outcomes-based approach for creating change and the importance in thinking about sustainability.

Establishing a point of contact

One way to initiate a DAT is to identify and establish a relationship with department members interested in effecting change. These department members may become champions of the DAT model and help its formation. A DAT champion can emerge from a different audience for each department: department members, chairs, or administrators. Often departmental champions of change have specific ideas that they bring to initial conversations around forming a DAT, which can be beneficial for moving the conversation about a DAT forward. In these moments, it is critical that facilitators be clear about the importance of equitable and diverse participation in DATs and how this value leads facilitators to intentionally start DATs without any defined focus or project (unless an initiative had already been started by the entire department). DAT application forms can be written in ways that allow interested members to explain their ideas, without promising that the DAT will enact them.

Regardless of the path you follow to initiate a DAT, outline to your audience the benefits that a DAT can bring to the department. Articulating what a DAT can accomplish and the resources that will be gained by following the DAT model will help potential champions understand the DAT model.

Here are specific strategies for connecting with different stakeholders who may become DAT champions and the benefits that these connections can bring to a DAT.

Starting with department members. DATs can be initiated by a department member(s) who is interested in making sustainable changes. These department members may already be acting as change agents within the department. Often, this department member already has an idea for what the DAT should focus on. In early conversations with a department member who is interested in starting a DAT, try to gain a broad understanding of the department and department members' views on undergraduate education. The department member you are working with can give you an insider's perspective on how change typically happens in the department. It is likely that the department member will also know the influential department members who may already be acting as change agents. Depending on how recruitment is approached for a DAT, the department member you are working with can help you to identify the appropriate stakeholders and potential DAT allies in the department. Typically, the person who initiates the process of beginning a DAT serves as the point person between the DAT and the facilitators and is considered the DAT champion. This person can also initiate the relationship between the DAT facilitators and the department chair.

Starting with department chairs. Department chairs may also be approached to determine if there is interest in starting a DAT in a particular department. Since department chairs are aware of the broader interests of the department and initiatives happening at the university, they are likely to have information that could shape the focus of the DAT's project. Having the support of the chair for a DAT can signify that the DAT is valuable to the department, and that those who participate in the DAT's work will be recognized for their efforts. When DATs are initiated by department chairs, however, it is important to ensure that those who are joining the DAT are doing so voluntarily. Participation in a DAT can have many benefits, but these may be overshadowed if participation is construed as mandatory.

Starting with university administrators. In some cases, it is beneficial to initiate support for a DAT with university administrators. University administrators can include deans, provosts, and others who are working outside of the department. Working with administrators to promote DATs provides the benefit of aligning DAT work with campus initiatives. An example of this kind of alignment is when campus initiatives focus on inclusivity and diversity, which coincides with one of the principles that guide the DAT model (see Chapter 1 for an in-depth look at the Core Principles). Departments that want to be at the forefront of campus initiatives may be perceived as proactive in working towards university goals if they start a DAT that aligns with these broader initiatives. If you can, plan to speak with relevant stakeholders who may later become champions or allies of the DAT model about how the DAT model can contribute in a unique manner to campus initiatives. University administrators also have access to campus-wide communication, which has the potential to reach departments that are interested in change but otherwise would not have known about DATs. Additionally, administrators tend to have greater influence on campus finances than department members. If administrators choose to advocate for the start of DATs on campus, they may be able to allot additional funding as a salary buyout or course release time to support facilitators or DATs in their work. In addition, administrators are in a position to offer non-financial incentives to faculty and departmental staff to encourage their participation. While the presence of administrators at some recruitment meetings can be productive, it is necessary to have additional meetings without the administrators present so that potential DAT members and allies can freely express whether they want to start a DAT and how it would be valuable to them.

Recruiting diverse DAT membership

It is important that DAT recruitment results in diverse membership along multiple dimensions (e.g., gender identity, race, ethnicity, sexuality, ability) and position within the department (e.g., tenure-track faculty, non-tenure track faculty, undergraduate and graduate students, and staff members). Having diverse perspectives makes it more likely that the group's work will equitably impact all populations within a department, a deeper variety of perspectives will be represented, and that all departmental populations will share the vision. There is also research showing that groups with diverse membership often develop more effective and creative solutions (Milliken et al., 2003).

In addition to considering formal title, it is also important to consider individuals' "informal" positions within the department. If one of the early DAT supporters is a person of influence in the department, this can aid in establishing the legitimacy of the DAT and its work. Having DAT members from different roles in the department (e.g., tenure-track and staff) ensures that multiple perspectives related to undergraduate education are voiced on the DAT. Since the entire department is responsible for the undergraduate program, it is essential that as many groups as possible are represented on the DAT. Ultimately, this will also ensure that the formation of the DAT has support from different groups within the department.

While recruiting diverse membership, it is crucial to discuss equity explicitly and to actively mitigate power dynamics. For example, avoid "tokenizing" members of marginalized groups. Tokenizing means making a primarily symbolic effort of inclusion when including a person who is a member of an underrepresented or marginalized group in order to give the appearance of equality. Marginalization impacts individuals in unique ways, so the perspective of a person from a marginalized group should not be taken as representative of all people of that marginalized group. For example, it is tokenizing to ask a woman in a predominantly male DAT to "speak about the woman's perspective in the department." Moreover, it is also necessary to consider the unique experiences of those who hold multiple, intersecting marginalized identities. Tokenizing has detrimental effects if a person from an underrepresented marginalized group is asked to serve on the DAT solely based of their identity, and not due

Principle 6:
Work is grounded in a commitment to equity, inclusion, and social justice.

to their interest in the work. Frequently, the act of tokenizing is not only inconvenient, but harmful to the emotional well-being of those being asked to represent the larger community of individuals with whom they share some common identity characteristics.

Strategize with stakeholders about the recruitment process. Once key champions have initiated the DAT formation process and DAT facilitators feel comfortable with the department's readiness, the DAT facilitators begin the recruitment process. There are a variety of ways that DAT members can be recruited. The success of specific recruitment methods is dependent on the department's culture. Collaborate with department chairs, DAT champions, and other interested department members to figure out which approach will work and which will be perceived as counter to the department's culture. If the chair has not yet been centrally involved in the process, it is necessary to bring them in at this stage. Setting up meetings between key champions (within the department or administrators) can help bring the chair on board. This is also the time to bring up the idea of having student participants on the DAT. How students are recruited to the DAT may differ from recruiting department members, but it must be considered with equal care.

Be explicit about the commitment to diversity and inclusivity. When engaging in the recruitment process, be transparent about the DAT model with potential DAT members and include a description of the six principles with a focus on diversity and equity. Keep in mind that there are many aspects of a person's identity that inform their experience with and perspective on the world, including ability status, race, ethnicity, class, sexual orientation, gender identity and expression, and their role within the department. Moreover, these categories are not independent—people at different intersections of these identities have unique experiences (e.g., the experience of a straight white woman and a gay Black woman are not the same). Use explicit language about the commitment to and advantages of diversity in membership, starting with announcements and advertising. The language used in outreach signals the DAT model's commitment to inclusivity.

Finding ways to share information about the DAT model and to be transparent about the experience for DAT members should permeate the recruitment process. To promote transparency, hold an introductory department meeting soon after the decision has been made to form a DAT. An example of how to share the information about the DAT's commitment to inclusivity is to invite several DAT members from other departments to speak at introductory faculty/staff/researcher meetings and to encourage them to share how their unique perspectives have been valued and their ideas promoted in an inclusive way in their DATs. Similarly, placing a high value on transparency is why facilitators work hard to explain the framework, goals, and expectations of the DAT model to chairs and champions before they decide to form a DAT. Being transparent about intentions will benefit the recruitment process and help set expectations for the emerging DAT.

Hosting an introductory meeting. If the champions and chair do not have major reservations about the DAT after the informal meetings, the next stage in DAT formation involves the larger department. Ideally, facilitators introduce the DAT model during a meeting using slides and handouts. In this meeting, facilitators must make sure that department members understand that while DATs are unique for every department and tailored for their needs, there are core components and principles which structure the membership and work of DATs. At first, many might misconstrue a DAT as a departmental committee. Articulate the differences between conventional departmental committees and the DAT model in order to properly set expectations for participation in a DAT. We often compare and contrast committees and DATs using the Collaborative Communities Chart, found in Chapter 1. The Core Principles and the theory underlying the DAT model should also be presented to relevant stakeholders, even if only in a brief manner. This helps departmental members realize the many roles that DAT facilitators play and that they do not impose their leadership or anyone's agenda on the group.

In the introductory meeting, strike a balance between explaining aspects of the DAT model and examples of its impact. Include examples of impacts DATs have had on departmental culture, climate, curricula, and teaching practices (outlined in Chapter 1). You may also wish to include examples of how DAT members will benefit individually from learning about change and developing as change agents.

Digital Toolkit
How-To Guide 4: Building Awareness of DATs, Slides 2.0–2.10: DAT Model Overview, Handout 2: DAT Project One-Pager, Handout 3: Collaborative Communities

Be explicit about the importance the DAT model places on diversity, inclusion and equity. Having examples of how the campus community has benefited from this type of commitment to equity and how it aligns with other campus inclusivity efforts is powerful as well. This opens the minds of department members to what is possible in terms of the change DATs can effect in the department. Facilitators can also open the floor for department members to discuss possible directions for the DAT during this meeting. Sometimes, potential DAT members will volunteer or sign up during this meeting. Sometimes, the department will vote on whether to proceed with the formation of a DAT, before facilitators begin recruitment.

If DATs already exist at your institution, consider asking if some of the DAT members would be willing to answer questions about participating in a DAT during the recruitment of new departments. Testimonials from existing DATs can be a powerful motivator for departments that are unsure about DATs and can contribute to building legitimacy for the facilitators and the DAT model.

Other methods for recruiting DAT members. There are many other ways facilitators may introduce the DAT project and recruit new members. Keep in mind that the typical department meeting may only reach faculty, and perhaps some staff and graduate student representatives. Facilitators can also ask to speak with education-related committees, at staff meetings, and at student group meetings. Recruiting within undergraduate and graduate student groups, clubs, and organizations are another way to ensure that a variety of departmental roles and important perspectives are represented in a DAT.

Principle 1:
Students are partners in the educational process

Recruitment can also happen via an email sent by the chair to all members of the department explaining the project or during the departmental meeting when the DAT model is outlined. In order to recruit and reach those who have limited access to certain kinds of communication methods, or those who need support with accessing materials, a facilitator should employ a variety of ways to disseminate information. Options should include digital documents that are screen-reader accessible, flyers for those who do not have regular access to computers, or word of mouth. In some settings, it may be helpful to have materials available in more than one language. In some departments, the recruitment process involves informal and simultaneous conversations between potential members and department champions and the DAT facilitation team.

To reach everyone in the department and allow for questions to be addressed, provide opportunities to have conversations about DATs and recruitment multiple times and in multiple ways. This could include conversations that occur as part of a Listening Tour. The effort to recruit multi-modally is at the heart of being inclusive. Furthermore, flexibility in membership allows people with other personal commitments to contribute in ways that may be less traditional. Oftentimes, individuals are not open to sharing their personal boundaries in fear of

Digital Toolkit
Slide 6.1: Inclusive Recruitment

being stigmatized. An example of adapting for inclusion is to allow members to attend meetings by video conferencing, in case their commitments or abilities do not allow them to meet in person. Including different configurations around recruitment and membership widens the possibility of participation for many individuals and sets the tone of transparent communication about DATs to the department.

Indicators of Success

Evidence that a DAT is likely to be successful in a department

As mentioned earlier, there are many forms of evidence that a department is ready for a DAT. The most fundamental is that the chair and champions of change engage in meaningful discussions about changing aspects of the undergraduate experience. A stronger signal is that interest in the DAT emerged from conversations that were already happening during faculty meetings. In addition, a high level of faculty engagement in meetings designed to introduce the DAT model to staff is a very positive sign. If these signs are present, the department is likely to benefit from a DAT, even if some department members are skeptical about its value.

If a department values and regularly reflects on its undergraduate education program, then it's likely that the department members are primed to continue talking about improving undergraduate education within the structure of a DAT. If the department chair is willing to offer incentives or special recognition for department members who participate in a DAT, interest and commitment to the DAT almost certainly will improve. Finally, if the potential members of the DAT demonstrate interest in becoming change agents or learning facilitation skills, it is likely they will be open to the DAT model.

If the recruitment process is successful, there will be a sufficient number of volunteers to begin a DAT (typically 4–8 people representing diverse roles in the department). If there are not enough volunteers or the chair has not indicated support, the department is likely not ready to have a DAT.

Evidence that a department may not be ready for a DAT

Keep an eye out for red flags that indicate a department is not ready to have a DAT yet:

- Insufficient number of DAT allies can impede both the formation of a DAT and the influence of DAT work on the department.

- If multiple department members are unwilling to talk about their perspectives on undergraduate education or do not seem to value time spent on improving undergraduate education, the DAT will struggle to gain support for its work.

- Department members' preconceived ideas about how change occurs in departments may conflict with the DAT model. As a result, they will be unlikely to view DATs as a potential pathway to bring about change.

- Department members are often overburdened with obligations. If department members are unable to commit to regular DAT meetings, it will be challenging to make progress on the DAT work.

- Sometimes departments are in the midst of making big changes (e.g., hiring a new chair, introducing a degree program, revamping teaching loads, developing a strategic initiative). When this is the case, it might be best to hold off on starting a DAT until these changes have taken effect.

In such cases, the DAT team should work with champions to assess why the department is not ready and what steps the department may want to take to prepare themselves for a DAT in the future. The DAT team and champions can then support the department through consulting and follow-up assessments.

IC Map: Structural Characteristics of a DAT

Digital Toolkit
How-To Guide 1:
Using Innovation
Configuration
Maps

The IC Map included in this chapter outlines four structural characteristics that are important for a DAT to have to some extent. This IC Map can be used by facilitators and department members interested in forming a DAT. Facilitators can use the IC Map to communicate the structural characteristics that are necessary for a DAT. IC Maps, their uses, and guidelines on how to read them are covered in detail in Chapter 1.

The group has a diverse membership across roles in department.

Faculty, staff, undergraduates, and/or graduate students are members of the DAT, as relevant to the focal issue. Members are recruited through an inclusive process.	The DAT members do not represent all relevant roles within a department, but information from relevant department roles informs work on a regular basis. Members are recruited through both inclusive and word-of-mouth processes.	The DAT members do not represent all relevant roles within a department and do not collect information from other relevant roles. Members are only recruited through word of mouth.	The DAT members represent only one role within a department and may or may not collect information from other roles. Members are only recruited through word of mouth.

The group has external facilitation.

The group has two external facilitators, and group members recognize them as facilitators.	The group has one external facilitator, and group members recognize them as a facilitator.	The group has no external facilitation. Instead, one or more group members serve as facilitators.	The group has no external facilitation. Instead, the group self-facilitates as a whole.	The group has no external or internal facilitation.

The group meets regularly on an ongoing basis.

The group meets at least every two weeks for at least one hour per meeting.	The group meets monthly for at least 1.5 hours per meeting.	The group meets monthly for less than 1.5 hours per meeting.	The group meets regularly, but less frequently than every month.	The group does not have a regular meeting schedule.

The group's membership is consistent.

It is clear who is a member of the DAT, and membership is stable on the timescale of a semester. All DAT members make strong efforts to attend every meeting.	It is clear who is a member of the DAT, and membership is stable on the timescale of a semester. A core group of members make strong efforts to attend every meeting. Those who can't attend consistently follow the meeting minutes and contribute to action items.	Some DAT members make no or weak efforts to attend every meeting. They do not follow the meeting minutes or contribute to action items when they miss meetings.	There are some individuals for whom it is not clear whether they are members of the DAT.	The membership of the DAT changes significantly on timescales shorter than a semester.

Recommended Reading

Reinholz, D. L., Pilgrim, M. E., Corbo, J. C., & Finkelstein, N. (2019, September 24). Transforming undergraduate education from the middle out with Departmental Action Teams. *Change: The Magazine of Higher Learning, 51*(5), 64–70.
https://doi.org/10.1080/00091383.2019.1652078

> This article presents the DAT model as a mechanism for change. Included in the article are examples of different DATs in departments. This article is a great resource to provide a general overview of DATs, their potential impact, and some lessons for supporting a DAT. Facilitators should consider giving this article to departmental leaders and other administrators to increase understanding and support for the DAT model.

Reinholz, D. L., Corbo, J. C., Dancy, M. H., Finkelstein, N. (2017). Departmental Action Teams: Supporting faculty learning through departmental change. Learning Communities Journal, 9(1).

> This paper compares and contrasts the DAT model to Faculty Learning Communities using an Activity Theory perspective. It also provides an extended example of the DAT model, in which a department develops a vision for a more integrated undergraduate curriculum, and ultimately creates three curriculum coordinator positions. This paper is useful for outlining the differences between DATs and other faculty groups, as well as a more detailed example of a DAT.

CHAPTER 3

Preparing to Facilitate DATs

The DAT model relies on facilitators to guide teams in achieving ambitious goals. This chapter describes the four roles that facilitators play in DATs and how facilitators can prepare for their jobs. We describe why the DAT model includes external rather than internal facilitators, and why it is ideal to have two facilitators support a DAT. We explain the qualifications needed to be a facilitator and how facilitators can develop their skills.

We focus on the practice of reflection as critical to the development of skilled facilitators and explain how facilitators use reflection in making choices around guiding DATs. We explain how to create structures to support reflection, including journaling and building a facilitator community.

We also describe how facilitators prepare to form a DAT by learning about the DAT's department and by taking that context into account in their work. We examine why it is so important for the work of facilitators to be legitimized by DAT members and what facilitators can do to cultivate that legitimacy.

KEY MESSAGES

- Skilled facilitators are responsive to each department's needs and context.
- The success of DATs rests on the capacities of skilled external co-facilitators who are viewed as legitimate in the eyes of DAT members.
- Facilitators support change by enacting four key roles that elevate team effectiveness and the change agency of individual DAT members.
- Reflective practices and continuous development of facilitation skills are critical to the successful facilitation of DATs.

Theory of Change Context

This chapter covers Outcome 3D: Facilitators are ready to run a DAT. Facilitators must prepare in several ways before facilitating a DAT. In order to determine how a DAT might operate and what its focus will be, facilitators must understand the department's needs and context. The needs and context are likely to have a significant impact on how the DAT functions, at least in the early stages. Understanding a department's needs and context are critical so that facilitators can adapt their approach to a new DAT.

Facilitators must also have the skills, knowledge, and resources to successfully facilitate a DAT. If, for example, a facilitator does not have enough time to develop the agenda for DATs, they will have difficulties in supporting the DAT. If facilitators do not have the capacity to support a DAT, taking on this responsibility could lead to a negative DAT experience for DAT members.

Even if a facilitator does have the capacity to support a DAT, the facilitator might not be perceived as qualified. In order for a facilitator to have an impact on a department or DAT, their perspectives must carry weight. There are many ways that facilitators can build legitimacy and convey that they are qualified to guide a team.

Prior facilitation experience both increases the capacity of those proposing to facilitate DATs and builds legitimacy. Facilitators are ready to run a DAT when they fulfill the three sub-outcomes of Outcome 3D. These three sub-outcomes reinforce each other; for example, prior facilitation experience both increases the capacity of those proposing to facilitate DATs and builds legitimacy. Facilitators should continuously attend to these sub-outcomes, even after a DAT has begun.

OUTCOME 3D

Facilitators are ready to run a DAT

Facilitators understand departmental needs and context	Facilitators have the capacity to support a DAT in the department	Facilitators have legitimacy in the eyes of potential DAT members and department leadership

---

Sufficient progress in Outcome 3D enables facilitators to fulfill Outcome 5, which outlines the different roles facilitators serve for the DAT. Effective facilitation involves four major types of activities: helping manage DAT logistics, supporting the development of a high functioning team, providing support that is customized to the DAT's goals and needs, and cultivating an environment external to the DAT that is conducive to the DAT's success. These activities are taken on simultaneously to support the DAT in its work and to demonstrate the value of the DAT to relevant external stakeholders. Understanding the different roles facilitators play and how to prepare for these roles is the primary focus of this chapter.

OUTCOME 5			
Facilitators support DAT members in creating change and developing as change agents			
Help manage DAT logistics	Supports the development of a high functioning team	Provide support that is customized to the DAT's goals and needs	Cultivate an environment external to the DAT that is conducive to the DAT's success

What Does It Mean to Be an External Co-facilitator?

A facilitator plays a primary role in helping DATs operate as high functioning teams. Our model intentionally relies on facilitators who are external to the DAT's department. When a facilitator resides outside the power structure of the department and is not directly impacted by the DAT's work, they are in a unique position to offer an outside perspective. Because they are not members of a department's community, external facilitators can ask questions of DAT members that help the group explore the underlying assumptions about their department and work. As they listen to their peers explain things to an outsider, DAT members are better able to reconsider the ideas they hold about their departments and consider new ones.

External facilitators are also better able to identify habitual, unproductive discourse patterns that DAT members may not be aware of. Because they are "outsiders," external facilitators can introduce new ways of communicating that disrupt existing patterns, without being viewed as directly attacking a community member. The establishment of new conversational patterns can open the door for more productive interactions (Corbo et al., 2015). However, DATs are not externally facilitated forever. As a DAT matures, a transition to internal facilitation or self-facilitation is often both necessary and appropriate. This is addressed in Chapter 8.

Our work with the DAT model has typically relied on co-facilitation, with two facilitators that co-plan and attend each DAT meeting. We do this for several reasons. Co-facilitation provides increased capacity to support a DAT across the four DAT facilitator roles, because facilitators can take on more tasks at the same time. This is especially important during discussions, because both facilitators can monitor the flow of conversation, and this distributes the cognitive load. Co-facilitation is also more resilient to scheduling constraints. If one of the facilitators cannot make a meeting, the other facilitator can run a meeting solo or with a temporary substitute.

Principle 5:

Continuous improvement is an upheld practice.

Most importantly, co-facilitation supports ongoing reflection on a DAT's progress. Reflection allows facilitators to identify areas where they need to improve. Being mindful of what happened in the meeting and reflecting on how participants responded to facilitation can provide insight about what is and isn't working. It can also point to the next steps a DAT needs to take. Co-facilitators should continually reflect on equity within the DAT and ask themselves whether they are applying inclusive practices in their facilitation. It is well worth the time to reflect together and discuss issues or problematic interactions that occurred.

Engaging in effective external co-facilitation

Using the co-facilitation model effectively requires several considerations. Positive co-facilitation relationships allow for candid communication that supports learning and growth. Good co-facilitators have frank discussions about their strengths and their co-facilitators' strengths, allowing them to leverage those strengths as a team. Co-facilitators come to consensus in the planning stage before a DAT meeting, help the DAT team reach agreed-upon goals during the meeting, and afterward, reflect openly about which facilitation choices were productive or unproductive, and suggest alternative facilitation techniques.

Co-facilitators keep a common journal for each DAT and add to it as soon as possible after each meeting. Journal reflections help facilitators examine their ideas, remember their insights, and build upon ideas over time.

Although we have typically relied on a co-facilitation model, we recognize that this may not be possible in all contexts, due to cost and personnel. If possible, it is immensely helpful for new facilitators to train by co-facilitating a DAT in their first year. In a context with a single facilitator, it may be beneficial to have DAT members learn more quickly how to help run meetings. For more information on this, see the section in Chapter 8 about developing internal DAT facilitation.

Digital Toolkit
How-To Guide 5:
Documenting
and Reflecting
on Meetings

What Are the Roles of DAT Facilitators?

The facilitator is responsible for the care of the team during and in between meetings, and this will look different for every team based on their needs. We break down "what facilitators do" into four major roles that are mutually reinforcing:

- Helping manage DAT logistics
- Supporting the development of a high functioning team
- Providing support that is customized to the DAT's goals and needs
- Cultivating an external environment that is conducive to the DAT's success

Helping manage DAT logistics

Facilitators ensure that there are mechanisms for DAT members to communicate, keep information organized, and meet regularly. Facilitators also bring supplies to support meeting activities. Accessible, easy-to-use communication mechanisms, such as shared meeting minutes, allow DAT members to exchange information fluidly with one another. Groups also need to organize information in an understandable, easily retrievable way. To make continuous progress, groups need to have regularly scheduled meetings (Garmston & Wellman, 2013). All of this logistical work is necessary for the group to function efficiently. Logistical support provided by DAT facilitators includes:

- Setting up the meeting schedule
- Coordinating the reservation of a meeting room
- Setting up a shared folder for documents
- Setting up a group mailing list
- Purchasing and bringing snacks and supplies to meetings
- Bringing A/V equipment, as needed
- Guiding meetings through an agenda
- Recording meeting minutes
- Emailing the group meeting reminders
- Following up meetings by emailing lists of action items
- Checking in with individuals about critical action items

(See Chapter 6 for a detailed look at these logistical elements)

We use the phrase *"help* manage" intentionally. While the facilitator ensures that all these tasks happen in an effective manner, they do not necessarily take charge of all of them. For example, we almost always ask a DAT member to support the facilitators in scheduling meeting rooms in their building. We encourage groups that have organizational capacity to take on some of these tasks. This will help them in the transition to self-sufficiency in future facilitation.

Logistics management is an ongoing activity. Effective facilitators continually reflect on and improve upon these mechanisms as needed. This contrasts with seeing logistics as a one-and-done task that is only considered during the group's inception. We encourage facilitators to continually reflect on the group's ability to communicate, organize information, meet, manage supplies, and create new mechanisms as necessary. In Chapter 6, we describe in more detail how facilitators help support the logistics of DATs.

Supporting the development of a high functioning team

Facilitators work to continuously improve team functioning. Team support provided by facilitators includes:

- Introducing process skills
- Developing community standards with the group
- Supporting equitable participation, so every member is heard and decisions are made thoughtfully
- Managing conflict in the group, and growing through it
- Developing mechanisms for shared governance

Facilitators use many tools to support these areas of team functioning. They monitor and analyze group dynamics. They ask questions, intervene in conversations, and make sure all voices are heard during meetings. They model behaviors and skills that promote a high functioning team, so that the group can see how these behaviors fit into conversations and meetings. They explicitly teach such "process skills," which is an umbrella term we use to refer to any kind of concept, knowledge, or activity that supports the functioning of a group. We will describe many different process skills throughout this book. Facilitators sometimes also "go meta" and talk explicitly about team functioning, creating opportunities for group members to reflect on how they are working, effectively or ineffectively, together.

Facilitators apply reflective practices to successfully address team functioning. This reflection involves multiple approaches: journaling, reflective meetings between co-facilitators, informal coffee hours with DAT members, and meetings where facilitators discuss successes and challenges with their facilitator community. Within these spaces, they can document observations of what happened, develop multiple interpretations of what may be occurring, choose from multiple approaches or facilitator moves, and judge the effectiveness of various facilitator approaches or moves. Reflecting within a community supports facilitators in thinking deeply, seeing things from multiple perspectives, and drawing on others' prior knowledge. In Chapters 4 and 6, we describe in more detail how facilitators use these reflections to improve team function and guide the team through their projects.

Providing support that is customized to a DAT's goals and needs

All DATs are unique, so a "one size fits all" approach limits the progress of DATs. Facilitators provide support that is customized to an individual DAT's goals and needs. Facilitators are well-positioned to take on these support tasks because they are less embedded in the work and can focus on the "bigger picture" of the group's trajectory. Custom support provided by facilitators includes:

- Assembling agendas to help the group progress toward their goals

- Guiding activities that support the group in team building and encouraging equitable contributions to the DAT's work

- Providing means for accessing resources, including information, expertise, individuals in positions to support the DAT, and data relevant to the DAT's project

A facilitator sometimes provides customized support by drawing on their own expertise. However, this is not necessary for someone to be a successful facilitator. Facilitators often bring expertise to DATs by fostering relationships with other on-campus entities. They can bring experts on topics relevant for the DAT to the group or introduce DAT members to professional networks that can further the DAT's work. For example, we have helped DATs make connections with other DAT members who have done similar projects and with campus staff from Career Services, Institutional Research, Student Affairs, and from offices focused on Diversity and Inclusion.

Skilled facilitators think about each DAT's work holistically and provide customized support to DATs both in and outside of their meetings. Facilitators can help prime the environment around DATs to achieve change in several ways. They can encourage DATs to spread awareness about their work and the impact it can have on the department by teaching them principles of change management and effective communication. They can help their DATs determine the kinds of support they may need to succeed. When appropriate, facilitators might speak with department chairs and administrators to request their support for changes envisioned by the DAT. It is important for DAT members to take responsibility for these types of actions in the long run, but they are often initiated by facilitators in the early stages of the DAT.

It's common for facilitators to have prior experience in managing nd completing projects, and when they are invested in the DAT's success, it can be tempting to take on the role of the project manager. However, there is a fine line between offering customized support and doing project work that could be meaningful for DAT members to accomplish. When the latter occurs, DAT members may not develop a strong sense of ownership around their project. A good rule of thumb for facilitators is to always ask if a DAT member is available to volunteer to complete work, or to ask the group how they would like to accomplish the set of tasks under discussion.

Principle 2:

Work focuses on achieving collective positive outcomes.

Facilitators should regularly reflect on the DAT's progress and needs in order to effectively offer customized support. This involves monitoring the group's progress toward their goals, identifying upcoming roadblocks, and considering what the group needs to do to move forward. In Chapter 6, we describe in detail how facilitators guide DATs toward determining and achieving their goals.

Cultivating an external environment that is conducive to the DAT's success

Facilitators can support the DAT in ways that are external to the DAT meetings. In order for the DAT's work to be supported and sustained by the department, the environment outside of the DAT must be prepared for the desired changes. Facilitators can help prime the environment for change in several ways, both within and outside of the department. Within the department, facilitators can talk with the department chair and other potential allies about how change happens and how it is supported through a DAT; they can spread awareness of the DAT's work and the impact it can have on the department; and they can share information on the DAT model and how it guides change efforts. This will start preparing department members for the changes that the DAT will make, as well as set expectations about the timeline for change to take place. While this relationship-building will ultimately become the responsibility of DAT members (Chapter 7), facilitators can model how to use communication to prime the environment for change. This will contribute to DAT members' growth as change agents (Chapter 5).

Facilitators can also prepare the environment external to the DAT's department so that the DAT's work is more likely to be positively received. Facilitators may have more access to stakeholders outside of the department and can leverage these connections to build awareness and support. Generating this awareness and support can ultimately lead to increased value and legitimacy placed on the DAT's work. In these ways, the department and the institution will be better prepared for the DAT's work.

How Can a Facilitator Develop Their Skills?

We do not expect facilitators to begin with all the skills for guiding DATs. While some kinds of prior experience and knowledge are helpful, a new DAT facilitator can become very skilled in each of their four roles while on the job.

DAT FACILITATOR HIRING CRITERIA

When we hire facilitators, we include the following in the job description:

Required qualifications:

- Master's degree from an accredited university
- Ability to quickly understand and adapt to working with people from various disciplines
- Excellent communication, collaboration, time management, and presentation skills
- Experience with facilitating the work of groups and collaborating with a project team

Preferred qualifications:

- Earned Ph.D. or ABD in a relevant field
- Experience with all or some of:
    - Organizational/institutional change
    - Teaching and effective education innovations
    - Quantitative and/or qualitative education research and methods
    - Program/project management

Use this as a starting point for thinking about your own basic criteria for DAT facilitators.

Ideally, DAT facilitators should have enough experience in academia (e.g., through earning a graduate degree) to understand how academic departments typically work. It is also valuable for facilitators to have expertise in collecting, visualizing, and interpreting education-related data. These skills are often used to support DATs in using data to inform decision-making.

However, facilitators do not need to have deep expertise in the departmental discipline or even with the DAT's focal issue, as this can be provided by DAT members and other members of the campus community. They also do not need specific kinds of skills to handle teams from different disciplines on campus. A general toolkit of skills is sufficient for supporting many kinds of teams.

One skill that is very important for effective facilitation and not usually found on an applicant's resume is the ability to consider the perspectives of others. This allows facilitators to see the complexities of an issue from different vantage points. We discuss how to develop the abilities needed for becoming a skilled facilitator in the next section.

Building individual facilitation skills

To develop a facilitation approach that is centered on seeking to understand others, it is helpful for facilitators to be oriented toward learning about others' perspectives. A DAT facilitator should seek this understanding with humble curiosity, bringing a desire to support the work of the group, even if that work moves in a direction they may not have expected (Garmston & Wellman, 2013). To learn from others effectively, a DAT facilitator must listen intently and document interactions thoroughly to support later reflection. Skilled DAT facilitators contribute to DAT meetings more by asking questions than by making suggestions and comments.

Principle 6:

Work is grounded in a commitment to equity, inclusion, and social justice.

A facilitator's skill in perspective-taking is enhanced when they engage deeply in learning about equity and diversity around many spectra of difference (such as race, gender, nationality, ability, and neurodiversity) and when they confront inequity in their daily life. Pursuing campus professional development in equity and inclusion, and specifically in the realm of guiding conversations around issues related to equity, will help a facilitator guide DATs in discussing aspects of equity that impact their projects.

There are many resources available for developing specific facilitation techniques. We highly recommend reading *The Adaptive School*, by Bruce Wellman and Robert Garmston (2013), along with the suggestions in the Recommended Reading section at the end of each chapter in this book. We will go into detail about how specific facilitation techniques from *The Adaptive School* can be used to support a DAT in Chapters 4 and 6. We also describe many facilitation techniques and activities in the DAT Digital Toolkit.

External facilitators benefit from bringing their expertise from prior work experiences to DATs, particularly in the areas of coaching, counseling, issues of diversity and inclusion, working in an academic field, and team collaboration. We recommend that facilitators educate themselves on how work cultures vary across a university and differ from other industries (Schein, 2010).

As you read and learn about being a facilitator, it is beneficial to practice new skills so that they become second nature when you are facilitating a group. For example, as you converse with others, challenge yourself to ask questions rather than give ideas. Note what went well while practicing these skills, and what did not. Some techniques may come more naturally than others, so focus on practicing skills that are more challenging for you. Ask coworkers to allow you to practice facilitating meetings within your own group (where the stakes are lower) and ask if they would be willing to provide you with feedback.

An excellent resource for self-checking is the *Facilitation Skills Inventory* (Bens, 2009). You will benefit from periodically reviewing the inventory for skills you have learned and for the skills you have implemented in your DATs. During your reflections, note the skills you frequently employ and those that you have not yet used. As you build your own skills, consider asking other members of the group to take on some of these facilitation tasks, so you can practice handing off the role of facilitator to others.

You can also prepare yourself by thinking about how the "DATs in Real Life" segments we share throughout the book may arise in your own DATs. Compare the DATs described to the challenges you faced when facilitating. What are the similarities and differences? How would you respond to them given the unique contexts of your DATs and university? What other challenges are you encountering? Regularly reflecting on and analyzing challenges will help you anticipate ways in which DATs may respond to challenges and/or successes and help you sort through different ideas about how to support them.

Building an effective facilitator community

A facilitator community is a set of facilitators who learn from one another. A facilitation community creates opportunities for facilitators to build competence through open discussion of practice. These discussions support facilitators' learning because members of the community draw upon and share their diverse experiences. This is especially valuable when facilitators encounter challenges with their teams, because other facilitators may have encountered similar situations or may see the situations from different points of view. Facilitator communities are also important spaces for facilitators to further their self-education through discussing literature, facilitation experiences, and attending trainings. Self-education includes using resources that challenge and inform the facilitator community to think about diversity, equity, and inclusion within the DAT structure, or going through trainings that help a facilitator feel better prepared to understand this perspective in their work.

Facilitation communities help build facilitator motivation and confidence. Validating challenges can help facilitators feel like they are less alone in their struggles and can affirm that some problems are universally challenging. It's important for community members to celebrate facilitators' insights and implementation of successful strategies, as this helps build facilitators' feelings of self-efficacy and confidence.

Principle 4:
Collaboration among group members is enjoyable, productive, and rewarding.

Nurturing an effective facilitator community requires a regular schedule of meetings, consistent sharing of experiences, and reflection on challenges and best practices. It is helpful to create routine practices that support sharing. This can include designating a coordinator for the community, engaging in community building practices, holding discussions of readings (such as those found at the end of this chapter), and discussing the progress, challenges, and successes experienced by teams that members of the community are coordinating.

How Do Facilitators Learn About the DAT's Departmental Culture?

It is natural for facilitators to make educated guesses about how a DAT may operate, based on their prior knowledge or experience. To some extent this can be useful, but it is critical to keep in mind that every department has a unique culture, identity, and history (Schein, 2010). Thus, effective facilitators understand departments' individual needs, contexts, and cultures. They also pay special attention to what issues of equity and inclusion are present within each department.

Understanding the local context and the department's history of education reform projects supports facilitators in helping the DAT enact meaningful change by leveraging existing cultural features. It also helps facilitators to understand department-specific challenges, which can range from historical divisions, to staff workload, to communication, to climate issues among stakeholder groups. Understanding cultural aspects of a department helps facilitators customize their support of a DAT. Finally, being able to adapt communication styles to a given department helps create strong relationships with DAT members.

Understanding a department's needs and context

Strategies for understanding departmental needs and contexts overlap with strategies for assessing departmental readiness (Chapter 2). Facilitators' understanding of a department's needs and context often begins through informal interactions. When talking with individuals or groups in an unfamiliar department, facilitators ask questions to better understand the department's culture and history, particularly around undergraduate education. These informal conversations can help facilitators gather information about potential challenges and opportunities a DAT may encounter in the department.

An effective technique for exploring departmental needs and context with a DAT in its early stages is the Strengths, Weaknesses, Opportunities and Threats (SWOT) analysis (Orr, 2013). This analysis helps facilitators learn about the department and can enable DAT members to take more of an outsider's view of their knowledge and experiences. Ideally, this will help set the stage for the DAT members to make thoughtful choices about their work.

Principle 3:

Data collection, analysis, and interpretation inform decision-making.

Other mechanisms for understanding a department's context include using surveys and interviews with department members. The facilitator can ask how their department approaches change and what kinds of changes they would personally like to see in undergraduate education. It is also helpful to ask how typical meetings and committees in the department operate. It is important to keep in mind that each member of the department will perceive the departmental culture differently, so it is valuable to seek out a diversity of perspectives. Further, facilitators can use interviews to get a sense of the collective identity that departments may have, and how such identity may be related to their fields of study. The Listening Tour provides an excellent baseline for characterizing the department with respect to the current state of its undergraduate education. Listening Tour Interview Questions can be used as is or modified by facilitators to learn more about a department. Even if interviews cannot occur until a DAT has begun to meet, a Listening Tour will still provide valuable information for facilitators

Digital Toolkit

How-To Guide 2: Conducting a Listening Tour

For the purposes of characterizing departmental culture around undergraduate education, we have developed the DELTA survey (Ngai et al., 2020). Responses to this survey can provide facilitators with information about the climate around instruction, social networks related to teaching in the department, and department members' perceptions of how the department culture aligns with the six Core Principles. This information is useful for facilitators and can be shared with DAT members to inform their work. In a department with a supportive chair, the DELTA survey can be administered soon after a DAT has formed. It can also be administered after a DAT has completed a major project to assess whether change has occurred in the department.

Digital Toolkit

How-To Guide 6: Using the DELTA Survey

As facilitators begin to understand the departmental context, they and the DAT members should be able to articulate how the department perceives undergraduate education and what points of tension exist around education in the department. This can be represented through cultural maps and diagrams, as described by Schein (2010).

Finally, it is helpful for facilitators to reflect on whether they need additional capacity to support a department's unique needs. It is common for facilitators to seek additional training. For example, a facilitator who has worked predominantly within physical sciences may seek out deeper knowledge of the social sciences' department culture before initiating a DAT in the social sciences. A facilitator working with a DAT that is analyzing a great deal of institutional data might reach out to colleagues in the university's Institutional Research office for support. A facilitator unfamiliar with inclusive practices may seek additional training through the institution's Human Resources department or Office of Diversity.

DATS IN REAL LIFE

What if a DAT delays student participation due to concerns about faculty climate?

In a DAT we recently formed, faculty member participants alluded early on to the department's rocky history. The department had just been assigned an external chair, and this person was starting to work with the faculty on moving forward from the department's recent challenges. The group had an excellent proposal and good energy around forming a DAT. Facilitators thought that the department seemed to be in good hands with the external chair, and that the prior challenges were distant enough from the focus of the DAT to not matter, so they chose not to press for details.

However, when the facilitators described the student recruitment process to the group, some faculty members seemed uncomfortable. They proposed delaying including students in the DAT until after the group had planned out a project. When facilitators explained the principle of Students as Partners, the group revealed that they were concerned that the kinds of free-form discussions that were needed to arrive at a project might inadvertently reveal to students too much about the department's "dirty laundry". The faculty and staff on the DAT proposed doing visioning among all of the faculty in the department as a way to build community and support for the DAT. Facilitators agreed this was a good idea, and began to think about ways to gain student input early in the process.

The external chair contacted the facilitators after the "dirty laundry" comment was made and offered to inform them about the nature of the challenges. The chair met the facilitators in a public but quiet area of campus, saying they would not want to be seen meeting with facilitators within the departmental building, for fear of stirring up rumors.

Without going into details, the chair explained that there was a faculty member who created a toxic, hostile atmosphere, and another faculty member was moving to another university in response. There had also been a power struggle over who would be the next chair, and one of the DAT members had been turned down by the Dean for this position, opting instead to appoint the external chair. The facilitators were relieved to learn that students had not been involved in these challenges and understood that the faculty were still working hard to build trust among themselves. The external chair indicated that students generally felt that helping the faculty body build trust among themselves was just as important as completing an education project.

Once facilitators understood the departmental context, it was much easier for them to work with the faculty's proposal to delay student participation. After the full faculty body participated in visioning, the DAT faculty and staff summarized the visioning ideas and generated a set of desired student outcomes from them. Towards the end of their first semester working together, they felt comfortable enough to recruit students. The facilitators began the second semester with the students and faculty reviewing data that had been gathered from students in previous years and relating these to the desired student outcomes. Students were able to provide valuable insights in this and all future DAT processes. They now appear to be on track to have high student involvement and sense of ownership among all DAT members.

Digital Toolkit
Slide 6.1: Inclusive Recruitment

Adapting facilitation to different contexts

In this book, we offer many strategies that facilitators can employ to support effective group work. Our intention is not to be prescriptive, because situations with DATs are always context-dependent and often ambiguous. All groups have unique features and idiosyncrasies that impact the success of any particular facilitator move. DATs benefit from facilitators that embrace the tension that precedes resolution and resist the sense of urgency to find quick solutions.

Skilled facilitators use situational context and knowledge of the group culture when judging which strategies to employ. Therefore, we advocate that facilitators take an approach that involves careful judgment and in-the-moment decision-making, along with periodic revisiting of previous decisions. Such an approach is supported by reflecting in ways that allow facilitators to anticipate what individuals and the group might do (Garmston & Wellman, 2013).

Being reflective involves regularly trying to understand a situation and embracing that deeper understanding to better adapt to different departmental contexts. Facilitators can ask themselves questions to assess a DAT's development and consider multiple strategies for a given scenario. Using the set of reflective questions provided, facilitators can look at a situation through multiple lenses, consider multiple responses, and then intentionally choose a facilitation strategy. Facilitators can reflect on these questions by themselves, with co-facilitators, with others in their facilitator community, or even with a member of the DAT.

REFLECTIVE QUESTIONS FOR FACILITATORS

Shared Vision
What are the short-term and long-term goals that the DAT is working toward?
What would support the DAT in making progress toward those outcomes?
What kinds of resources would be useful in helping the DAT achieve its outcomes?
Do all members act in ways that indicate they feel ownership over the goals and work?

Developing Members' Knowledge and Skills
Do DAT members understand the six Core Principles?
Do DAT members recognize unique aspects of participating on a DAT?
Do DAT members seem to be growing in their skills and contributing to a team?
Do DAT members seem to be growing as agents of change?
Are DAT members deepening their knowledge about the DAT's focal issue?

Collaboration
What patterns occur in this DAT's conversations?
Are conversations alternating productively between divergent and convergent formats?
Is it necessary to balance out participation in the DAT's conversations in some way?
What can the DAT members learn about high functioning teams to help them be a more effective group?
Are members adhering to their community standards?

Addressing Conflict and Tension
What are the areas of disagreement? What is the nature of the disagreements (e.g., in priorities, values, interpersonal conflict)?

What underlying dynamics and history might be at play in the group's interactions?

Are there any underlying tensions that need to be addressed or monitored?

How is power distributed in the DAT?

Does the DAT operate in equitable ways?

What is not being said, heard, or acknowledged?

Is more information needed to address a situation? How can we get it?

How can we work in partnership with DAT members to resolve the situation?

Achieving Successful Outcomes

How well does the group align with the DAT Core Principles?

Is the DAT building legitimacy within their department?

What assumptions is the group making about their work?

Is the DAT considering the sustainability of their work?

How do external/internal pressures on the group impact their work?

Do individuals have the capacity to carry out their tasks? How can they be supported?

Is the group using an inclusive lens while reflecting and designing their work?

Metacognitive Facilitator Questions

How do facilitators engage in reflection?

Are facilitators using strategies in a balanced way?

Do DAT members understand the strategies that facilitators are using?

Is the timing appropriate to apply a particular facilitation strategy?

Do I have time to employ a strategy in a meeting?

What are indicators that will show a facilitation strategy has been effective?

DATS IN REAL LIFE

What if facilitators need to adapt their approach?

In the most recent DAT that we formed, we noted during our reflections that the group was very task-oriented and unusually well-organized. We anticipated that the group might express some impatience with the DAT Model's "Go Slow to Go Fast" approach. Indeed, after their third meeting, the chair of the department, who was a member of the DAT, emailed facilitators to relate that a few members had told him they thought the pace of work was too slow. However, the facilitators remembered that after that same meeting, another member had commented on how much they were learning about process skills. The facilitators decided to report both pieces of feedback during the next meeting. They then offered to limit process skill time to five minutes and asked the group if they would like to discuss some outside-of-meeting processes that might work for them. The group eventually made both a Slack channel and two subgroups to work on different projects, and the pace of work naturally increased.

Digital Toolkit

Slide 2.8: Go Slow to Go Fast

How Can Facilitators Develop Legitimacy?

Developing legitimacy as a facilitator in the eyes of the DAT members is important for your and their success. We define legitimacy as the respect, authority, and capability that is ascribed to an individual or a group by others. An individual can become *legitimized* through the recognition by others as having expertise or value. Legitimacy allows people to express their views and take action while having trust from others. As with credibility, legitimacy is bestowed by the DAT and is a perception the DAT forms about the facilitator (Garmston & Wellman, 2013).

Lack of legitimacy will limit a facilitator's effectiveness. DAT members are more likely to follow the process put into place by facilitators if they perceive that the facilitators have experience and knowledge of how work gets done in academia. Therefore, it is critical to establish a certain threshold of legitimacy before a DAT begins its work, and continue to build that legitimacy while working with a DAT. This concept is also central to DAT effectiveness: the DAT needs to have sufficient legitimacy within a department to enact change.

DATS IN REAL LIFE

What if DAT members have mismatched expectations about the DAT model?

One of our DATs was initially skeptical of the value of facilitation, then rejected facilitation entirely. In initial meetings, DAT members openly questioned the value of talking about process skills. After a few meetings, a DAT member told us privately that they thought we were not making enough progress during the meetings.

In response, the facilitators reduced the amount of time spent on process skills. After a few more meetings, DAT members requested that they be allowed to create the agenda and structure the meetings themselves. We interviewed DAT members in order to better understand their perspectives.

The interviews revealed that DAT members had concerns about participating in the research portion of the DAT project. In meetings, they had expected to focus on solving individual problems, rather than setting out a vision and outcomes to work toward. They also were used to a designated committee leader that would tell the group what to do. We had explained how DATs work differently than committees in early meetings, but this did not increase our legitimacy among the DAT members. The one-on-one interviews served to inform us and alleviate some tension, but in this case, did not significantly change the course of the DAT.

The remainder of the meetings were organized by DAT members, and they did not discuss process skills. They completed a relatively simple project and disbanded after meeting for one academic year.

Upon reflection, we realized that if we had learned more about the leadership expectations of DAT members and how departmental committees were run, we may have been better able to address subtle signs or statements of concern. Additionally, a couple of months had passed between the initial information session and first DAT meeting. We concluded that important information about the rationale and structure of the DAT project had either been forgotten, or in some cases may not have been received and understood by DAT members.

We used this experience to develop a more explicit process for forming and informing new DATs (see Chapter 2). We found that making more inquiries in advance and providing DAT members with information in multiple ways helped us set clearer expectations about participating in a DAT and supported facilitators in establishing legitimacy. We also found that providing time for DAT members to reflect on the impact of facilitated activities and process skills allowed members to articulate their value to others. Members of subsequent DATs still frequently need repeated explanations for why we set aside time for process skills, but they now tend to do so with a tone of curiosity rather than mistrust or displeasure.

Building legitimacy as a facilitator

Legitimacy is a quality that the group members must ascribe to you. The amount of legitimacy you hold when you start working with a group will vary, due to past experiences that group members may have had with facilitators, the group members' perception of your own experience and qualifications, and their understanding of your role as a facilitator. Your legitimacy will vary from person to person within a DAT, so strive to recognize subtle signs that you have been granted legitimacy. You should not expect this to be an overt move or proclamation, but rather, legitimacy may be ascribed to you through actions (DAT members' willingness to work with you) or verbal comments. When these moments arise, it is important that you accept legitimacy as it is offered. Legitimacy may be established through several pathways early in the DAT process:

Legitimacy gained from others. Other people, within or outside of the DAT you are working with, can legitimize you as a facilitator by speaking about their interactions with you. This is especially beneficial when the person who legitimizes you is recognized as a person respected by the group. For this reason, it is beneficial to ask the chair of the department to formally introduce you to the department and describe why they value the resource of external facilitation.

Legitimacy from your experience. Remember that DAT members may not have an opportunity to read your CV or resume, so you should tell them about your relevant experience when you introduce yourself. Be sure to describe your degree credentials when introducing yourself to the group. Postgraduate work is particularly important in the eyes of faculty, whereas staff and instructors will appreciate hearing more about your experiences with students. If you have previously worked with the department or in their field, briefly outline that experience and describe your role and the impact of your work.

Mention your experience or credentials supporting equity, diversity and inclusion, or how you are seeking training in this area. Talk briefly about your experiences with facilitation and supporting change, and especially why you are motivated to be a facilitator of this particular DAT. This indicates to the group that you are invested in their work and success.

As you work with a DAT, it is likely that you will be able to draw from your experiences and expertise to guide them. Explicitly share this with the group and provide a context for where this knowledge or experience comes from (e.g., "When I was doing my graduate degree, I learned something that may apply here..."). This demonstrates that you have valuable experience to lend to the group, which can build legitimacy as the DAT members come to view you as a contributing member of the team.

Legitimacy gained from interactions with the DAT. You will build legitimacy as a facilitator as you start working with the group. Being highly professional, listening carefully, and responding quickly to all potential or active DAT members sets a tone for developing a relationship with the group. Your work will be trusted when it is conveyed in a gracious, thoughtful, clear, and concise manner, and one that shows your respect for the time DAT members are volunteering with their participation. It is especially important to comfortably say, "I don't know, but I can work to find out for you" when you don't know an answer.

Principle 6:
Work is grounded in a commitment to equity, inclusion, and social justice.

Individuals will have different initial perceptions of you—and you of them. Get to know the individuals in your DAT and show them that they are individually important to the DAT. Treat individuals with sensitivity to their unique background and personal characteristics. Be flexible around their individual needs, and work hard to include everyone to the degree they are interested in being involved. Be aware of how implicit bias can affect your treatment of individuals, and work to counter those biases in yourself and how they are expressed by others. The legitimacy you gain from this approach will create a "brave space" within which the group can thrive.

It is important to match your contributions to the needs of the group. This includes the "process skills" that you teach at the start of each meeting and the activities you suggest for making progress on their work. Before you begin teaching a skill or activity, explain how it relates to their work to date. That will help them see the value your facilitation brings to the team's progress and functioning. In Chapters 5 and 6, we describe how to match relevant process skills and activities to specific group challenges, in both the formation of an effective team and in making progress on a project.

Interactions with DAT members outside of regular DAT meetings are a good opportunity to build legitimacy. When departments that have a DAT or that are interested in a DAT are hosting an event, you can show support with your attendance. If there are departmental initiatives to which you can contribute, even in a small way (e.g., making a connection on campus, sending literature about relevant research), making an effort to do so can go a long way towards building your relationship with DAT members. Establishing a standing coffee hour that any DAT member can attend, inviting DAT members out to coffee to discuss their work in the department or their thoughts on the DAT, and sponsoring cross-campus DAT celebrations are other ways to interact with DAT members outside of meetings.

What if you need to develop legitimacy with a new DAT member?

In one DAT, a staff member we call Jordan joined the DAT after the DAT had been working together for about 18 months. We noticed that Jordan frequently rejected facilitator's proposals, interrupted, and talked over other DAT members. The derailing commonly happened when the group was discussing complex issues in depth. During those times, Jordan would often advocate to move forward with making decisions and delegating tasks. In response, we observed that other group members were withdrawing from conversations. We hypothesized many issues that could be at play: Jordan could have specific expectations about DAT meetings that they disagreed with, or the power struggles between Jordan and the facilitators could also have left Jordan feeling unheard. We decided that one of us would invite Jordan to coffee to learn more. Jordan enthusiastically accepted.

At coffee, the facilitator confirmed that Jordan didn't comprehend the DAT's purpose or life cycle. This was understandable, as we had not introduced Jordan to the DAT model when they joined the DAT. The facilitator shared why things may feel slow in a DAT, as we are encouraging team building and thoughtful consideration of all voices. The facilitator also learned more about where Jordan was coming from—they were used to a fast paced, high production environment in a K–12 school situated in a large city. Jordan related that they could see their task orientation was different than others in the group, and offered to help facilitate, so more could be accomplished. The facilitator acknowledged that Jordan's executing skills were very valuable, but also encouraged them to allow the group to proceed at its own pace and to respect when other people were holding the floor. After reflecting on the conversation, we thought that Jordan's helpful energy could be redirected to a specific facilitation role. We invited Jordan to support the facilitators in collectively taking notes, which they gladly did in future meetings.

Together, these strategies helped Jordan engage much more successfully in the DAT. It also strengthened the amount of trust between Jordan and the facilitators and increased the legitimacy both Jordan and other DAT members gave to the facilitators.

Indicators of Success

Evidence of facilitator readiness

First, in conjunction with their colleagues, facilitators can assess whether they have the knowledge and skills to run a DAT. Some indicators include completion of DAT-specific training, study of published resources around facilitation and DATs, completion of a self-assessment using the *Facilitation Skills Inventory* (Bens, 2009), and involvement in a community of other facilitators.

Facilitators can assess whether they have a sufficient understanding of departmental needs and context. Indicators include being able to map or articulate cultural features of the department, understanding a range of department member views on undergraduate education, being able to explain what department members want to accomplish by forming a DAT, having knowledge of how the department currently operates, and confirming these conceptions with department members.

Evidence that facilitators have been granted legitimacy

Your interactions with DAT members and department members can indicate whether they view your authority as legitimate. Department members may ask you as a facilitator for your opinions or feedback or may acknowledge the value the facilitator role brings to a meeting. DAT members may indicate that they appreciate the time facilitators devote to process, or request that the facilitator spend more time on process or structuring the meeting. Department members may show they value your understanding of equity, diversity and inclusion issues by engaging in conversations on these topics with you. DAT and/or department members may also include facilitators in conversations outside of the DAT work, which can indicate they consider you to be a valuable member of their community.

IC Map: DAT Facilitator Behaviors

This IC Map describes the variation in which the four key roles of facilitation and the key practice of reflection may occur. Ideal facilitator behaviors are found to the left of the dotted line, and acceptable behaviors are found to the left of the bold line. This IC Map can be used by facilitators in a reflective process of self-assessment and can help highlight areas where facilitators might develop their skills. IC Maps, their uses, and guidelines on how to read them are covered in detail in Chapter 1.

Digital Toolkit
How-To Guide 1: Using Innovation Configuration Maps

Facilitators help manage the DAT's logistics.

Facilitators ensure that there are mechanisms for DAT members to communicate, keep information organized, meet regularly, and bring supplies. They continually reflect on and maintain these mechanisms.	Facilitators ensure there are mechanisms for DAT members to communicate, keep information organized, meet regularly, and bring supplies. They don't regularly maintain them or reflect on them.	One or more logistical functions is not working well.	Facilitators do not handle logistical functions with clear, concise, inclusive and professional communication.	Facilitators do not handle logistical functions in a timely fashion.

Facilitators focus on developing a high functioning team.

Facilitators reflect on all areas of team functioning. They apply appropriate techniques to establish and continually improve (1) community standards and a positive culture, (2) equitable leadership, (3) equitable participation, (4) effective conflict management, and (5) the development of change agency in individuals.	Facilitators reflect on most areas of team functioning. They apply appropriate techniques to establish and continually improve functioning in 3 of the 5 areas.	Facilitators apply techniques without having invested enough time in reflecting on the needs of the DAT, resulting in few improvements to group function.	Facilitators apply techniques, but not frequently or appropriately enough to influence team or individual behavior.	Facilitators do something to worsen team dynamics.

Facilitators provide support that is customized to the DAT's goals and needs.

Facilitators regularly reflect on team progress and needs. They provide resources (information, relationships, data, and guidance), assemble agendas, and lead activities that are highly customized to support the DAT in moving from vision to sustainable structural and cultural change, in ways that are specific to the DAT's needs.	Facilitators lead useful activities and provide resources that are partially customized to support the DAT's progress.	Facilitators lead activities and provide resources, but they are not sufficiently customized to effectively meet the DAT's goals and needs.	Facilitators lead activities, but do not offer resources.	Facilitators do not offer resources or lead activities, or they lead activities that are misaligned with the DAT's goals.

Facilitators cultivate an environment external to the DAT that is conducive to the DAT's success.

Facilitators continuously reflect on opportunities for and barriers to change.	Facilitators sometime reflect on opportunities for and barriers to change.	Facilitators do not engage in reflective practice around opportunities for and barriers to change.

Facilitators provide support that is customized to the DAT's goals and needs.

Facilitators help the DAT communicate with all relevant stakeholders. They spread awareness of the DAT's work so that it is received positively within and outside of the department.	Facilitators help the DAT communicate with some stakeholders. They are not as proactive as they could be in spreading awareness of the DAT's work.	Facilitators do not provide guidance to support DAT members in communicating with relevant stakeholders.	Facilitators share negative impressions of the DAT's work with relevant stakeholders.

Recommended Reading

Garmston, R. J., & Wellman, B. M. (2013). *The Adaptive School: A Sourcebook for Developing Collaborative Groups*. Rowman & Littlefield.

> *The Adaptive School* contains a comprehensive description of best practices for facilitators in academic institutions. We reference many of these best practices throughout this book. A third edition was released in 2016.

Dismantling Racism Works (2016). *Dismantling Racism Works Web Workbook.* www.dismantlingracism.org

> The resources created by Dismantling Racism Works support deep analysis of racism and the development of action plans for dismantling racism within institutions. The Digital Toolkit Slides 4.1–4.16 are derived from Dismantling Racism Works' article *White Supremacy Culture* by Tema Okun.
> (https://www.dismantlingracism.org/uploads/4/3/5/7/43579015/okun_-_white_sup_culture.pdf).

Kaner, S., & Doyle, M. (2007) *Facilitator's Guide to Participatory Decision-Making*. Second edition. Jossey-Bass.

> This book contains chapters on understanding group decision-making, the role of a facilitator, listening skills, facilitating open discussion, dealing with difficult dynamics, setting agendas, building sustainable agreements, and reaching closure with groups.

Binkhorst, F., Poortman, C. L., McKenney, S. E., & van Joolingen, W. R. (2018). Revealing the balancing act of vertical and shared leadership in Teacher Design Teams. *Teaching and Teacher Education, 72,* 1–12.
https://doi.org/10.1016/j.tate.2018.02.006

> This study illustrates how vertical leadership (top-down) and shared leadership can be combined effectively by teacher teams.

CHAPTER 4

Building a High Functioning Team

This chapter describes how facilitators and DAT members work together to build effective teams that co-create the DAT's culture. The DAT culture supports the behaviors of a high functioning team and supports DATs in making change. As part of the DAT model, DAT members gain skills in communication and collaboration. They learn to contribute to equitable team functioning by paying attention to the strengths in their differences and including everyone's voices in their work. In order to be a highly effective team, members learn skills in regulating their conversations and creating a positive community. The culture that DAT members and facilitators co-create can be applied outside of the DAT context.

KEY MESSAGES

- The DAT model provides opportunities to intentionally build the culture of a high functioning team.
- It is important for DAT members and facilitators to co-develop norms and practices for equitable intergroup collaboration and engagement.

Theory of Change Context

In this chapter, we describe in detail how facilitators and DAT members work together to build effective teams. The effectiveness of a team is largely influenced by its team culture. Thus, this chapter focuses on Outcome 6A: DAT members and facilitators co-create the DAT's culture. By using specific techniques to support development of behaviors and values unique to the DAT, facilitators help DAT members create a microculture that intentionally shares processes, values, and behaviors designed to support DAT members to initiate change in the larger department. Once established, the DAT culture can support DAT members in sustaining change and effecting change in the future.

OUTCOME 6A

DAT members and facilitators co-create the DAT's culture

DAT members and facilitators co-create the DAT's

1. Observable behaviors
2. Underlying values

What Role Does Culture Play for the Functioning of a Team?

Cultures are defined by implicit values and processes, as well as explicit rules, rituals, and routines, which are highly variable and unique to any given group (Schein, 1985). In a DAT, culture is created by the interactions of the facilitators and the DAT members, based on the histories, experiences, intentions, and expectations that they bring to the group. While the culture of many newly-formed groups develops in an undirected way, the facilitators of a DAT take care to support the development of a culture that will be aligned with the DAT Core Principles and that will help the DAT engage in the other components of its work. Ideally, this DAT microculture will be perpetuated by its members even after external facilitation has ceased.

A DAT forms a microculture within its department that has the potential to be more inclusive, equitable, and productive than its larger departmental culture. The DAT's external facilitators provide the modeling and experiences that support the development of these cultural features. This inclusive microculture results, in part, from the DAT's intentionally "flattened" power structure, a more collegial discourse pattern, norms of collaboration that allow for inclusive discourse, and the intention for equitable membership.

In order to nurture such a microculture, a team focuses on its own development and self-care. Self-care as a team and individual self-care are fundamental to a successful DAT. Honoring team members and using an ethic of care toward individuals supports group identity development and excellence within a team. Goals become broader than completing a project: they begin to extend to the goal of becoming a high functioning team. As a facilitator, you are in the position to recognize when teams are pushing beyond the tenet of self-care to move a body of work forward, or when they are exhibiting less care for individual team members than they could. In that case, a potential facilitator move could be to focus the DAT on self-care. Collective identity as a team is an aspiration worth striving for. Working hard with a group of people while also taking care of them allows you to develop a team identity.

The development of a positive community runs deeper than collegiality; rather, it extends to honoring every member and examining practices that have historically led to inequities or marginalization of individuals. The honesty and trust that can come from this collective work is a feedforward loop. In other words, members anticipate that they will be supported by the team. It provides a foundation so the team members can be vulnerable with one another. This allows them to work transparently and put forward ideas that might be unpopular or stretch the group. It also allows members to deeply influence each other's views of education, enabling them to implement thoughtfully designed, ambitious projects that result in substantive departmental change.

Over time, DAT members become able to articulate key elements of their DAT culture and feel capable and motivated to use their skills to enact positive cultural and structural changes in their department.

WHAT WE MEAN BY "DAT CULTURE"

Following Schein (2010), we think of culture as consisting of three layers:

- the observable behaviors in which a group engages
- the articulable values that motivate those behaviors
- the unconscious/inarticulable beliefs that underlie those values and typically go unquestioned (we won't address these further here)

By "observable behaviors," we mean the ways people act, speak, and move with respect to each other; the rituals and processes that people engage in; the ways that people organize their physical space; and the tools that people use to accomplish their work. In short, these are things that an outsider would notice about a group they encounter for the first time, even though they may not understand the reasons for the behaviors. In a DAT meeting, these behaviors may include having snacks, inserting deliberate pauses into conversation, sitting in a circle, making an analogy using jargon from the DAT members' discipline, or using a decision matrix. These behaviors may be introduced by facilitators or DAT members, but to become part of the overall DAT culture, they must be taken up and reused by multiple people in the DAT over time.

By "underlying values," we mean the beliefs, principles, attitudes, feelings, frameworks, and interpretations that underlie the observable behaviors and are articulable by the people exhibiting those behaviors. In other words, if an outsider were to ask members of a group to explain why they behave in the ways they do, these are the answers they would give. In the context of a DAT, the Core Principles are an example of underlying values that the facilitators bring to the group. The department can also have its own underlying values that DAT members bring to the group. For example, the values may be related to academia in general (e.g., "We must respect academic freedom"); their discipline (e.g., "Scientists are only swayed by data"); or their particular department (e.g., "We are very friendly and open in departmental communication").

How Do Facilitators Support Positive Interactions in a DAT?

It can take time, community engagement, and explicit attention to many aspects of the group to develop an effective team. As we will explore in this section, facilitators introduce "process skills" during each meeting to support the DAT in: (1) creating and following community standards; (2) learning and engaging in practices that confront oppressive situations and favor equitable participation and leadership; and (3) helping teams manage conflict and determine a productive leadership structure.

Principle 4:
Collaboration among group members is enjoyable, productive, and rewarding.

Setting appropriate expectations within the DAT is equally important and should be a goal early in the formation of the group. Terrell Strayhorn's book, *College Students' Sense of Belonging* (2019) stresses that in order to allow individuals to feel like they belong, it is vital to know their expectations.

Creating community standards

An important element of teams that work effectively together is that everyone knows and agrees to standards of behavior and professionalism they expect of one another. Establishing community standards gives everyone an opportunity to express how they like to work and be treated. This builds trust and can prevent problems before they start. There are many ways for a group to define and adopt a set of community standards. DAT facilitators usually lead members in developing community standards in the very first DAT meeting. In the second meeting, members adopt the summarized standards, and in subsequent meetings, they are posted on the wall. Periodically, but especially when new members join the DAT, the community standards are reviewed and are opened to revision. When behaviors that counter a DAT's community standards occur, facilitators open up a conversation space for reflection, whether in the DAT or in individual consultation.

Digital Toolkit
Slide 6.3:
Community
Standards

Engaging in rituals

Globally, humans build community over rituals, food, and in small talk about each other's lives. One important way DAT facilitators support this is by providing an abundance of both healthy and indulgent snacks, including chocolate. They provide finger food snacks, along with tongs, paper plates, and napkins to allow DAT members to easily and hygienically manage them. DAT facilitators also begin most meetings with a quick community builder—an inclusive conversation unrelated to the work world.

Attending to leadership structures and power dynamics

Digital Toolkit

How-To Guide 7: Building Community

Facilitators often use process skills to encourage DAT members to consider different models of leadership and their underlying power dynamics—and to think through how incorporating these different models could benefit the DAT. While there are several types of leadership compatible with the DAT model, this model emphasizes equitable, distributed leadership that involves all members. Distributed leadership is emphasized because academic cultures are often based on shared governance. Change within an academic culture is unlikely to be sustainable unless all stakeholders feel like they or their representatives have had a meaningful seat at the table, which includes input to decision-making. DAT facilitators avoid weighing in on decisions, unless they relate to their areas of expertise. In doing so, they avoid making alliances that could affect group cohesion, and they gain members' trust in that they, as outsiders, will not hold undue influence on a project that is "owned" by the department.

DAT members may have a strong sense of how a leader behaves and acts as a result of their departmental culture. For example, in some departments, faculty may be accustomed to being told what to do by their department chairs and may not have experience with processes involved in working on a consensus-based team. This could result in a mismatch of expectations with the DAT model.

Digital Toolkit

Slide 5.5: Facilitation vs. Leadership

One way to mitigate a mismatch in leadership expectations is to be explicit about the roles that facilitators do and do not play. Leaders develop a vision and set agendas in line with that vision. Facilitators help the group develop a shared vision and assemble agendas based on the group's input and goals. Leaders advocate for paths and make decisions when the group is at an impasse. Facilitators stay neutral to paths and help the group make decisions. Leaders specifically attend to productivity and delegate when necessary, whereas facilitators attend more to process and help group members delegate among themselves. It is important to remind the group of these differences, as well as make it clear why facilitators don't take on leadership roles.

Considering leadership also requires reflecting on the organizational structure as a whole. Some DAT groups embody more networked structures where power is decentralized and there is no clear leader. Networked structures can be beneficial because everyone has a say in decisions and there is no single point of failure. Other groups are more hierarchical or top-down. These structures are beneficial toward getting work done quickly and having a clear division of roles.

Digital Toolkit

Slide 9.1: Hierarchical vs. Networked Organizations

In some cases, it is necessary to moderate power centers. Facilitators can do this by inviting DAT members to reflect on the spectrum between two organizational structure models (flat and hierarchical) and to consider what structures align with their values and goals. Facilitators also can discuss how flatter organizational structures align with the DAT's principles: "Students are partners in the educational process" and "Work is grounded in a commitment to equity, inclusion, and social justice." Deliberately emphasizing that the work is a result of a collective, not an individual, effort will encourage members to consider a flatter structure.

Managing conflict

When needed, facilitators support teams and individual members in managing both chronic and acute conflicts. One of the first steps in dealing with conflict is to accept conflict as a normal part of a team's work. Facilitators communicate this fact to the team in various ways, including with the deliberate attention paid to the "process skills" at the beginning of each meeting and by referring back to process skills previously introduced as they come up during subsequent meetings. There are several examples available in the Digital Toolkit of how to manage and reduce conflict using process skills, including "knowing who makes decisions," paying attention to the six Core Principles and the eight Norms of Collaboration, and understanding and recognizing the "Anti-Norms." These resources will be covered in more detail later in the chapter.

It's natural that team members bring diverse perspectives and opinions. Such differences in ideas can often be productive for teams, as it helps members learn from one another and see things from others' points of view (Garmston & Wellman, 2013). We refer to conflict that stems from substantive differences in ideas and leads to learning as cognitive conflict. Dialogue is key for ensuring that cognitive conflict leads to productive outcomes. While productive conflict can feel uncomfortable for team members, this discomfort is an important part of learning.

A less productive form of conflict is affective conflict, where conflict becomes personal and emotional. Such conflict can often lead to aggressiveness or apathy. Having productive norms for communication can support teams in avoiding affective conflict. In some cases, one or more group members can approach conflict from an affective perspective, which can hold back groups and block progress. Creating opportunities for one-on-one dialogue with members (e.g., taking them out to coffee) can help identify root causes of a conflict, help them feel heard, and help them understand different perspectives.

When conflict happens, it is important to identify the root concerns underlying the group members' discomfort—these could include concerns over scarce resources, power, diversity, task avoidance, or privacy (Garmston & Wellman, 2013). When attempting to resolve conflict in a group setting, it is important to articulate the root causes, underlying assumptions, and whether the conflict is largely cognitive or affective. In these situations, it is particularly helpful to be an external facilitator, as you can offer an outside, big-picture perspective. The "9 Whys" activity from Liberating Structures (www.liberatingstructures.com) or "The 5 Whys for Inquiry" prompt from the National School Reform Faculty (www.nsrfharmony.com) can be used in a group or individually to help uncover root causes. Holding group members accountable to community standards and productive norms can also help the team engage in more cognitive conflict, as opposed to affective conflict.

Effective teams do not fear open conflict, but rather value the examination of hard issues. Facilitators should avoid emphasizing or reinforcing "politeness" as a cover for conflict avoidance within teams. Instead, they should affirm those who raise hard issues. Social norms often avoid discomfort, which can reinforce oppressive systems and eschew change (Dismantling Racism Works, June 2020). Effective teams do create opportunities for reflecting on conflict. This reflective time allows members to name and learn from mistakes, give apologies and respond with forgiveness, as well as develop ideas for how conflict can be handled differently in the future.

What if the DAT looks to facilitators for leadership?

In one DAT, members expressed a need to be told what to do and looked to the facilitators to provide this kind of leadership. This most likely arose from a departmental culture in which committees were given specific charges and committee chairs were responsible for tending to them. This DAT eventually chose to put one of the members in a leadership role and asked the DAT facilitators to take a lesser role in guiding the group.

For DATs working within top-down leadership cultures, the emphasis on shared governance in the DAT model may be particularly challenging. These DATs benefit from facilitators being explicit about their roles and how shared governance supports the DAT model Core Principles. They also benefit from introducing topics of leadership early and having open discussion about the kind of leadership structures they want to have in place.

How Do Facilitators Ensure Equitable Participation in a DAT?

DAT facilitators pay close attention to equity in participation and decision-making. When DAT members solicit equitable participation from one another and empower everyone to engage in decision-making, they ensure that they make one another feel heard and valued. Projects arising from teams with equitable participation tend to be stronger and are more likely to succeed because they are developed with a diversity of ideas (Schein, 2010).

Equity is a concept that is often misunderstood. One definition of equity is that it means providing resources and access to those whose position in society is marginalized. On a high functioning team, all members feel equally valued, even though they naturally differ in their abilities, experiences, and contributions to the team. To achieve equity, specific actions can be taken to reduce bias and favoritism, whether unconscious or conscious, implicit or overt. Academia is a hierarchical system which places staff and students below faculty, and non-tenured faculty below tenured faculty. The United States has a hierarchical culture and political system which still places white people above people of color (Dismantling Racism Works, 2016). Individuals carry these biases within themselves and express them in their patterns of speech, attention, and action. Therefore, we can expect these and other biases to be present in every DAT.

DAT facilitators draw on an extensive set of tools to guide a team toward more equitable participation. They observe the personalities of members and levels of participation—and they step in to regulate the flow of conversation or advocate for hearing from quieter voices as necessary. They also raise awareness of the strengths that different personalities and minds bring to the table: internal and external processing; extroversion and introversion; and aptitudes for strategic thinking, influencing, relationship-building, and execution.

Tools available to facilitators for implementing equitable participation represent entire fields of study. Here, we focus on: (1) confronting oppressive and non-equitable situations, (2) valuing strength in difference, (3) being intentional in conversation, and (4) enduring equitable participation of students.

Confronting oppressive and non-equitable situations

Equitable participation can be encouraged and supported through a concerted effort to confront history and power dynamics that are at odds with equity. Although there can be no "safe spaces", facilitators can establish "brave spaces" where members intentionally confront challenging perspectives, share their truths, and approach working on a diverse team with openness and honesty.

A powerful way to teach DAT members about equitable participation is to ask them to consider what it is not. To do so, we have developed process skills from the Dismantling Racism Works Web Workbook, which presents a framework for understanding white supremacy and other oppressive cultures (Dismantling Racism Works, 2016 and June 2020). This framework draws attention to how qualities emphasized in oppressive cultures, such as perfectionism, defensiveness, and power hoarding, inhibit positive and equitable collaboration and maintain oppressive structures. For example, defensiveness causes criticism to be viewed as inappropriate or unwelcome, which makes it challenging to deal with existing concerns or to raise future ones. In DAT meetings, we call these qualities Anti-Norms, as they work to degrade positive group function. Slides we use to illuminate these topics for the DAT members are found in the Digital Toolkit. As an extension activity, DAT members could form a reading group focused on the workbook created by Dismantling Racism Works or similar resources to further the group's understanding of oppressive cultures.

It is important that facilitators address oppressive and non-equitable situations and interactions that may happen in the DAT as soon as they occur or shortly thereafter. Although it is not inevitable that these moments might arise, it is probable, and therefore it would serve the facilitators well to be as prepared as possible. These types of situations allow members to learn from one another. Facilitators should proactively seek opportunities to gain skills in this area before working in a DAT. Studying and training will help develop judgement, as will talking to other facilitators who have experience in navigating these issues.

Micro-aggression is a term for the commonplace interaction in which someone knowingly or unknowingly marginalizes a member of a non-dominant group. Depending on the situation, facilitators can choose to address the situation as it happens or after it happens with one or more of the group members. One framework for confronting microaggressions is called "Open the Front Door" (OTFD), a mnemonic name which stands for Observe, Think, Feel, and Desire. In using OTFD, a facilitator might say, "I noticed that you referred to female students as 'girls' (*observe*). I think that such language is infantilizing to women (*think*) and it makes me feel uncomfortable (*feel*). I would like us to use more age-appropriate language when we talk about female students (*desire*)."

Other forms of oppression that facilitators may find useful to explore with DATs are implicit and explicit bias, cultural proficiency, stereotype threat, and privilege. Ideally, DAT members will learn to self-monitor their contributions, make inquiries about one another's ideas, and take into account variation in individual personalities, experience, and ability, as they strive for more equitable participation.

Principle 6:
Work is grounded in a commitment to equity, inclusion, and social justice.

Digital Toolkit
Slides 4.0–4.16: Common Organizational Pitfalls

DATS IN REAL LIFE

What if power dynamics lead to conflicts between DAT members?

One of our DATs worked together for a semester and a half before a conflict between a faculty member and a graduate student came to light. A graduate student had joined the team about six weeks prior to the conflict. They had jumped right into the project work, taking the lead on developing a tool that could provide useful data for the DAT's project. They had clearly invested some time in their work.

After the graduate student presented their work in a meeting, one tenured faculty member pointedly criticized this work and stated that it wasn't relevant. Another tenured faculty, one of the founders of the DAT, pointedly disagreed with the criticism. Multiple DAT members contributed thoughts to soften the criticism or direct conversation toward a different topic, but the critical faculty member was quite persistent. Facilitators had already been working to manage the dynamics this faculty member introduced to the group, due to their tendency to interrupt and push for decision-making before all ideas were on the table.

To defuse tension in the moment, facilitators used paraphrasing and acknowledged each member's varied contributions to the project. After the meeting, facilitators learned that the faculty member was the graduate student's major advisor. Therefore, the typical faculty-student power dynamics were heightened in this situation. Facilitators feared that the graduate student would be upset, or that the graduate student's DAT activities would affect their relationship or work with their advisor. They also were concerned that one or the other member would drop out of the DAT.

Digital Toolkit
*Slides 4.2–4:
Either/Or Thinking
and Sense of
Urgency*

For the following meeting, DAT facilitators prepared process skills that were related to the tone of the criticisms made by the faculty member: either/or thinking and sense of urgency (Dismantling Racism Works, 2016). A facilitator checked in with the graduate student to see if they were comfortable discussing those process skills, and they said that it sounded productive. The facilitators also checked in with the two tenured faculty members who had engaged contentiously in the conversation for their input and shared with them that they were concerned about power dynamics between the DAT members. Specifically, the facilitators sent this email (names have been replaced with letters):

> Hi X and Y,
>
> We noticed that the conversation about Z's work was more combative than most DAT meetings so far, particularly between you two. This concerns us because it puts Z in a difficult position, as a graduate student, to respond to critiques from those who have seniority.
>
> Do you have suggestions for how we can keep the conversation tomorrow constructively critical? While we think that disagreement about ideas/ implementation is productive toward making progress, we would like to keep

the conversation less tense.

A draft agenda for tomorrow's meeting is available for you to review. We welcome your ideas.

Best,
DAT Facilitators

The critical faculty member did not attend the next meeting. The facilitators built two opportunities for reflection into the meeting agenda: one to introduce the process skills, and another to reflect on the "fact that there was disagreement on the project". During the DAT meeting, the facilitators emphasized that conflict is a normal part of groups and solicited DAT members' ideas on how to productively deal with conflict using the prompt: What are tools around handling conflict and expressing criticism constructively? Faculty, graduate students, and undergrad students all contributed to this discussion.

The DAT did not see tensions rise to this level during future meetings. The group continued making rapid progress on their projects. The graduate student at the center of the conflict continued to take a leadership role on several aspects of the project, and later presented some of the work they did for the DAT at the university's annual symposium for education research. A couple of months later, the critical faculty member left the DAT amicably at the conclusion of the academic year, citing too many administrative duties.

Valuing strength in difference

Human variation is endless and wonderful. But when people view difference as a deficiency or barrier rather than a source of strength, they struggle to work effectively. A powerful framing that facilitators apply to these situations is to view differences as a source of strength. The more dimensions of difference a group contains, the more the group benefits from the particular strengths that come along with each dimension. However, these strengths can only be leveraged if the group values the differences which generate them. In this section, we focus on developing the concept of Strength in Difference by examining differences in personality. The Strength in Difference concept includes many other dimensions, including gender, race, ethnicity, and disability.

Principle 6:
Work is grounded in a commitment to equity, inclusion, and social justice.

Here, we want to address some of the personality variations among people that frequently affect group dynamics and can even lead group members to conclude they cannot work together. For example, group members may identify as introverts and extroverts. In U.S. culture, extroversion is valued over introversion, so extroverts and introverts may enter the room expecting to be listened to or to be ignored, respectively (Cain, 2013). These personality traits can carry with them certain patterns of interaction and talk. Extroverts may dominate conversation or distract the group with social talk since they gain energy from social interaction. Introverts may not share their excellent ideas or struggle to enter the conversation and may take some time to integrate into the DAT community. Another way group members differ is in how they think through information and ideas. Some prefer to have time to think on their own before discussing—they are *internal processors*. Others, *external processors*, prefer to think things through in conversation with someone else.

Another dimension of personality are the cognitive strengths members bring to the table (Rath, 2007). Rath describes 34 evidence-based traits that people draw on in navigating the world, which are grouped into four domains: Strategic Thinking, Relationship-Building, Executing, and Influencing. While most people's prevalent traits fall into several domains, they usually have a domain of greatest strength. Group members with different dominant domains may struggle to understand one another. However, strengths in each of the four domains are essential for a group to succeed in a project of the scale that Departmental Action Teams take on. It's a facilitator's job to inform group members about how they are dependent on one another's strengths to accomplish the project, and to generate understanding of the tension that naturally arises.

Principle 4:
Collaboration among group members is enjoyable, productive, and rewarding.

DAT members may engage with the DAT model differently due to their varying strengths. For example, some members will strongly appreciate the time spent on processing and group function. Others who like to think about big picture, lofty outcomes, may resonate with the activities focused on developing a shared vision. Still others who enjoy problem solving might most appreciate the conversations around planning and implementing a project. Asking DAT members to reflect on their own strengths, lived experiences, backgrounds, level of comfort, and how these characteristics will affect their engagement in DAT activities can draw attention to the types of activities DAT members prefer and make them aware of the tension that could emerge when engaging in DAT activities they do not prefer. Recognizing that certain activities may cause feelings of discomfort can help DAT members become aware of these feelings, and either go outside of their comfort zone or mitigate them throughout a meeting.

How do facilitators help a group to view differences as strengths? Typically, short conversations on the topic are woven throughout several meetings. For example, as members settle in for a meeting, small talk naturally arises and people learn a little bit about each other's lives. Facilitators teach members about types of personality and cognitive differences and explore the strengths that each brings to the group. They solicit conversation about group members' personal experiences with these areas of difference, discuss whether the DAT as a group has particular strengths, and invite members to consider how they can use their understanding of these strengths productively. This activity can help to explore and understand how each person is unique and allow people to feel valued and included within a diverse group. A slide that can be used to support these conversations is found in the Digital Toolkit.

Digital Toolkit
Slide 6.2: Strength in Difference

In their journals or reflections, facilitators think about the strengths that members exhibited during meetings and use this understanding to make guiding suggestions. For example, a facilitator might observe that an individual is comfortable in the influencing domain and might therefore ask if they would be interested in taking a role of being the group's liaison to the department. If members are interested in exploring their individual differences more deeply, a facilitator could refer the group to trainings focused on strengths that are offered by some institutions. To build group identity around strengths, facilitators periodically gather input from members about their accomplishments, tensions, strengths, and areas of need—and summarize it in a way that invites discussion. The *Using DAT Member Input How-To Guide* offers a structure for this activity.

Digital Toolkit
How-To Guide 8: Using DAT Member Input

Once concepts and vocabulary related to personality differences have been introduced, facilitators can reference them in the flow of a meeting. For example, a facilitator might say: "Let me check in with the internal processors—does anyone have another idea, or need some time to think?" or "There were a lot of ideas in there! You are a great external processor. Can I try to summarize the key idea, and if I didn't get it right, will you let me know?" Or, "We are at the point in this project where we will need to draw on your strengths in execution".

While it is important that groups leverage individuals' strengths, it is also important to encourage individuals' growth in other areas. Qualities of individuals are not innate; they are honed and practiced. Skilled facilitators notice individuals' areas for growth and support their learning in areas that may feel unfamiliar or uncomfortable. If a group member tends to take on roles in one domain, facilitators can invite them to take on a role in another domain as a learning opportunity.

Facilitators need to constantly tie a group's explorations back to the core concept of Strength in Difference by asking members to reflect on why difference feels challenging to navigate for both individuals and groups; how they distinguish between identifying and judging difference; and what goals can be set for exploring differences that they may not understand or feel comfortable with. By emphasizing the notion that drawing on the Strength in Difference concept will make for a more successful endeavor, facilitators channel the group's attention to difference in a productive way. This focus helps the group develop an identity that is more cohesive, yet still honors individual differences, backgrounds, and lived experiences.

Being intentional in conversations

Euro-American culture tends to value expediency, a quick pace, and fast decision-making. Other cultures value the inclusion of everyone's voices ahead of these values. Facilitators can help DAT members broaden their notions about conversations, recognize that all forms of conversation can advance sharing and understanding, and learn which strategies are more productive at which times.

As a facilitator, you should be careful not to inadvertently privilege one culture's preference for communication over another. Keep in mind that group members may hold different sets of shared assumptions. As facilitators, it is our job to help the work of the DAT to be productive and for interactions to be respectful—while facilitating conversations between potentially different cultures with contrasting communication norms. For example, conflicting communication can arise due to differences between direct and indirect communication styles, informal and formal speaking styles, task-oriented approaches and those that focus on first establishing a relationship, or cultural tendencies to take words at face value and tendencies to infer a deeper meaning.

There are several concepts about conversation that are helpful for facilitators to introduce and later reference in subsequent meetings. High functioning groups talk in ways that are different from the ways we might typically speak. In particular, the discourse of high functioning groups is planned, intentional, and attentive. Facilitators pay special attention to whether discourse is benefitting the group. One technique that facilitators use to help a team practice this kind of monitoring is called W.A.I.T.: Why Am I Talking? W.A.I.T. encourages members to internally reflect on the purpose of a contribution before voicing that contribution, in order to promote more intentional conversation. Facilitators may also "go meta" to ask the group whether a particular conversation is productive, and whether any member might like to take it in a different direction.

Norms of Collaboration, Additionally, the Norms of Collaboration are a set of conversation tools and standards that help participants engage in positive and equitable group processes (Garmston & Wellman, 2013). There are eight norms, each starting with a "p" for mnemonic purposes. We find it useful to group them into two categories: those focused on regulating the conversation and those focused on creating a positive community. All these norms serve the goal of making the group inclusive and equitable. Ideally, groups will come to naturally employ all the norms during their meetings. We typically introduce one or two norms per meeting for the first four to eight meetings. After describing the norms using a slide or handout, we invite DAT members' thoughts.

Digital Toolkit
Slides 3.0–3.9:
Norms of
Collaboration,
Handout 4:
Norms of
Collaboration

NORMS OF COLLABORATION FOR REGULATING CONVERSATIONS

Pausing slows down the conversation. It provides for "wait time," which has been shown to dramatically improve thinking. It signals to others that their ideas and comments are worth thinking about, dignifies their contributions, and implicitly encourages future participation. Pausing enhances understanding and questioning, and greatly increases the quality of decision-making. In cultures that don't often promote introspection, pausing inherently changes the rhythm of discourse. Requesting a pace change (e.g., "could we take a minute to think more about this before responding") can be helpful over time in promoting pausing.

Paraphrasing involves recasting another's thoughts into one's own words. Paraphrasing helps to reduce group tension by communicating an attempt to understand another member. Paraphrasing can advance the conversation when it is used to: (1) acknowledge and clarify what has been said; (2) summarize and organize ideas; and (3) shift the focus of the conversation to a higher or lower level of abstraction (e.g., providing examples, making generalizations, or observing crosscutting themes). Using different types of paraphrasing helps members of a team hear and understand each other as they evaluate data and formulate decisions. It is helpful when the speaker signals their intention to paraphrase ("So, you're suggesting…", or "I think I'm hearing . . .") and focuses the paraphrase to a level that helps further the group's thinking.

Probing for specificity seeks to clarify terminology, information, ideas, feelings, or perceptions that are not yet fully understood. Probing can be either specific or open-ended, depending upon the circumstances. One might ask, "Tell me more about. . ." or "What makes you say that?" or "I didn't understand what you meant, could you explain?" Recognize that care is needed in probing, as the tone of voice used could feel supportive, harsh, or intimidating. It is helpful to ask for clarification of vague nouns and pronouns (e.g., "they"), action words (e.g., "improve"), comparators (e.g., "best"), rules (e.g., "should"), and universal quantifiers (e.g., "everyone").

Pursuing a balance between advocacy and inquiry helps balance these two necessary components of collaborative work. The intention of advocacy is to influence the thinking of others by sharing your point of view. The intention of inquiry is to better understand others' thinking by asking questions. Highly effective teams consciously attempt to balance these two components. Inquiry provides for greater understanding. Advocacy leads to decision-making. Maintaining a balance between advocating for a position and inquiring about the positions held by others helps create a genuine learning community and the synergy needed to accomplish great work.

Putting ideas on the table and pulling them off provides grist for collaborative progress. Ideas are the heart of a meaningful conversation. Members need to feel safe to put their ideas on the table for consideration. To have an idea be received in the spirit in which you offer it, label your intentions: "This is one idea…" or "Here's a thought…" In advanced functioning groups, once an idea is "put on the table," it is often owned by the group and examined for utility on its merits, rather than connected to specific individuals and evaluated on that basis. Recognizing when an idea may be blocking dialogue or derailing the process is equally important. In this case, it's helpful to suggest the group "consider taking this off the table". A "parking lot" or holding area in the meeting minutes can be used to document ideas that are temporarily taken off the table for members to return to later. This signals to members that all ideas are valued.

NORMS OF COLLABORATION FOR COMMUNITY BUILDING

Presuming positive intentions is the assumption that other members of the team are acting from positive and constructive intentions, even if we disagree with their ideas. Presuming positive intentions is not a passive state. Instead, it involves seeking out disagreement in the spirit of greater understanding and it can be expressed through speech patterns like "yes, but." Presuming positive intentions is a foundation of trust: it promotes healthy disagreement and reduces the likelihood of misunderstanding and emotional conflict. A useful way to frame this is to ask, "Why would a reasonable person do this/think this?" (See "Crucial Conversations" in the recommended readings section at the end of this chapter.)

Paying attention to self and others involves bring aware of how information is shared, how it is said, and how others are responding to it. As we pay attention to someone else's way of processing information, we are better able to communicate with them. When we pay attention to self and others, we recognize when we may have been speaking too much or too little. When others may not have had equitable opportunities to share, we invite them to do so. It is helpful to be curious about other people's impressions and understandings, but not to be judgmental. A helpful question to ask is, "What am I pretending not to notice?" (See "Crucial Conversations" recommended reading at the end of this chapter)

Practicing cultural proficiency involves seeking perspectives, knowledge, and skills in order to promote inclusion, equity, and social justice. Individuals and teams developing cultural proficiency recognize that multiple viewpoints enrich group expertise and they seek out viewpoints that are not represented. Cultural proficiency is grounded in the understanding that none of us is ever fully culturally proficient. Those who work toward cultural proficiency recognize their learning is never complete and that their way may not be the best or the only way. They recognize the systemic nature of oppression and the need to take small and large actions that advance an equitable society. Practicing cultural proficiency requires individuals to understand their own cultures and identities, and to recognize they may have societal privileges which disadvantage others. People practicing cultural proficiency seek out and honor the histories, perspectives, and cultural practices of others. They regularly reflect on their own progress toward being more informed, skilled in action, and inclusive. These concepts can be put into action by asking questions and displaying curiosity about people's lived experiences and unique perspectives, practicing self-reflections, and seeking out professional development in inclusive meeting practices.

DATS IN REAL LIFE

What if DAT members are not following community norms?

Digital Toolkit
How-To Guide 8: Using DAT Member Input, How-To Guide 2: How to Conduct a Listening Tour

One of our early DATs had a lot of member turnover over a year and a half. Members developed habits of derailing the agenda, pontificating, and interrupting one another. It was clear that they were not listening intently to one another. After completing a Listening Tour with several DAT members, the facilitators decided to present the feedback to the members. They identified two areas of tension in the group: purpose and interactions. During the process skill portion of the meeting, the facilitators summarized what they heard (making sure individuals remained anonymous) and some of what they had observed that members had not mentioned.

The facilitators were concerned that a whole group discussion following these observations might spark blaming or complaining. To foster more productive behavior, facilitators handed out notecards and asked DAT members to respond to the prompt "How would you like us to work together?" They asked members to specifically write down group norms to adopt and how they would like facilitators to support them. The facilitators then synthesized all the input into seven core values, which they wrote on a big post-it note. They reviewed this note at the following meeting and asked for edits. They then displayed this note during every subsequent meeting. This process allowed all members of the group to express themselves more freely than they might if they had to state their responses via a process that attached their name to their comments.

We have collected feedback on notecards in many DATs. At other times, we have asked DAT members for input when we have had a chance to talk with them one-on-one after a DAT meeting, at one of our weekly open coffee hours, or in a short email. All these methods help facilitators know what is important to DAT members about the group's functioning and inform the process skills that facilitators choose moving forward.

Digital Toolkit
Slides 6.4–6.6: Convergent and Divergent Conversations

Function of Conversations. Another concept that facilitators typically introduce early in a DAT's formation is whether a conversation is convergent or divergent.

Divergent conversations focus on generating lots of ideas, exploring contingencies, and encouraging different perspectives. Conversations stay positive when group members bring a "yes, and" attitude to such discussions and trust that the strongest ideas will be selected later. Facilitators often use brainstorming activities to guide these conversations in an equitable and efficient way. These and similar techniques are preferred for guiding divergent conversation, especially in large groups, because dominant individuals can tend to crowd out the voices of others and cause fewer ideas to come to light. Repeated experience with a dominated divergent conversation can lead those with quieter voices and personalities, or those with less power in the institution, to self-censor. Nonetheless, despite their shortcomings, there are occasions when short, whole-group divergent conversations are needed.

In contrast, the goal in convergent conversations is to narrow down options and make decisions. For such conversations to be equitable, it's important for facilitators to pay attention to how group members are exercising leadership and to take steps to give all members a chance to be a part of the decision-making. Facilitators often do this by soliciting information about members' opinions or priorities using sticky notes or notecards and compiling that input to display to the group. They might then ask open-ended questions that frame a discussion: "What are decisions we need to make? How might we come to a decision about this?" When it appears that a group has implicitly accepted a decision, facilitators use questions to the entire group to clarify the nature of the decision and determine whether the group is, in fact, in consensus.

Facilitators can bring awareness to which type of conversation is intended for a particular meeting segment by labeling it as convergent or divergent right in the agenda. They can also inquire whether members agree with the types of conversation that are planned and invite changes to the agenda. Conflict can emerge when members disagree about whether they are having a convergent or divergent conversation. In that situation, facilitators can use questions to keep the conversation in bounds. If someone pushes for a decision during a dialogue, facilitators can ask if people are ready for deciding. On the other hand, if someone starts to bring up tangential ideas during a focused discussion, facilitators can ask if that is an area on which the group wants to focus their time. If it is not, facilitators can ask if they would like to put the new ideas in a "parking lot" in the group's meeting minutes document.

Digital Toolkit
How-To Guide 5: Documenting and Reflecting on Meetings

Both of these conversation types are critical for effective group communication. It can be very productive to alternate between divergent and convergent conversation within one meeting, or across several meetings. It also works well for facilitators to alternate between divergent idea generation with the larger department (perhaps via surveys or focus groups) and convergent processing of those ideas within the DAT.

Ensuring equitable participation of students

Empowering undergraduate student voices is important if students are going to be well-served by their undergraduate education. It is important for DATs to elicit student voices by actively asking for their perspectives and avoiding assumptions about how a student will react, what they are feeling, or how they will be impacted by decisions about their program of study. It is also important to recognize that student DAT members may be searching for their place on campus as they are also seeking their sense of belonging within the DAT. Facilitators should be sensitive to this dual struggle while respecting their perspective as valuable. Just as it is important for facilitators to gain legitimacy with a DAT, student DAT members also must gain their legitimacy within the group. Students can provide valuable insight about their own experiences (e.g., with faculty, with advisors, and with classmates). Very often, they can also provide the most accurate information about the impact of a program of study and how it is experienced by its participants.

Principle 1:
Students are partners in the educational process

It is important for DAT members to value contributions from students. While non-students may make assumptions about factors that may influence the student experience, they will have limited knowledge about these factors and how they impact students. The Ideal Student Visioning activity (see Chapter 6) can help highlight what DAT members may be missing in regard to the student experience. This activity can be coupled with self-reflection, with members reflecting upon their involvement in factors tied to the undergraduate experience.

What if participation on the team is inequitable?

We had new graduate student members join one of our DATs after about a year. Another graduate student had joined at the beginning and took a very proactive role in the project. One of the strengths of this member was that they could envision the big picture in the future and articulate a detailed path to get there. However, facilitators noticed that this person was unintentionally dominating the conversation and the direction of the group. We were particularly concerned because the new graduate student members were not contributing as many ideas as they potentially could and one of them showed signs of disengagement.

Digital Toolkit
How-To Guide 8: Using DAT Member Input

The facilitators decided to apply two interventions to the situation. During process skill time, the facilitators collected feedback on notecards. DAT members were given the following prompt to respond to: "I feel motivated to collaborate on a project when…" They were also asked to include any other comments they had. Notecards were digitized and anonymized. The following meeting, facilitators displayed the list of comments, which included the statements "…I feel my opinion is valid", "I can contribute", "People rely on me", "Working with rather than for someone", and "Whole team is bought in". The group was invited to discuss their reflections on the feedback. Then, facilitators introduced the process skill Step Up / Step Back, which guides members to consider how much they are contributing and takes steps to correct any imbalance on their own. Alternatively, they could have engaged the group in looking at the collaborative norm "Paying attention to self and others".

Digital Toolkit
Slide 6.7: Step Up / Step Back

It is important to recognize that when some members dominate and others are reticent, these behavioral patterns feed into each other and can create a negative spiral (Tannen, 1987). It's valuable to introduce corrective process skills for inequitable participation as soon as they appear and be prepared to re-introduce them when new members join the group.

How Do Facilitators Teach Process Skills to DAT Members?

Devoting meeting time to process skills is valuable for many reasons. Facilitators can make connections between team skills and the outcomes that the DAT is trying to produce. Facilitators often explain that process skills help the team to "Go Slow to Go Fast." Taking the time to learn to work together effectively and equitably allows for much more efficient teamwork later. The facilitators can deepen the team's expertise by selecting some skills to practice more intentionally, and by being more explicit in explaining how process skills work and how they are chosen to fit a particular situation. Over time, DAT members become equipped to enact these skills in other settings and grow as effective change agents.

DAT facilitators spend less than ten minutes of each meeting discussing process skills. They may devote a segment of the agenda to a single skill, or they may distribute discussions of skills throughout a meeting as relevant opportunities arise. These generative and purposeful opportunities to reflect on ways of working are not prescribed; instead, they are tailored to the immediate concerns of the DAT. In planning process skills to introduce, facilitators pay attention to the department's context, including resource allocation, size of department, team members' collegiality, and any other relevant history.

The Index of DAT Activities and Process Skills on page 158 lists specific skills and activities that facilitators can use to guide a DAT during different stages of the DAT life cycle. It divides activities into three categories: enhancing group functioning, guiding project work, and engaging the department. It is a useful tool for facilitators to reference when they are thinking about skills and activities they might use to provide customized support to DATs.

Indicators of Success

Evidence of an effective DAT culture

When an effective DAT culture has developed, DAT members will begin to employ facilitation techniques that have been introduced or used by facilitators. For example, a DAT member might verbalize their use of a norm (e.g., "To paraphrase…") or facilitation strategy ("Let's have divergent conversation first."). DAT members or facilitators can validate the use of these norms, (e.g., "nice paraphrasing!"), which reinforces them as features of the DAT culture. Note that a major goal of DAT co-facilitators is to foster the development of a self-sufficient "DAT culture". The work of facilitators presented in this chapter covers the development of DAT culture, but not of self-sufficient DAT culture. That level of development is described in Chapter 8.

Evidence of an effective DAT culture in development

There are two intermediate indicators that demonstrate a DAT culture is developing. The first is the ability of DAT members to describe features of the DAT's process and culture. This is revealed when DAT members accurately explain the DAT's ways of working, structure, and goals to other people, including new members and each other. We have found this often occurs when we meet DAT members for open coffee hours (a practice we established to encourage communication between and within DATs) and they talk to people who are not on the DAT. We also hear statements like these during interviews and focus groups.

Further evidence that an effective DAT culture is developing emerges when DAT members reference any of the six Core Principles. As DAT culture becomes more adopted, conversations, actions, and dispositions related to the principles can be observed in a DATs work. Of primary importance is the principle acknowledging the commitment to equity, diversity and inclusion, and its use as a lens to ground thinking and action.

The second indicator is that DAT members value the DAT process. This is revealed when DAT members indicate they learned something valuable from the process skills facilitators presented, when they positively reference process skills, or when they positively reflect on how the DAT's approach contributed to the success of their endeavors. They may also reveal that they value the DAT when they show appreciation for the community the DAT has formed and how facilitators support the DAT with logistics, expertise, guidance, connections, and even food. Facilitators can also gather information about how members value the DAT by conducting Exit Interviews, when external facilitation is winding down.

IC Map: DAT Member Participation

Digital Toolkit
How-To Guide 1:
Using Innovation
Configuration
Maps

The Innovation Configuration (IC) Map for this chapter covers DAT member participation. This map highlights DAT member behaviors that reflect their participation in the group and its work. Facilitators might refer to this map if the DAT appears to be stalling. It can help identify areas to jumpstart the group's progress. IC Maps, their uses, and guidelines on how to read them are covered in detail in Chapter 1.

DAT members feel that facilitation supports the DAT in accomplishing its goals.

DAT members view most or all facilitation strategies as aiding them in accomplishing their goals.	DAT members view a handful of facilitation strategies as aiding them in accomplishing their goals.	DAT members do not view facilitators as aiding them in accomplishing their goals.

DAT members engage in process skills.

DAT members take responsibility for practicing process skills during meetings (e.g., one group member keeps track of process skills used during the meeting).	DAT members actively learn about and use specific process skills with the goal of integrating them into the DAT work.	DAT members express interest in learning about and using process skills, but there is no follow through.	DAT members dismiss the value of learning about or using process skills.

DAT members engage in learning about models of change.

DAT members have a fluent understanding of change models and know how to relate them to their work.	DAT members are well-versed in various change models and can sometimes relate them to their work.	DAT members have some familiarity with change models, but they can't relate them to their work.	DAT members are interested in knowing more about change models, but they don't make time to do so.	DAT members feel they don't need to learn about change models.

DAT members engage in activities led by facilitators.

DAT members welcome facilitator-led activities and eagerly engage in them.	DAT members engage in facilitator-led activities.	DAT members engage in facilitator-led activities with pushback or difficulty and often need prompting or direction.	DAT members express, either verbally or nonverbally, that facilitator-led activities are a misuse of time. DAT members don't value or understand the purpose of facilitator led activities.

DAT members are inclusive.

All DAT members are recognized as having unique expertise, contribute fully to decision-making, meaningfully share power with other DAT members, and see themselves as legitimate partners in the DAT.	All DAT members see themselves as partners in the DAT, but some are not consistently treated as if they have relevant expertise, are only sometimes given opportunities to share power, or only sometimes contribute to decision-making.	Students or staff are not included in the DAT. However, the DAT seeks input from students or staff as relevant, to inform its work (e.g., via surveys or focus groups).	Some DAT members (e.g., students) are not seen as having expertise, do not share in decision-making, and do not see themselves as true partners in the DAT.	DAT members do not include and do not seek input from all relevant groups in the department.

The DAT engages in community building rituals.

The group engages in community building rituals on a regular basis without prompting from facilitator (e.g., interacts through icebreakers, celebrates progress, and has snacks).	The group engages in community building rituals only when prompted by the facilitators.	The DAT goes through the motions of community building rituals without truly engaging in them. The group does not initiate any rituals.	The DAT does not allow community building rituals.

Recommended Reading

Patterson, K. (2002). *Crucial conversations: Tools for talking when stakes are high.* Tata McGraw-Hill Education.

Fisher, R.; & Ury, W. (1981). *Getting to yes: How to negotiate without giving in.* Arrow.

> These books have good strategies for communicating with others when important decisions need to be made, for managing strong emotions and opinions, and for dealing with personal and professional conflicts.

CHAPTER 5

Developing DAT Members' Change Agency

Building a DAT that is capable of implementing and sustaining change in a department will require the development of team members as change agents. Change agents are fundamental to the DAT model, and their actions and behavior will influence all outcomes of the DAT work. The aim of the DAT model is to equip DAT members with the knowledge, skills, and resources necessary to act as change agents after the DAT's initial work is completed. Facilitators can empower DAT members to take on the change agent role and help DAT members develop as change agents while the DAT works on its project.

KEY MESSAGES

- As DAT members' knowledge of the DAT model and supporting theory deepens, they begin to better understand change and how change happens.

- The DAT model increases members' change agency by developing their capacity as change agents and their sense of change agency.

- DAT members can apply the knowledge, skills, and resources related to change agency beyond the DAT's work, setting the foundation for future change efforts.

Theory of Change Context

One of the main goals of a DAT is to grow DAT members as change agents; that is, to develop their skills and confidence to create future change after the DAT ends (Outcome 6B). We see this development as involving two components: the DAT members' capacities as change agents and their internal sense of change agency. We define "capacity" to be the skills, knowledge, and resources that are necessary to a domain. In a DAT, capacities are developed through solving meaningful problems together (Garmston & Wellman, 2013). By "internal sense" we mean the ability of DAT members to see themselves as capable of creating change.

OUTCOME 6B

DAT members grow as change agents

DAT members increase their capacity around	DAT members increase their sense of
1. Collaboration	1. Capability to create change
2. The local context	2. Opportunity to create change
3. The DAT's focus	3. Motivation to create change
4. Change	4. Identity as a change agent

The development of these capacities and internal senses are co-conditions that exist in a positive feedback loop. The development and use of capacities that make them more effective change agents help DAT members build a stronger internal sense of themselves as change agents; an increasing internal sense of their own change agency encourages them to develop their capacities.

How Do DAT Members Develop Capacity as Change Agents?

Facilitators support the development of DAT members' capacity to be change agents, the skills, knowledge, and resources that are used to make change. These capacities are developed as DAT members:

- Experience being a part of a high functioning team and completing a change project
- Observe how facilitators organize and support the team
- Learn about change in higher education
- Practice skills related to change management

Additionally, capacities can be developed through solving meaningful problems together (Garmston & Wellman, 2013). While department members are specialists in their areas of study, most of them are infrequently called upon to make meaningful changes in education, and as a result, many feel poorly equipped to tackle these types of challenges. Yet to make meaningful change in education, the department's culture and its participants must be supportive of the change and committed to its sustainability. Creating this type of meaningful and sustainable change requires different skills and knowledge than are typically cultivated within a traditional academic position. Department members must become problem solvers in the context of higher education and the change the DAT is trying to achieve. Thus, it is important for DAT members to deliberately cultivate department members' capacities as change agents in order to support the work of the DAT. Team members are recruited into the DAT for their willingness to both enact change and to build their capacities as change agents. If they are more interested in achieving other types of goals, then they may be more suited to participate in more traditional, project-based committees.

Change agent capacities are relevant beyond the work of a DAT. Department members can use these capacities to promote change in other contexts: their classrooms, research groups, or other collaborative settings. They can offer assistance to other change initiatives, whether in the department or elsewhere in the institution. As DAT members develop their capacities, it may even lead them to start their own change efforts. Ultimately, development as a change agent has the potential to impact many different areas of the institution.

CHANGE AGENT CAPACITIES

There are four capacities that we see as relevant to growing as a change agent:

1. Capacity related to **collaboration** involves the knowledge, skills, and resources that are necessary to productively work together as a team. This includes knowing and using explicit norms for collaboration, using tools and strategies for decision-making, navigating the politics of one's department, managing group dynamics, and resolving conflicts. This capacity also includes the ability to assess the team's and one's own processes for collaboration.

2. Capacity related to **local context** involves having knowledge, skills, and resources that are necessary to create change within the department and the institution. This includes knowing how decisions are typically made within a department and knowing enough history to understand what approaches tend to be successful or unsuccessful in working with a department.

3. Capacity related to the **project focus** involves the knowledge, skills, and resources that are necessary to deeply understand and address the issue that the DAT is working on. This involves gathering and analyzing data, drawing from the literature, connecting to experts, conducting small-scale pilot tests, and seeking out specialized training.

4. Capacity related to **change** is the knowledge, skills, and resources to enact large-scale change within an organization. This involves knowledge of different change models (e.g., Kezar's change models, discussed later in this chapter), knowledge of change strategies (e.g., Prosci, discussed later in this chapter), and the experience gained from engaging in previous change efforts.

Learning about collaboration

Since a collaborative group culture is supportive of change (Garmston & Wellman, 2013), change agents should develop their communication and collaboration skills in order to foster this type of culture. Understanding explicit norms for collaboration, which are covered in Chapter 4, is central to developing capacity as a change agent. Change agents should also learn about and be able to use tools and strategies for decision-making, navigating departmental politics, managing group dynamics, and resolving conflicts. Additionally, change agents should seek out and learn more about diversity and equity initiatives and social justice issues. Ideally, change agents will learn about equity and diversity continually and build a mindset that seeks out contributions from a wide range of individuals. These skills ultimately support change by helping a team communicate the visions, opinions, and concerns of its members. Change agents can also use these skills to help DAT members and others resolve conflicts and reach agreements. As a facilitator, you can incorporate collaboration into the DAT and explicitly tie collaborative behavior to change agent behavior. Inform DAT members that a high functioning team that operates with a collaborative culture is more likely to succeed in promoting positive change (Garmston & Wellman, 2013; Quan et al., 2019).

Principle 4:
Collaboration among group members is enjoyable, productive, and rewarding.

Understanding the local context of the DAT

To become change agents, DAT members should develop capacity related to the local context, including initiatives on campus, information on whether these initiatives have been successful, and the demographics of the student body, faculty, and staff. This can involve obtaining knowledge (e.g., departmental history of change initiatives), developing skills (e.g., instructional or research-related skills specific to the department), and obtaining resources (e.g., knowing who to contact to learn more about students in the major). Developing capacity related to the local context will enable change agents to move change efforts forward in several ways. For example, by understanding context, change agents will be able discern what types of communication between the DAT and the rest of the department are helpful and necessary. In some cases, departments may prefer to share news and seek input via faculty meetings, whereas in other departments email is considered to be a more efficient and preferred method of communication. Developing this capacity also contributes to identifying potential allies for the DAT's work within and outside the department. This is an essential step in moving DAT work forward, and is covered in more detail in Chapter 7, Effectively Engaging the Department.

The local context can be as broad as the DAT's entire institution. Understanding the institutional culture is important even when change efforts are localized to a department, as research has shown that change agents are typically more successful when their efforts align with institutional culture (Kezar & Eckel, 2002a). Institutional culture includes the values, mission, and history of the institution (Kezar, 2014). Knowing the decision-making processes of the institution and the institutional stakeholders can also inform DAT change efforts, as these can directly support or inhibit the DAT's work.

Partnerships can offer great value to change efforts. Often, departments and groups at an institution are siloed, which prevents mutually beneficial partnerships from forming. Change agents should build partnerships when possible to advance the work of the DAT. Facilitators should help DAT members investigate if the campus has groups dedicated to teaching and learning, student affairs, or other student-related initiatives. Once the subgroup of students the DAT is targeting with its work is identified, facilitators can guide DAT members in discovering if initiatives and opportunities to support these students already exist on campus. The office of scholarships, office of diversity, and student affairs office are all good places to make connections. Change agents recognize that there may be relevant initiatives and resources already in existence and will investigate what is already available and can contribute to the DAT's work, rather than have the DAT build the same toolset from scratch.

Time, money, and energy are other important resources that contribute to change efforts. By learning about other initiatives on campus, it may be possible to find and apply for sources of funding for DAT work. This can contribute money and possibly recognition to a change initiative. Change agents should speak with the department chair and other DAT allies to identify ways to locate time, money, and energy to the DAT's work. Ultimately, identification of resources that can contribute to a change initiative will inform the plan of action.

Developing an understanding of the DAT's focus

The initiatives that DATs choose to take on are typically rooted in undergraduate education. As part of their everyday work, DAT members are infrequently provided with training or resources to tackle such initiatives. In order to become change agents, they need to develop a deeper understanding of the DAT's focus, set appropriate goals, and design proper plans of action. Developing a deeper understanding may require change agents to collect and explore sources of data they don't typically work with. Data collection can include:

- Exploring literature on education
- Attending workshops or seminars (e.g., learning how to uncover unconscious bias)
- Reading reports on institutional or departmental data (e.g., department exit surveys for graduating seniors)
- Engaging with groups on campus that have knowledge of student affairs or educational best practices (e.g., some universities have teaching and learning centers that offer personalized support)

As a facilitator, it is likely that you are more familiar with the types of data that DAT members might need for their change work. Guiding DAT members on how to find and interpret data to inform their work will help them grow as change agents.

Developing an understanding of the DAT's focus for change is essential to constructing appropriate strategies for creating change. Additionally, it is likely that some data and resources that can inform change initiatives already exist and using these data as a launching point for the DAT work will contribute to its success. These baseline data will also help change agents to evaluate if they need to refine the initiative based on existing work and to evaluate if it's likely to be effective.

Principle 3:

Data collection, analysis, and interpretation inform decision-making.

DATS IN REAL LIFE

What if DAT members think they already have all the information they need about the focus of their work?

One DAT we worked with wanted to make changes to their department to improve inclusion and teaching in the undergraduate program. When they initially brainstormed ideas of what to change, the undergraduate student member of the DAT interrupted the conversation and shared that the ideas that were being discussed were not changes that would benefit them as a student. This was an important turning point for the other DAT members, as they were confronted with the knowledge that they were unaware of the needs of the undergraduate students in the department. The DAT subsequently decided to conduct two rounds of focus groups; the first targeted underrepresented students in the department and a second group that was open to all students. The questions posed to the focus groups were informed greatly by the perspectives of the undergraduate DAT member and the DAT member from the student affairs department. Ultimately, the focus group interviews informed the direction of the DAT work.

Facilitators will often recognize when a DAT may be missing important perspectives or knowledge related to their work. Facilitators must carefully consider how to introduce new perspectives to DAT members. In this case, the facilitators and the DAT members had created an environment where the student member felt comfortable bringing up a diverse perspective. Cultivating an environment where diverse perspectives are encouraged is an important job for facilitators.

Gaining knowledge about change and how it happens

An important capacity for change agents to develop is the knowledge of types of change and how they may occur. To understand how institutions change, organizational learning theorists distinguish between two types of learning: single-loop and double-loop (Argyris & Schön, 1996). Single-loop learning is organized around making small changes or adopting new practices, while leaving underlying assumptions, beliefs, and norms unchallenged. Single-loop approaches are often quick fixes that are typically guided by a student deficit perspective and, as such, are unlikely to be effective at addressing equity issues on a campus (Bensimon & Malcolm, 2012). In contrast, double-loop learning is organized around the root causes of a problem, and requires an organization to change its values, beliefs, and operating practices. This type of learning is more desirable, because it results in meaningful changes that are likely to be sustained.

When change agents match their strategies for change to the type of change that may be needed and the context of the change, they are more likely to build support for the change effort (Kezar, 2014). Current knowledge of organizational change can shape how change agents understand and approach changing behavior within a department and can inform how change agents should situate their change efforts within the context of the entire institution. Thus, understanding different change theories, models, and strategies is an important foundation for designing the DAT's current (and future) change effort. Even once a change strategy has been identified and fleshed out, it must continually be examined to determine if it is (still) a good fit to achieve the desired changes. There are many models of change, but for the purposes of this book, we describe change generally and summarize change models that have been developed for and used in higher institution settings.

First, we present Adrianna Kezar's findings that outline the characteristics of different types of change efforts. These characterizations are general and can be used to understand and guide a diversity of change efforts. Next, we provide an example of a model of change (Multicultural

Organization Development) that was designed with a specific outcome in mind—producing a multiculturally-responsive environment. Finally, we include examples of change management practices that have been developed based on theories of change and include strategies that can be directly employed in change efforts. When appropriate, facilitators should incorporate this content knowledge about change into DAT work and guide DAT members through applying what is already known about change to their own change effort.

Kezar's change models. Adrianna Kezar outlined six models of change that broadly apply to change efforts in institutions of higher learning. These change models characterize the logic, mechanisms, and products of change efforts (Kezar, 2001). Table 5.1 briefly summarizes the different types of change and articulates the relationship between Kezar's findings and the DAT model for change. For a richer understanding of the change models outlined in table 5.1, please refer to *Understanding and Facilitating Organizational Change in the 21st Century: Recent Research and Conceptualizations* (Kezar, 2001) or *How Colleges Change: Understanding, Leading, and Enacting Change* (Kezar, 2014).

Table 5.1.
Characteristics of Kezar's change models and their influence on the DAT model.

Change Model	Influence on DAT model
Scientific management: Incentives and rewards used to influence behavior, top-down approach, linear and purposeful, often first-order change	DAT model promotes changing teaching incentives and guidelines
Evolutionary: System is considered holistically, change driven by responses to external factors, change happens gradually and via adaptation, change is often unplanned and first-order	DAT model promotes implementing flexible structures that can be adapted in response to changing external forces
Social cognition: Underlying beliefs (mental maps) guide change, focus on second-order change that is prompted by cognitive dissonance that comes through sense-making and shifting paradigms	Interviews and surveys are used to understand how department members think about change and to align DAT change efforts with the department members' existing mental maps or to develop strategies to shift how they think about change
Cultural: Shift underlying culture of department, resistance can occur if changes do not align with values, slow and unpredictable process, often unplanned change	Since change occurs through a shift in values, surveys and interviews can be used to understand the history and existing culture within a department and to situate proposed changes in this context
Political: Use groups to support strategic collective action, leverage existing power structures in the institution, may encounter resistance if individuals don't perceive it benefits their interests, can be first or second-order change	DAT members seek to align work with existing university initiatives when possible and support for the DAT work is sought from those in positions of power
Institutional: Leverage existing external structures that apply pressure to institutions, changes to institutional norms which are generally unplanned and tied to an external environment	The DAT model was developed using funding from the National Science Foundation, and this funding source carries a certain amount of prestige and power, which can influence change

The change models outlined in Table 5.1 can be applied in a variety of ways. First, they can be used to identify and understand the change efforts that are typical in a department or institution. Using the change models to characterize change efforts that have succeeded or failed can provide change agents with a better understanding of how they should structure their own initiatives. Second, these models can be used to structure thinking around multiple aspects of change efforts, such as where the motivation for change comes from and the types of resistance that are likely to occur. Finally, if a planned change initiative is not succeeding, change models can help diagnose the situation and offer paths forward. Slides and a handout about Kezar's change models are found in the Digital Toolkit.

Digital Toolkit
Slides 7.0–7.13: Models of Organizational Change, Handout 5: Change Models, Handout 6: Change Alignment

Multicultural Organization Development. Multicultural Organization Development (MCOD) was developed to inform the efforts of organizations that are working towards becoming more multiculturally responsive (Jackson, 2006). In this model of change, the organization is considered to be the unit of change. MCOD identifies three types of change agents that play a role in the change efforts necessary for an organization to work towards being multicultural: the internal change team, external MCOD practitioners who act as consultants, and the leadership team. MCOD theory and practice are guided by several assumptions (Jackson, 2006):

1. Individual consciousness raising and training activities for individuals may be necessary but are not sufficient to produce organizational change

2. Organizations are not either "good" (multicultural) or "bad" (mono-cultural)

3. The change process needs to be pursued with a clear vision of the "ideal" end state, or the multicultural organization, in mind

4. The picture of the real should be derived from an internal assessment process

5. Ownership of the MCOD process is a key to success

6. Significant organizational change in social justice and diversity will occur only if there is someone monitoring and facilitating the process

Principle 6:
Work is grounded in a commitment to equity, inclusion, and social justice.

Articulating the assumptions guiding the change effort and knowing how they influence its implementation can help the change agents understand the limitations and affordances of that change model. Understanding these assumptions can enable change agents to determine whether a change model is a good fit for the goals they are trying to achieve. For example, knowing that an assumption of MCOD is that a person needs to monitor and facilitate the process in order for change to occur means that an outcome of the change agents' work needs to include the creation of this role, if it does not already exist.

Practically, MCOD can be used to identify where an organization is relative to achieving the goal of becoming more multicultural and to guide the work the organization's members must take on to continue moving towards this goal. Products of MCOD include activities that organizations can perform to move from one stage to the next and recommendations of different types of data that can be collected to help organizations evaluate their progress. Change agents play an important role in identifying indicators of the organization's current state in the developmental process.

Since DATs serve to inform and influence departmental culture, MCOD offers many insights into how organizations experience change and the types of resistance that may occur. The reflection activities that MCOD recommends for evaluating progress can be useful for DATs to assess their own efforts (Jackson, 2006). Articulating the different types of change agents and their associated responsibilities, as done in the MCOD, can be helpful for DAT change agents to consider. When a DAT's work is specifically related to increasing diversity and becoming more multiculturally responsive, MCOD can play a direct role in shaping the DAT's goals and action plan.

Change Management. Change management refers to a body of practices that organizations can engage in to help change proceed smoothly for their employees and clients. Just as projects are often guided by a dedicated project manager, the change aspect of a project can be guided by a change manager. Both project and change management should be supported by the active involvement of leadership. The three elements of project management, change management, and leadership can be imagined as a three-legged stool. When projects are not successful, it is often due to a failure to attend to change management. Conceptions of change management first emerged from the field of business (Hiatt, 2006). Some best practices in change management include (Hiatt & Creasey, 2012):

- Dedicate resources to manage change, in addition to managing the project
- Identify a leader to champion each change project
- Support the project's champion in communicating to the organization about the change
- Encourage the participation of all stakeholders in the project
- Communicate with all stakeholders frequently and openly
- Ensure that change management is integrated with project management and the work of middle managers

Digital Toolkit
Slides 8.0–8.3: Change Management

In the world of DATs, either the facilitators or the DAT members can play the role of change managers. Change managers are more successful when they approach change from the perspective of each individual (Hiatt & Creasey, 2012). Change occurs as individuals move through a predictable cycle: awareness, desire, knowledge, ability, and reinforcement (aka ADKAR). When change managers diagnose where an individual is in the cycle, they can better determine actions to help that individual move to the next stage (Hiatt, 2006). Slides that can be used to introduce change management concepts to DATs can be found in the Digital Toolkit.

How Do DAT Members Increase Their Sense of Change Agency?

Cultivating the capacities of a change agent is not the only component to becoming a change agent; DAT members must also develop their sense of change agency. To behave as a change agent, DAT members need to not only believe that they can promote change, but also be motivated to do so. Research has demonstrated the value that self-efficacy and motivation contribute to the success of change agents (Bandura, 1997). Even if change agents believe they can create change and are motivated to do so, they might not take action if they do not believe the opportunity exists for them to act as a change agent. These qualities all contribute to cultivating an identity as a change agent, which is an important role for DAT members to embrace if they plan to engage in future departmental change efforts.

```
SENSE OF CHANGE AGENCY
```

There are four components that comprise an "internal sense" of being a change agent:

1. DAT members feel **capable** of making future change when they believe that they can accomplish more changes in the future. This belief is a form of self-efficacy and can be driven by mastery experiences (success on prior similar tasks), vicarious experiences (seeing peers complete similar task), or social persuasion (exposure to verbal judgements by others about one's ability). All of these are relevant sources of capability feelings for DAT members.

2. DAT members feel that they have **opportunities** to create change when they can recognize situations where they could productively work towards change. The more experience DAT members gain in working on change efforts, the more accomplished they will become. As DAT members develop this capability, they may see opportunities for change in contexts they hadn't previously considered or see ways to apply their capacities that they hadn't previously recognized. In other words, it's not that there are more opportunities around them in an objective sense, but rather it is that they are more likely to recognize and pursue these change opportunities than before.

3. DAT members feel **motivated** to make future change when they have a desire to engage in future change efforts. When DAT members are intrinsically motivated to engage in change work, they typically do so because they find the work meaningful and interesting. DAT members can be extrinsically motivated as well, when pursuing a change initiative satisfies a need that is separate from change itself (e.g., meeting accreditation standards, fulfilling responsibilities for tenure).

4. 4. DAT members feel a stronger **identity** as a change agent through two mechanisms: their own self-recognition as people who create change and their recognition by others as people who create change. Both forms of recognition can influence whether and how they engage with change work.

Feeling capable of creating change

Feeling capable of making future change is related to self-efficacy: the belief in one's ability to accomplish tasks (Bandura, 1977). It is important to develop self-efficacy as a change agent, because those who do not believe they can accomplish tasks are more likely to avoid tasks or put minimal effort into them; conversely, those with a high sense of self-efficacy are likely to persevere and succeed when facing challenging situations (Britner & Pajares, 2006).

It is possible to increase self-efficacy when it comes to making change in many ways. These include (Bandura, 1997):

- Mastery experiences: Acknowledging success on prior similar tasks

- Vicarious experiences: Seeing peers complete similar tasks

- Social persuasion: Being exposed to positive verbal judgements by others about one's ability

- Internal states: Learning to not interpret negative physical and affective states caused by failure as indicative of lack of ability

Facilitators can create many opportunities for DAT members to participate in these experiences to build self-efficacy. For example, working towards creating change through the DAT's project can be considered a mastery experience. Working with other change agents in the department or institution can vicariously build self-efficacy in DAT members as they observe how change agents operate and learn from their behavior. Facilitators can provide feedback on an individual's work as a change agent and relay how others perceived a change agent's ability to build self-efficacy. Finally, change agents can increase their self-efficacy by monitoring their own reactions and feelings while they operate as change agents. Engaging in this self-reflective practice helps change agents recognize when they have reached the limit of their abilities, which can help prevent failure in a particular task (Mauer et al., 2017). Allocating time during DAT meetings to reflect on the change the team members are promoting and their abilities to advance the work can foster this behavior.

Having the motivation to create change

Even if a DAT member has the skills to make changes, they will not act as a change agent without motivation to take on change initiatives. This motivation leads to a desire to engage in existing and future change efforts and can come from both intrinsic and extrinsic factors.

When change agents are intrinsically motivated and feel that they have social support, they engage in an activity for the inherent satisfaction of completing the work. Intrinsically motivated change agents are more likely to show interest and excitement in their work, which leads to better performance, persistence, and creativity, as indicated by self-determination theory (Ryan et al., 1991). Intrinsic motivation can be influenced by the environment, and the right conditions can support the development and maintenance of intrinsic motivation. When change agents feel that they are competent in their work and have a sense of autonomy, their intrinsic motivation is supported (Ryan & Deci, 2000).

One type of intrinsic motivation comes from change agents feeling that their work is meaningful. DAT members are typically recruited or volunteer to join the DAT because of their interest in the DAT's work. Part of the DAT model is DAT members identifying projects that work towards their shared vision, as will be discussed in Chapter 6 on DAT work. Creating a shared vision together helps all DAT members to find meaning in their work, because they believe in and contribute to the overarching goal. Ultimately, when change agents who are intrinsically motivated feel that their tasks are significant and that their efforts will result in the desired outcome, they are more likely to invest their time and energy to the change effort. In essence, they believe that their behavior will be effective. Facilitators can help to cultivate this feeling of significance in many ways: for example, facilitators can situate the DAT's work in existing institutional change efforts to show how the DAT is advancing the institution as a whole. Or, facilitators can make inferences about the impact the DAT's work can have on educational practices outside of the department.

Change agents might also be intrinsically motivated by a desire to help others (Specht et al., 2018). Change agents who are motivated in this way often help a group establish an identity and provide a social orientation for participants in the change efforts (Specht et al., 2018). This supports the change efforts because participants connect with a group identity that is built on a desire to help others. In the case of DATs, DAT members who are motivated by the desire to help others may also identify strongly with the DAT and its mission and can provide and support the identity of the DAT as a team.

Extrinsic motivation can come from many sources and leads to the completion of work for reasons that lie outside the individual (Ryan & Deci, 2000). For example, some DAT members may be extrinsically motivated by a desire to satisfy the department chair's needs or a need to uphold standards set by their discipline. Extrinsic motivation can lead to behaviors that range from autonomous to controlled. When extrinsic motivation is accompanied by feelings of autonomy, greater engagement and better performance are likely (Connell & Wellborn, 1991; Miserandino, 1996). For more details on the continuum of external motivation, please see Ryan and Deci's (2000) work.

When change agents are not motivated, they are considered to be in a state of amotivation (Ryan & Deci, 2000). When this occurs, change agents do not feel any autonomy over the work, and are unlikely to value the work or its completion. This can lead to change agents simply going through the motions, rather than acting with intention.

Historically, department members who join DATs are often driven by intrinsic motivation to improve undergraduate education. DAT members generally have a desire to help others and find the DAT's focus meaningful. This is often noticeable in their history of service for the department. However, DAT members can be supported by extrinsic motivation as well, such as recognition of service from the department chair. Change agents who understand the factors that motivate them and others to accomplish DAT work will be able to better predict and influence the conditions under which the work will be successful. Facilitators can engage the DAT in conversations about why each DAT member elected to participate in the change effort, which can lead to a feeling of unity over shared motivations and identification of strengths due to differences in motivation.

Recognizing opportunities to create change

Even if a change agent has the capacity to behave as a change agent, they may be constrained by external factors (Michie et al., 2011). For example, there may be social constraints in place, such as an implicit hierarchy where non-tenure track faculty may not be given the same social status and power as tenure-track faculty, which would reduce the opportunities for a change agent to act. Physical constraints also may exist, such as a lack of meetings or committees that bring together the department to implement change efforts. Thus, the environmental conditions must also be conducive for change agents to use their skills.

Identifying as a change agent

Identity is who a person considers themselves to be, and the construction of identity as a change agent is a dynamic process that is dependent on context (Moore, 2008). As Holland and others (1998) note, identities are "lived in and through activity and so must be conceptualized as they develop in social practice" (p. 5). Self-efficacy, motivation, and opportunity all contribute to identity as a change agent. Thus, this identity may be developed by behaving as a change agent through the DAT model and being seen in the department as a change agent. Helping DAT members to recognize how they are acting as change agents, on any scale and in any context, can help to construct their identity as change agents.

Principle 5:
Continuous improvement is an upheld practice.

Indicators of Success

Evidence of change agent attitudes

While there are few tangible indicators that DAT members may have begun to identify as change agents, it is possible to note changes in behavior and attitudes. A DAT member may show an increase in self-efficacy by providing extra support for the DAT's work. They may speak positively about the DAT culture to others, and advocate for DAT practices outside of DAT meetings. Finally, DAT members may show confidence and excitement in continuing to work on change efforts both in the department and across the institution, which indicates a willingness to take on a role as a change agent.

Facilitators can also directly ask DAT members how they feel about their change efforts and their own agency. This can take place through a short feedback activity. This type of examination can raise DAT members' awareness of their own capacities as change agents. They might be surprised to realize that they feel very capable of making change in the department after their work in the DAT!

Digital Toolkit
How-To Guide 8:
Using DAT Member
Input

Recommended Reading

Hyde, C. A. (2018). Leading from below: Low-power actors as organizational change agents, *Human Service Organizations: Management, Leadership and Governance, 42*(1), 53–67. https://doi.org/10.1080/23303131.2017.1360229

> This article provides information on how change agents with low positional power were able to enact change. The examples provided in this article are useful for understanding how change agents may operate successfully.

Ryan, R. M., & Deci, E. L. (2000). Self-determination theory and the facilitation of intrinsic motivation, social development, and well-being. *American Psychologist, 55*(1), 68.

> Self-determination theory provides insight into human motivation. In this seminal article, Ryan and Deci define human motivation and what factors impact motivation.

CHAPTER 6

Guiding a DAT through a Project

In this chapter, we describe how facilitators work with DAT members on projects, which progress in conjunction with the development of the DAT's group functioning (Chapter 4), and support the DAT in engaging the wider department in their work (Chapter 7). A major goal of a DAT is to achieve sustainable change on a broad-scale issue related to undergraduate education in their department. We conceptualize "issue related to undergraduate education" broadly: it might be related to curricular change (e.g., alignment of learning goals between courses, assessing disciplinary skills across the major) or cultural change (e.g., building a sense of undergraduate community, improving equity and inclusion of marginalized groups). Successful DATs choose a scope of work that can have a broad impact (i.e., beyond a single course or instructor), but is manageable given the scale of available or cultivated resources.

Much of this chapter covers the logistics of DAT meetings and moving the DAT work forward. Initially, we look at preparations for the first meeting, the activities around the development of a shared vision of undergraduate education, and the visioning associated with the DAT and its emerging culture. Several activities around visioning are presented and explained in depth.

The remainder of the chapter provides an in-depth examination of the processes involved in linking the vision with the goals, outcomes, DAT projects, and assessment of projects. In addition, we discuss the variety of data types a DAT might generate or examine in its work and how facilitators can guide the DAT in using data to inform and move the work forward.

KEY MESSAGES

- Facilitators have many logistical tasks to attend to before the DAT meets for the first time and many ongoing activities as the DAT meets and engages in its work.

- DATs initially develop a shared vision around who they are as a group and a vision of what undergraduate education should look like in the department.

- Linking the vision with the goals, outcomes, projects, and assessments is crucial in accomplishing the DAT's work and implementing sustainable change in the department.

Theory of Change Context

This chapter revisits and elaborates on the roles that facilitators play for a DAT, as articulated in Outcome 5. These roles set the foundation for a facilitator's work in guiding and supporting the DAT's project work.

OUTCOME 5

Facilitators support DAT members in creating change and developing as change agents

Help manage DAT logistics	Supports the development of a high functioning team	Provide support that is customized to the DAT's goals and needs	Cultivate an environment external to the DAT that is conducive to the DAT's success

The remainder of this chapter focuses on the DAT engaging in a change effort, Outcome 6C. A precondition for successfully engaging in a change effort is for the DAT members to create a shared vision for undergraduate education and the undergraduate experience in their department. Not only must DAT members share in the understanding of the vision, they also must share in its creation. DAT facilitators help the DAT construct a shared vision through various prompts and activities, like the "ideal student exercise" described later in the chapter.

Once the DAT has a shared vision, it engages in the actual change process. The process that the DAT engages in to create change is cyclic (see the Change Cycle for the expanded version). Finally, the DAT will achieve outcomes as a result of the change process.

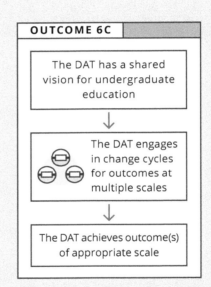

OUTCOME 6C

The DAT has a shared vision for undergraduate education

↓

The DAT engages in change cycles for outcomes at multiple scales

↓

The DAT achieves outcome(s) of appropriate scale

The Change Cycle

The Change Cycle has three phases, each of which has an action/outcome-focused component and a data/analysis-focused component that are mutually reinforcing. It involves: (1) developing desired outcomes while analyzing the state of the department, (2) planning activities to engage in while analyzing challenges, opportunities, and departmental capacity, and (3) implementing activities while monitoring and reflecting on its progress. A DAT can spend a while "swirling" between the components in one phase before moving on to the next phase. That's expected and fine, as long as they are being productive.

At any given time, a DAT may engage in more than one of these change cycles. For example, the DAT might split into subgroups with "parallel cycles," each of which is focused on a subset of the DAT's overall vision. Or, the DAT may have a "cycle-within-a-cycle": a short-timescale cycle focused on a more immediate outcome that is a component of a long-timescale cycle with longer-term outcomes. What matters is that the DAT engages in its work through cyclic processes that incorporate the steps in the change cycle and that the outcomes that are driving the cycle are appropriately scaled. Typically, this means that the DAT will have some long-term outcomes driving it in a big-picture sense, and some related short-term outcomes that are guiding its immediate work.

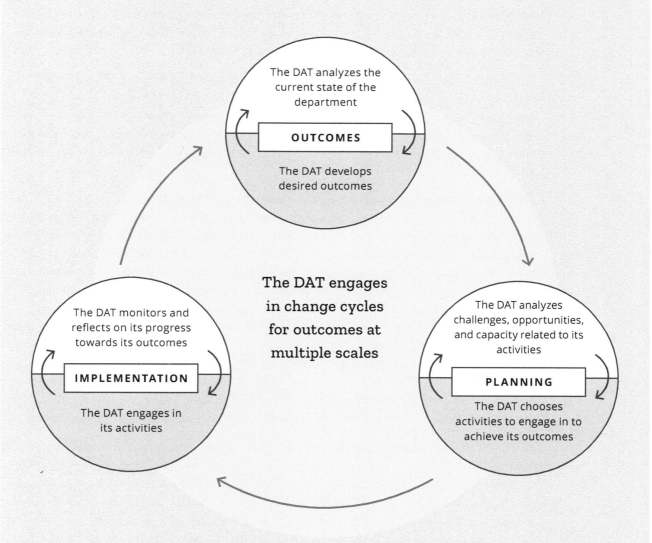

How Do Facilitators Prepare for DAT Meetings?

Alongside the group development work described in previous chapters, facilitators direct a variety of logistical and organizational activities that guide the DAT project. Even before a DAT has its first meeting, facilitators direct a number of activities which set the stage for the project, including:

Meeting Scheduling. During the first DAT meeting, or early on in communication with DAT members, prioritize scheduling regular meetings out as far as is reasonable (typically one semester or quarter in advance). If possible, attempt to build a schedule of next semester's meetings before the end of the current semester. Faculty and student course schedules get locked in early and will usually determine meeting times and days.

DATs usually meet once every two weeks for about one hour. Less frequent meetings can harm the continuity of the DAT work and development of the DAT culture. However, high functioning subgroups that are doing small group work between meetings may be able to meet less frequently than the whole group. The one-hour length is variable as well. Shorter meeting times are not workable, but longer times of up to two hours have been adopted when member schedules allowed.

Creation of a Shared Online Working Environment. During regular meetings, the facilitators keep detailed minutes while the team examines and discusses data, creates documents, and assembles pertinent literature. The creation of a cloud-based drive is essential for organizing and sharing information and documents. All DAT members have "read and write" access to this drive and are encouraged to use it during their work. We have used Google Drive, but there is a myriad of other options. It is a good idea for the facilitators to preload commonly used documents and folders before the first DAT meeting. This will help keep the drive organized and make resources easy to find. For example, a running meeting minutes document should be created and placed at the top level of the drive (see the "Anatomy of an Agenda" on page 101 for a more detailed look at meeting minutes). Sub-folders which may be needed include: Data, Literature, Founding Documents (such as a Request for Proposal) or Directives from Upper Administration. Other folders will be required given the specific work of the DAT. Strive to keep the content that doesn't fit well into any category at the top level of the drive to a minimum.

While facilitators set up this collaborative workspace, it's expected that DAT members will make active use of it. During the first DAT meeting, present this shared space as a resource you recommend they use—but do not assume all members will be familiar with working in a cloud-based environment. Ask members if the format will work for them and be open to switching to another cloud-based solution if any member is uncomfortable with your choice. Most of our DAT members have been open to learning how to use the shared drive functions. Facilitators can assist members or, often, DAT members will have the necessary skills and be happy to help other members navigate and use the shared drive.

Room Reservations, Requirements and Accessories. Reserving a consistent meeting room will help the meetings to be efficient, reliable and predictable. Ideally, meetings will be held in a departmental space. Check to see that the room is big enough, has appropriate furniture, whiteboards or tables, appropriate technology, and is accessible. In short, you are looking to reserve a room fitted and arranged to promote collaboration. Strive to make room adjustments that facilitate the work, but remember that typically you won't have much control over the room layout or furniture. For each meeting, bring the "go bag" of dry erase markers, sticky notes, large permanent markers, giant sticky notes, notepads, "consensus cards" (see Prioritizing Goals and Projects later in this chapter), appropriate cables and adapters, and any other supplies to support the agenda and planned activities for the day.

CONTENTS OF A DAT "GO BAG"

There are several items that DAT facilitators should bring to all meetings—some of them will be used at every meeting and some will be used as needed. We always suggest maintaining a packed bag of these materials, so that it is easy to grab it on the way to your next DAT meeting:

- Writing tools: pens, sharpies (for sticky-note activities), dry erase markers and erasers (for whiteboards)
- Stickies: Standard-sized post-its, 4"x6" size, flip-chart-sized
- Index cards
- Consensus Cards
- Cables/adaptors for connecting your laptop to projectors
- Non-perishable snacks, serving utensils, small plates and/or napkins

---

Technology. It is preferable to project meeting minutes and other relevant documents on a screen or TV for all to see, so that people engage in the shared space rather than being immersed in their individual computer screens. Arrive early to ensure the technology works. Often, you will have to switch connections or string your own cables to make things work. Encourage DAT members to bring their own laptops or devices, so they may access working documents on the shared drive. This practice will vary by group. In some instances, DATs may determine through their community standards that devices should not be used in order to encourage member engagement. However, it should be kept in mind that some members may need devices or other accommodations to access the work. As in all things regarding DAT facilitation, be prepared, yet be flexible and adaptable.

Food and Meetings. Typically, DAT facilitators supply snacks for meetings. The addition of snack food helps create an environment which encourages collaboration and builds community. Bring a wide variety of items that can be easily distributed with cups, small plates, or napkins. At the first meeting, inquire about member allergies, food sensitivities, and preferences. This attention to their wants and requirements builds member trust and a sense of facilitator legitimacy. In interviews with past DAT participants, they consistently mentioned how much they appreciated snacks at meetings.

DAT Journals. Facilitators keep an online journal for each DAT that is not shared with the DAT's members. This document is used to plan future meetings, to record reflections immediately after meetings, and to store copies of important emails. It also contains a parking lot of ideas that facilitators are interested in exploring with the DAT. Within the journal, an agenda planning template includes spaces for necessary materials, meeting goals, process skills, and project work. A reflection template contains spaces for a general reflection on the meeting, meeting goals and focus, distinctive moments, and evidence of the Core Principles. As described in Chapter 4, reflections are an invaluable tool for facilitators to map the direction and progress of both the DAT's project and their own facilitation.

Meeting Agendas. Thoughtful agendas are crucial to DAT success. Facilitators typically prepare a draft agenda in the DAT's journal prior to each meeting (see Figure 6.1 for example). To promote DAT member ownership of the project, it helps to explain agenda development in one of the first meetings and to point out that the group will increasingly structure their own agendas as the project matures. We think of facilitators as assembling agendas based on ideas expressed by the group, rather than creating agendas.

Digital Toolkit
How-To Guide 5:
Documenting
and Reflecting on
Meetings

The culture which develops within the DAT will determine how agenda writing is approached. Typically, the DAT should spend several minutes at the end of the meeting deciding on topics for the next meeting. Sometimes, facilitators write the agenda with input from the lead members between DAT meetings, or solicit input from the DAT generally. Agendas are always reviewed with the group at the opening of the next meeting, so any items that were overlooked may be added and modifications may be suggested.

Facilitators play an important role in tracking meeting time and making sure progress continues according to the agenda. It is not uncommon for agenda items to take longer than anticipated and encroach on other agenda items' time. Facilitators generally handle these situations on a case-by-case basis. If it comes up, remind DAT members about the time allocation on the agenda and ask how members would like to proceed; otherwise, seek to conclude the conversation on that item to mutual satisfaction. In other situations, the facilitator may feel it appropriate to remind the group of the time and suggest tabling the current conversation to be revisited in a future meeting. It is the facilitators' role to put tabled conversations on the agenda for an upcoming meeting.

Figure 6.1: An example meeting agenda

4.30.19

Attendees: Alanna, Chris, Clara, Courtney, Dan, Gina, Joel, Karen, Mary, Sarah

Norm of Collaboration: Presuming positive intentions

Norm Checker: Sarah

Meeting goal(s): 1. Review feedback about facilitation from DAT members 2. Outline how this feedback will influence the DAT model

Topic and Purpose	Conversation Type and Notes	Decision/Action
Welcome and announcements 12:00-12:10	We have two DAT team meetings left this semester Icebreaker: What is one activity you love to do during the summer? Courtney and Dan presented about DATs at a conference, Joel was invited to speak about DATs at a departmental seminar Go over meeting goals: is this what we want to accomplish today?	
Norm of collaboration 12:10-12:15	**Presuming positive intentions** This is the assumption that other members of the team are acting from positive and constructive intentions, even if we disagree with their ideas. Presuming positive intentions is not a passive state. Disagreement, in the spirit of greater understanding, is sought out and often shows up in a "yes, but" or "yes, and" format. Presuming positive intentions is a foundation of trust. It promotes healthy disagreement, and reduces the likelihood of misunderstanding and emotional conflict.	
DAT member feedback 12:15-12:30	Read through the feedback silently. Write down what themes are most salient to you and write them on sticky notes (one theme per note) Categorize the themes that the group recognized in the feedback. What are some ways we can prioritize these themes?	
Feedback plan 12:30-12:50	What changes are possible to make to the DAT model in response to the feedback? How and when will we implement these changes?	
Next steps 12:50-12:55	What needs to be accomplished by our next meeting?	
Norm check 12:55-1:00	How did we do with today's norm?	

METADATA

OPENING

PROCESS SKILL

BODY

CLOSING

ANATOMY OF AN AGENDA

Typical DAT agendas have a number of components, as described here. We like to use a three-column format for keeping agendas, with the first column for the agenda item topic/purpose and timing, the second column for detailed information and notes, and the third column to call out action items or specific decisions.

Metadata: The information that teams want to consistently collect will vary. We have found it useful to track attendance, the norms that are used for the meeting, and the goals for the meeting. Other items you might want to track include: who is taking notes for the meeting, the date of the next meeting, and future work for the team. Talk with your DAT about the value in tracking these different pieces of information (e.g., keeping track of attendance allows you to look back at meetings where decisions were made and to know who contributed to the decision-making process).

Opening: Create space at the beginning of the meeting for team members to make announcements, share exciting news, and participate in a community building activity – but try to limit this activity to no more than a few minutes. Preserving this time at the beginning of the meeting for the team to interact with each other sets the stage for the rest of the meeting.

A typical agenda begins with a "check-in" or a community builder. If community builders are used, facilitators should select them carefully and be sensitive to everyone's individual situations. Keep in mind that these are meant to build community, so if someone feels marginalized or uncomfortable by an activity, then it is not meeting its goal. Some members might feel that these activities impede progress on the "actual work" of the DAT. We feel that for a DAT to be a high functioning team, group connections and personalization are important and community builders are a quick, simple way for the DAT to make progress in this area. Facilitators use community builders selectively and mindfully.

Process skill: By consistently spending a few minutes on a process skill or activity, the team develops the habit of thinking about team functioning. Putting the process skill early in the agenda gives the team the opportunity to practice the selected process skill for the rest of the meeting. A table of process skills can be found in Chapter 4. Have a conversation about the value that process skills can provide for a team and consider strategies for supporting teams in engaging in process skills during a meeting.

Next, the facilitators can introduce a process skill which acts as a lens for the day's work. Process skills are described in detail in Chapter 4. An example is the selection of a Norm of Collaboration for the meeting. At times, a facilitator or a volunteer acts as "norm checker." The norm checker monitors the group's use of the norm during the meeting and reports out at the end of the meeting. Sometimes, in addition to a norm, facilitators may present a process skill that fits the meeting focus. In most meetings, time spent on group process is no more than 10 minutes and often less. Reporting out on a norm allows a DAT to analyze its conversational skills and recognizes that a major way to improve a skill is to get feedback. Where possible, the norm checker should provide explicit examples of how the productive use of the norm added to the discourse and offer other examples where the use of the norm was missed.

Digital Toolkit
How-To Guide 7:
Building
Community

Body: The bulk of the meeting is spent on DAT project work, and the content in this section will vary between meetings. Facilitators should provide structure to the content they plan to cover each meeting, and to look to different activities to engage teams in processes such as brainstorming or decision-making. Facilitators should also practice transitioning between topics and learn how to determine the amount of time to allot to each activity.

Closing: It is critical to allot a few minutes at the end of the meeting for the group to generate a list of action items, find volunteers for each item, and talk about what to accomplish at the next meeting. This will also provide an opportunity to discuss any work that needs to happen between meetings. The end of the meeting is also a good time to ask the team to reflect on the process skill that was chosen for the meeting, or to think about how they are functioning as a team when examined through a lens chosen by the facilitator.

The last few minutes of the meeting are spent with the norm checker reporting out and on "Next Steps" to be added as topics to the next meeting agenda. It is good practice to establish the norm of consistently starting and ending meetings on time.

Meeting Minutes. Accurate and detailed meeting minutes help a DAT achieve its goals. They are especially valuable to help a participant catch up after missing a meeting. A running meeting minutes document is kept at the top level of the DAT's shared drive and is accessible to all DAT members. Facilitators commonly take turns adding notes to the running minutes document during a meeting. Care should be taken to make notes as accurate as possible so they can be understandable to those who were not present at the meeting. A benefit of co-facilitation is in the ability to take nearly verbatim meeting notes. In circumstances where there is only one facilitator taking notes, it might be necessary to ask one of the members to assist in note-taking. If a facilitator is not able to attend a meeting, ensure DAT members are aware of this absence and recommend that a DAT member take notes in their place. During the meeting, the minutes are commonly projected for all to see and DAT members may contribute to them in "real time" as the meeting progresses. This helps the group track main themes, action items, or disagreements which may arise during a meeting. Facilitators can create a new minutes document when the initial one becomes too large, or at regular intervals (e.g., every academic year).

It is a good idea for facilitators to explain their note-taking routine during the first DAT meeting, as some members may have questions or concerns about this practice. Facilitators should make it clear from the outset that the minutes are taken this way to help with reflections, to plan more efficiently, and to inform members who miss a meeting. Facilitators should use professional judgement if a member starts to talk about issues that are sensitive or mentions the names of students or staff in the department. In these cases, it is important to not take verbatim notes. When appropriate, facilitators can ask how much of the discussion is acceptable to capture in the notes. Facilitators may later make note of these interactions in the confidential meeting reflection journal. That set of notes is accessible to facilitators only and is described in the following section.

Between-Meeting Work for Facilitators. One of the most surprising aspects of facilitation for new facilitators is the amount of preparation that is involved between meetings—although this can vary depending on the DAT, where they are in the DAT life cycle, and the facilitators' experience. If you are an experienced facilitator, it is helpful to explain to new facilitators how much time you spend on different activities between meetings; how you prepare for a meeting; and the value of debriefing and writing reflections after a meeting.

The amount of effort in planning conversational structures or activities for a meeting should not be underestimated. Specific structures and activities that can be included in a meeting are described in the DAT Digital Toolkit resources that accompany Chapters 4, 5, and 6. In preparation for the upcoming meeting, facilitators should copy the newly prepared agenda from the journal to the running meeting minutes document, and then email a link to the agenda, along with reminders to participants about any action items they agreed to do before the meeting.

BETWEEN-MEETING FACILITATOR TASK LIST

These are the typical tasks that DAT facilitators engage in before each meeting, with estimated lengths of time they should budget for each:

- Previous meeting debrief and reflection: **10–30 minutes**
- Email of previous meeting summary and action item list: **10–30 minutes**
- Meeting agenda planning: **30–60 minutes**
- Email communication with DAT members: **As needed**
- Collect resources for DAT: **As needed**
- Individual or small group meetings with DAT members: **As needed**
- Email of meeting reminder: **5–10 minutes**

Between-Meeting Work for DAT members. As the DAT project work commences, it will usually be necessary for members to carry out tasks between meetings. It can also be very effective for subgroups to meet (either face-to-face or virtually) between meetings to work on specific activities. Ideally, DAT members will propose specific tasks to complete between meetings, but even then facilitators will often need to put out a call for volunteers to take on tasks. This can occur either when an idea seems to have reached a consensus in a meeting, or during the time reserved for sorting out action items, in the last 5 to 10 minutes of a meeting.

DATS IN REAL LIFE

What if DATs are unable to meet in person?

In the spring of 2020, universities worldwide suspended in-person meetings to slow the spread of the novel SARS-CoV-2 virus. DAT facilitators responded to the situation by polling DAT members about their preferences on meetings going forward. Most DAT members chose to continue meeting via teleconference software. Because the situation had disrupted almost all routines, DAT facilitators adjusted their first online DAT meetings to emphasize reconnecting and to allow members to restate or revise their commitments to ongoing projects. At that point in time, many DATs had working subgroups. Facilitators found that subgroups which had a strong DAT member leader tended to be able to continue their work with minimal disruption. For other subgroups, facilitators helped identify new DAT member leaders, or assumed responsibility for the subgroup.

During this time, technology was the unsung hero, enabling everyone to work despite their drastically different circumstances. While previously facilitators had aided individual DAT members in teleconferencing into meetings, now everyone relied on teleconferencing to do their work. Facilitators found that certain teleconference features were particularly helpful: software that gave facilitators the ability to mute and unmute participants (to control background noise); the ability to set up breakout rooms in advance, and communicate to groups in breakout rooms; and the ability for facilitators and participants to share their screens with the group. Facilitators were also able to use features that allowed participants to virtually "raise hands" and make other nonverbal signals, which provided a good alternative for the consensus cards they previously used for decision-making. While the remote format was not a perfect or preferable replacement for in-person meetings, it worked well enough for DATs to continue to make progress and for DAT members to stay connected.

How Do Facilitators Help the DAT Create a Shared Vision?

Once the logistics have been arranged and meetings are on the calendar, you are ready to begin the work of guiding the DAT. The DAT process is built around a shared vision. This helps the DAT create goals, determine actions, and devise plans to assess progress. In subsequent sections, we examine the processes required for the DAT to move from developing a vision to implementing a project.

The DAT develops a shared vision for their work soon after its initial meeting. A shared vision is necessary to develop shared goals, which are the concrete objectives that will build toward enacting the shared vision. A shared vision, a shared dissatisfaction with the current state, and knowledge of resources are necessary for change (Garmston & Wellman, 2016).

Digital Toolkit

Slides 10.0–10.9: Visioning and Implementing Projects

A shared vision for undergraduate education is the long-term sense of what undergraduate education should be in the department. Focusing the work around a shared vision can lead to creative and flexible ideas. This contrasts with a focus on immediate problems, which tend to lead to narrower solutions. While it may be easier and more expedient to focus on individual departmental issues, a broader vision can help address the sources and causes of these problems or issues.

Facilitators help the DAT construct a shared vision through activities such as the "Ideal Student" exercise described in the following section. Questions that help a group develop a shared vision are: "What are we working toward in the long-term?" and "What justifies our continued existence?" We present several tools and strategies we have used to guide DATs toward a shared vision.

Development of a shared vision and associated goals for improving undergraduate education is aligned with the "Appreciative Inquiry" model of self-determined change. Appreciative Inquiry proposes collectively creating a vision of a compelling end state based upon the best attributes of the current situation. This model serves as a useful tool in the DAT work for several reasons: it moves the work away from deficit thinking, it engages people in the work creatively, it can generate results quickly, and it incorporates positive aspects of Constructivist Learning Theory (Cooperrider & Whitney, 2001).

This approach also closely aligns with the idea of "Backward Design." Backward Design is an educational development concept which encourages educators to design "backwards" by starting with the desired end-state, then focusing on curricular goals and objectives that align with the end state, and finally designing activities and assessments with those goals in mind (Wiggins & McTighe, 1998). Backward Design can be useful for facilitators to use when introducing a visioning activity, as many faculty are familiar with it, having applied it in designing their courses.

Developing a shared vision

Principle 2:

Work focuses on achieving collective positive outcomes.

There are several ways that DATs develop a shared vision, including activities that use methods and strategies that hone in on the DAT's underlying values as a group.

Ideal Student Visioning activity: This activity uses Backward Design in an innovative way. We commonly use this activity with DATs that are working on curricular student learning outcomes, though it is also applicable for generally defining an ideal state of an undergraduate program. The reference letter exercise was developed at Carleton College (Savina et al., 2011) to help faculty articulate tangible, concise student outcomes for their major. This method involves faculty writing a letter of recommendation for an "ideal student" exiting their program of study. Specifically, letter writers are asked to include answers to the following questions about their "ideal student":

- What kind of person will this graduate be?
- What will they be able to do?
- What will they know?
- What skills will they have?
- How will they behave?
- What will they value?
- What will this student attribute their sense of belonging to?
- What sense of purpose will this student have?

Used as a dialogue activity, analysis of these "letters" will produce lists of specific attributes that DAT members develop around their program of study. The resulting student characteristics and associated departmental behaviors and structures prove valuable and are referred to throughout the DAT project.

Once the letters are written or envisioned, the authors transfer main points onto sticky notes. The notes are arranged on a wall or table by themes, and the group discusses the overarching ideal student. By association, in the process of defining the ideal student, departmental characteristics can emerge. The group then develops a concrete list describing an ideal state toward which their work can be directed. This creates a distinct endpoint from which "backward design" may commence.

DAT facilitators have developed variations of the Ideal Student Exercise (Savina et al., 2011). Rather than write a reference letter, which few student DAT members are familiar with, DATs have been prompted to answer the question: "What would you like to be able to say about an ideal student graduating from your department?" or "What would characteristics of an ideal community be, for your department?"

Digital Toolkit
Slide 10.4: Ideal Student Activity

The KASAB Method of Outcomes Visioning: The KASAB approach comes from professional development literature and refers to the levels of learning that exiting students will have achieved in five specific areas: Knowledge, Attitude, Skills, Aspirations, and Behaviors (Killion, 2018). Similar to the letter writing exercise, the KASAB method has faculty envision the detailed KASABs students will possess upon completing their program of study. These characteristics then inform the development of specific learning outcomes for the major. This approach has the advantage of being more accessible to people unfamiliar with or unaccustomed to writing reference letters (e.g., student or staff DAT members).

Both of the referenced methods employ backward design. Once the ideal graduate and their characteristics are determined, the pedagogical elements that lead to that endpoint may be developed (e.g., activities and assignments which will guide the student toward that end and assessments to determine if these outcomes have been achieved).

Visioning is a specific type of brainstorming activity. The method of asking DAT members to respond to a prompt by writing as many ideas as possible on individual sticky notes and arranging these notes according to themes with affinity mapping can be used for any situation where it is beneficial for the group to convey and organize many individual ideas quickly. This exercise can be modified in many ways. For example, DAT members can write down questions rather than ideas. To better organize the ideas, DAT facilitators sometimes find it useful to have sticky notes of different sizes and colors.

Visioning for individual growth: Visioning work can also focus on DAT members and their perceptions of personal and professional growth through their participation in the DAT process. This exercise helps DAT members crystallize their role and potential for growth within the group. You can prompt this activity with questions such as:

- What would you like to gain from participating in the DAT?
- In what ways would you like your experience with the DAT to have an impact outside of DAT meetings?
- How do you envision an ideal change agent in your department?

How Do Facilitators Help the DAT Develop Achievable Outcomes?

Based on its shared vision, the DAT develops a list of desired outcomes. These are essentially the goals that the DAT is working towards, the achievement of which will help it move closer to enacting its vision. As such, these outcomes are more concrete than the components of the vision (e.g., they should be SMART: Specific, Measurable, Achievable, Relevant/Results-focused/ Rigorous, Time-bound) (Doran, 1981), although they could exist at a variety of scales. The development and prioritization of these outcomes should occur in coordination with an analysis of the on-the-ground state of the department. An unbiased analysis based on data is necessary to avoid outcome prioritization that is based on anecdotes or assumptions, rather than true departmental needs.

Principle 5:
Continuous improvement is an upheld practice.

Before a DAT begins to brainstorm possible goals, it is helpful to frame its thinking around changes that are sustainable for the department. Departmental culture and the DAT's activities both influence whether changes are sustained. Sustainable changes tend to use available resources to create adaptable mechanisms, which support enduring improvements (Garmston & Wellman, 2013; Kezar, 2014; Reinholz et al., 2019). Significant changes to undergraduate education are necessarily complex, requiring change to existing departmental structures, cultural symbols, and power relationships. It helps for DAT members to keep the Core Principle of continuous improvement in mind at all stages of their work. One-shot efforts are rarely sustained. If DAT members commit to engaging their department in a continuous cycle of planning, implementing, assessing their work, and altering their plans, it is much more likely their work will succeed and be sustained.

Digital Toolkit
Slide 1.5: Core Principle 5, Slide 10.5: SMART Goals, Slide 10.7: Continuous Improvement, Slides 10.8-10.9: Sustainable Departmental Change

DAT facilitators commonly have members create SMART goals at the onset of new endeavors of any significance. Progress toward goal attainment occurs when the team (and individual members) clearly know the desired end state and time points of progress. These goals are more concrete and short-term than the vision, and should be developed directly from the vision, but are broader than specific projects or tasks. If the plan of action is not connected to goals and vision, the project is unlikely to result in effective change to undergraduate education. A slide related to choosing sustainable projects can be found in the Digital Toolkit.

Facilitators help the group to gain the knowledge they need to set goals by locating existing sources of data, such as those provided by the campus-based institutional research office. Facilitators can assist in locating resources the DAT could use to develop surveys or focus groups and also help with the search for pertinent literature. Facilitators should also familiarize themselves with the variety of campus contacts which the DAT may tap, if additional skills or resources become needed. As a DAT progresses closer to being self-facilitated, facilitators can start helping members to locate resources on their own as a step towards independence. In the following sections, we will explore ways in which facilitators may guide the DAT toward efficient and successful goal development.

Linking vision, goals, outcomes, projects, and assessments

DAT members sometimes mistakenly conflate elements of vision and goals with projects or activities. DAT members also might have difficulty aligning specific vision elements with specific goals, desired outcomes of those goals, projects or activities that may fulfill those goals, and ways to assess whether outcomes have been achieved.

A sticky activity can be used to help DAT members align these elements of planning. The outcome focus of this exercise prevents the promotion of projects and goals which are tangential to the group vision.

In this activity, facilitators write elements of a vision (or the element that the group has chosen to focus on) in a vertical column on the left side of a whiteboard. Along the top of the board, the following column headers are written: Goal, Outcome, Activity, and Assessment. This creates a matrix which has row and column headers, but nothing in the cells.

Vision Element	Goal	Outcome	Activity	Assessment
Vision element 1: Graduates will have professional skills	Students engage in learning about professional skills	Students report feeling prepared for a future career	Offer a professional skills seminar	A career preparation question on a student survey or exit interview
Vision element 2				
Vision element 3				

Table 6.1. A sample chart that can be used in a sticky activity for aligning different aspects of planning a DAT project. The first row is an example of how DAT members might complete the chart.

DAT members are then asked to write sticky notes to populate each cell. For example, if one element of a vision is for graduates to have professional skills, then one corresponding goal could be for students to engage in learning about professional skills; a corresponding outcome could be for students to report feeling prepared for a future career; a corresponding activity could be a professional skills seminar; and a corresponding assessment could be a career preparation question on a student survey or exit interview.

Some DAT members may focus on assessments, while others focus on goals or outcomes. The matrix is populated by the facilitator helping to direct each sticky note to its appropriate column. Alternatively, facilitators could offer to generate the matrix in a shared online document, and DAT members could populate it as homework. Once the matrix is populated, it is useful to have a discussion of the emergent patterns. Are there certain elements of vision that are more elaborated upon than others? Are there some goals that are difficult to assess? This discussion will help inform the next step of the group's work, which is to narrow down which goals and projects the group pursues.

Digital Toolkit
Slide 10.3: Vision, Goals, and Activities

DATS IN REAL LIFE

What if some DAT members are not engaged?

Facilitators sometimes struggle with the balance of ownership among DAT members. If a DAT has many members, individuals may not feel accountable to the group. Or, in some DATs participation could be unbalanced, with a few members consistently taking on more work than others.

One of our DATs had a membership change after its first year which led to such an imbalance. Three new graduate students joined to help the team develop an assessment for their majors over the summer. The seasoned DAT members working over the summer included one graduate student and two faculty members. The graduate student veteran was particularly engaged, frequently articulating a vision for the project and independently developing a software tool to support the assessment work. After a few meetings, one of the other graduate students appeared disengaged in meetings, and the timeliness and quality of their work was not as high as the others.

The facilitators suspected that the less engaged student, and perhaps others, lacked a feeling of ownership of the work. After all, they had not been engaged in the original design of the project. There was also little opportunity for their ideas to be heard, since two of the veteran DAT members were very vocal. Articulating ideas may also have been more challenging for the less engaged student because English was their second language.

The facilitators were not able to attend one of the upcoming meetings, and they leveraged that opportunity to invite the less engaged student to help them plan the agenda. The student accepted, and during the ensuing conversation they were able to confirm that the student felt like they were on the periphery of the project. They were able to incorporate the student's ideas into the design of the agenda, which the student seemed to appreciate.

The facilitators then decided to give all DAT members an opportunity to describe their thoughts about project ownership by writing their responses to the prompt: "I feel committed to this project when... and I feel valued when..." on a notecard. The facilitators digitized and verbally summarized the comments during the following meeting. Although the less engaged student left the group after that summer, the facilitators noticed that over the next year of meetings, other students began to take greater ownership of the project.

How Do Facilitators Help the DAT Prioritize and Plan a Project?

Now that goals and associated projects have been articulated, they can be narrowed down and an action plan can be developed. Facilitators play a crucial role in keeping the DAT focused on its goals throughout this process. The plan of action is the roadmap describing the efforts and activities the DAT will undertake on the path to achieve its goals. The various activities involved and facilitator roles are examined in the sections below.

Prioritizing goals and projects

Once the DAT has determined achievable, assessable goals and associated projects that are aligned with its vision, it is time for the group to prioritize goals. Once goals are prioritized, project priorities often fall more easily into place. Some DAT members may have ideas that are near and dear to their hearts and may attempt to sway the group by dominating a discussion. An activity that can provide a more equitable way to prioritize goals is known as 25/10 Crowdsourcing, a part of the Liberating Structures series created by Keith McCandless and Henri Lipmanowicz.

Digital Toolkit
Slide 10.6: 25/10 Crowdsourcing

To narrow down good ideas, a facilitator introduces an activity in which each participant is asked to write on one or two notecards what they see as the most important goal or goals of the DAT. The group members stand up and exchange notecards without reading them, so the author of each notecard is not identifiable. Pairs then form, they read their notecards aloud, and discuss the merits of what is written. Individuals then turn the notecard they received over and give it a rating from 1 (low) to 5 (high). The standing, pairing, discussing, and rating process is repeated three times. Individuals then sum the ratings on the back of the last card they received. Facilitators then ask if anyone has a card with a rating of 20 (the maximum). Anyone with such a card then reads out what is written on the card. Reporting out then proceeds for cards with slightly lower ratings. After the top three or four are read out, the facilitator collects all the cards to be digitized after the meeting. The group then discusses the top-rated goals that emerged from the activity, hopefully arriving at one or two to focus on as a DAT. This method can be modified to also help a group prioritize among projects and determine a single goal.

A more in-depth way to approach prioritizing goals or projects involves a Decision Matrix—which is created by listing goals or project ideas as row headers and criteria you want to use to evaluate the projects as column headers. Constraints that may impact projects can also be listed in the headers which allows for input on the feasibility of the projects. In this process, facilitators or DAT members do not typically assign different weights to columns. DAT members either work in pairs or individually outside of the meeting times to assess whether individual goals or projects meet the criteria that were agreed upon by the group. The decision matrix is then used to ground a discussion in which goals or projects best meet the priorities of the group. While it may take as many as two DAT meetings to complete a decision matrix, these matrices and the conversations about them have the advantage of helping DATs think through their priorities carefully and avoid bias in their decision-making.

Digital Toolkit
Slide 9.10: Decision Matrix, Slide 9.9: Decision Criteria and Constraints

A discussion of the constraints around specific goals and projects can often raise questions about whether the DAT has the power to implement the changes they seek. In some cases, faculty can answer these questions by clarifying the authority structures that the DAT operates within. In almost all cases, students will not be aware of these structures, so facilitators should ask questions to get clarification.

In other cases, the DAT will not be clear about who has the decision-making power needed to move their work forward. To determine that, the DAT members may need to arrange an appointment with the head of the department or Executive Committee to discuss their ideas. The concept of "Inform, Recommend, or Decide" can be helpful in preparing the DAT for these conversations. Decision-making power can be held by the chair, a committee, the DAT, or even on a subgroup within the DAT. However, it is crucial that all parties be informed which body has decision-making power to effect a change.

Digital Toolkit
Slide 9.2: Deciding Who Decides

Digital Toolkit

Slide 9.4: Gauging Consensus with Fist to Five

When groups have trouble choosing a reasonable number of goals, "Fist to Five" is a useful consensus-gauging technique that can be employed. It is best used with questions that can be answered with "Yes" or "No". The question is typed or written on the board for everyone to see, and the facilitator checks to see if the group wants to vote on the question. Participants then vote with a show of a certain number of fingers (or an equivalent method for anyone who has a physical disability that prevents them from doing so). Five fingers means the participant wants to see the work happen and will lead it. Four fingers means they support the work. Three fingers means they support the work, but have some minor concerns that can be handled later. Two fingers means they have a minor concern that needs to be discussed. One finger means they have a major concern that must be discussed. A fist means they will block the work because they have so many concerns. If everyone in the group shows three fingers or more, the item is voted in. If they do not, the group tries to address any concerns of those that voted with one or two fingers. Voting may occur a second or third time, as the group moves toward consensus. Alternatively, the group may decide to table that idea and move on to the next one.

Digital Toolkit

Slide 9.3: Consensus Cards

Facilitators have also used "Consensus Cards" with many DATs to help them make decisions as a group, or to indicate their thoughts or feelings quickly. Each member is given three cards that are different colors and shapes: octagonal red cards (like a stop sign), triangular yellow cards (like a yield sign), and square green cards (because squares are easy to make). The team can use these in two ways: during a discussion, members can hold up a card to indicate that they agree with what is being said (green square); if they would like to speak, raise a concern, or ask a question (yellow triangle); or if the conversation is going off track or the group is violating its norms (red octagon). The cards similarly can be used when the group needs to come to consensus on something. In that case, green means "I consent without reservation," yellow means "I have minor reservations that must be addressed before I can consent", and red means "I have major reservations that prevent me from consenting." After a consensus check, anybody who raised a yellow or red card explains their reservations, and the group can then work to modify the proposal to address them. The team will need to decide in advance whether consensus to move forward requires everyone to display a green card or whether a certain number of yellows are allowed. In either case, it is the responsibility of the dissenters to clearly explain their concerns, of the group to address those concerns to the best of their ability, and of everyone to operate in good faith.

Once a DAT has prioritized its goals, it can prioritize specific projects or activities that the team members have previously brainstormed and believe will achieve or contribute to those goals. This may take several meetings. When prioritizing projects, it is important that the DAT determines if there is a natural sequence to the projects that have been proposed, or if there are "short-term wins" (Kotter, 2007) that can be achieved early. Early successes, or "mastery experiences", can be important motivators because they increase self-efficacy for the longer-term work to come (Bandura, 2008). In fact, it is difficult to maintain group motivation unless significant evidence of success manifests in the first 12 to 18 months of an initiative (Kotter, 2007). In addition, the increased self-efficacy gained from these early successes has been shown to increase motivation for future efforts (Britner & Pajares, 2006). Early success also helps the group see the value of the DAT model and the value of the process work they are doing. Seeing processes result in measurable progress leads the DAT to view them as productive and worth nurturing.

Planning projects

Once the DAT has settled on desired outcomes, it needs to develop a plan of action that describes the activities that the DAT will engage in to achieve these outcomes. Typically, DAT members will have no problem brainstorming many possible activities. Their challenge will lie in narrowing this list down to an achievable plan. Helping the DAT members to align their outcomes and vision will increase the utility of their plan. Additionally, the DAT should work to identify potential challenges within the department that will hinder their plans and opportunities that might help them. They also need to understand departmental and institutional capacities that they can leverage as part of their efforts. By taking all these factors into account, they will be better equipped to choose a set of activities that will successfully lead to their desired outcomes. In addition, creating reasonable, achievable timelines and obtaining the necessary resources for each project, or subproject, is essential. Facilitators can assist this effort by keeping the group members focused on the outcomes they have decided upon and guide them through the following tasks:

Define Deliverables. The DAT will take each project and associated goal and determine the specific deliverable that will contribute to the desired outcome. Facilitators help the DAT identify what these deliverables will entail, whether they are concrete items such as formative assessment plans for the curriculum or less tangible goals such as improving the sense of community within the department.

Outline the tasks. Have the group take each outcome they have decided upon and break it down into the dependent tasks required for its completion. The SMART goals exercise might benefit the group in this effort.

Assess Resources: People, Time, Power, and Materials. DAT members will need to determine resource needs for each task in the timeline, as being able to gather and focus resources is a necessary capacity for change (Garmston & Wellman, 2013). Necessary resources may include funding, data, places to work, and any number of odds and ends, depending upon the specific tasks. Facilitators help by directing the DAT to campus sources of data and knowledge, and by suggesting that DAT members reach out to their departmental leadership for support.

Create a Timeline. Early in the planning process, DAT participants will need to figure out the order in which task completion should occur and time required to do the work, while keeping the end goal in mind. Facilitators can lead a sticky note or online exercise to help keep this activity manageable and organized. Setting up the timeline in software, on a whiteboard, or on a giant sticky note is an important final step. Allocating wiggle room within the timeline is advisable here, as well as setting milestones to help assess progress and occasions to celebrate successes. In this stage of planning, optimism bias can distort teams' sense of the obstacles which may delay deadlines (Lovallo & Kahneman, 2003). Having a visualization of the entire project from start to finish is helpful for the DAT to get the big-picture view of their project, as well as to make it easier to drill down to individual tasks and milestones. It is helpful to have the completed timeline readily available to the DAT online and as a hard copy at meetings.

Review DAT Life Cycle. At this stage in the planning process, the DAT is nearly ready to implement its project. Momentum starts to build in the group around this point, and it can become challenging to get the group to "zoom out" and consider longer term outcomes. It can be helpful to remind the group of the big picture using the DAT Life Cycle diagram (Figure 1.1.) Often, they will be surprised at how much work they have already accomplished, and this can be a moment to celebrate their successes.

Digital Toolkit
Slide 10.2:
DAT Life Cycle

Form Subgroups. Once tasks, resource needs, and limitations are articulated, groups are often ready to form subgroups to implement the plan. These subgroups work on their projects between the DAT meetings. Facilitators can assist subgroups by guiding and delegating the following tasks: forming the subgroup, subgroup meeting agenda making, reminders about homework and action items, reminders about subgroup meetings, creating subfolders for subgroup work in the shared drive, helping craft reasonable expectations around doing homework, defining subgroup deliverables, and prompting subgroups to report key information to the DAT. However, it is important that facilitators empower DAT members in the organization and delegation of this work, as it is easy for the DAT to over-rely on the facilitators to make these tasks happen.

Subgroups are effective because members have developed a high degree of trust in one another. The subgroups are motivated to do excellent work because they have a strong sense of belonging in the DAT and ownership of their component of the project. However, to keep members feeling valued and important, it is essential that certain roles do not always get relegated to certain members. For example, it is possible that students, women, or other members of minoritized groups could be relegated to note-taking or assessment marking. This leads to some DAT members feeling undervalued. Encouraging DAT members to rotate between groups or between roles within a group will allow all group members to learn about all the tasks that are related to the function of the group. Flexibility is key to inclusivity, especially when figuring out how all members can participate in and contribute to the DAT.

DATS IN REAL LIFE

What if the DAT has difficulty converging on a plan of action?

We have encountered groups who have had problems arriving at or developing an action plan. Three patterns or "types" of groups were encountered. These are described below, along with the efforts made by facilitators to help them.

Digital Toolkit

Slides 6.8–6.9: WAIT (Why Am I Talking?)

Several groups took up to a year to articulate their priority area or a concrete project. These groups often tended to have long discussions that were tangential to the agenda or had individuals who had a propensity to be long-winded. Facilitators tried several tactics to move the work forward. The introduction of skills such as WAIT (Why Am I Talking) were somewhat successful in minimizing the long-winded periods and redirecting the conversations, but they didn't solve the problem. In order to disrupt this pattern of whole group discussion, facilitators designed activities which allowed the group to collect many ideas from everyone quickly. Facilitators would then typically summarize those ideas in writing on the shared drive outside of the meeting. When a group was unaccustomed to activities, the facilitators would take time to frame the goal of the activity, explain how it related to their larger goals, and give clear instructions, both written and verbal, at the next meeting.

Facilitators also worked to disrupt ineffective whole group discussion by asking the group to reflect on those patterns during process skill time. They would return to key collaboration norms, collect feedback from the participants about their meeting experience (and summarize it for the group), and initiate periodic reviews of the community standards. When it seemed beneficial, facilitators offered to meet certain participants for coffee to talk about their ideas and concerns for the DAT, and in turn share concerns facilitators had about the ways that conversations were not well regulated.

There were other groups which were not overly divergent in their conversation, but needed time to come to a better understanding of their department. Initial meetings of these groups revealed many disparate concerns, or different perspectives on the same concern. When these groups had trouble finding departmental data that could help them arrive at a priority focus, some of them proactively conducted a survey on the issues that their department seemed to be struggling with. Other teams organized and wrote a review of their findings and ideas in report form and requested departmental feedback. Then, in the second year, they turned to change projects that they could implement. Facilitators made sure to celebrate all intermediate milestones these groups were achieving, whether it was organizing their ideas, producing a short report of their ideas, presenting their ideas at a faculty meeting, constructing or selecting a survey instrument, or summarizing the results of a survey. These groups did good work and made progress, though their time frame was more extensive than average.

Lastly, some groups were composed of personalities that were less inclined to take action. Often these meetings would be very congenial and include many great ideas, but participants did not take initiative to prioritize the ideas or volunteer to put them into practice. This placed an added responsibility on the facilitator to remind members of the importance of goal setting and action item creation during meetings. In these groups, facilitators focused on using consensus-based decision-making processes, such as Fist to Five and Consensus Cards. It was also important for time to be set aside for listing all the proposed action items and asking for a volunteer for each action item before the meeting ended. When action items were proposed, but did not have a volunteer, the facilitators would put the action item into the follow-up email, flagged with the name "someone" in a bright color.

Using data

One of the Core Principles of the DAT model is that "data collection, analysis, and interpretation inform decision-making." Data-informed decision-making may not be a part of the departmental culture, but it can become part of the culture of the DAT. The data used by DATs primarily come in two forms. First, DATs often draw upon the research literature in education and institutional change. Because most DAT participants are disciplinary experts, but not education researchers, they are unfamiliar with this literature. Facilitators can introduce them to the education and change research literature specifically related to their discipline.

Secondly, facilitators can help connect participants to institutional data collected either by the university or by their own department. Sometimes reports and surveys already exist, while at other times the DAT will need to collect meaningful data on their undergraduate population. Research data is particularly powerful for DATs to understand the context in which they are

Principle 3:
Data collection, analysis, and interpretation inform decision-making.

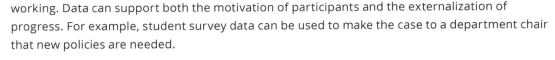

working. Data can support both the motivation of participants and the externalization of progress. For example, student survey data can be used to make the case to a department chair that new policies are needed.

Digital Toolkit
Slide 1.3: Core Principle 3, Slides 11.0–11.2: Data Analysis and Interpretation

A DAT may collect a variety of data that relate to its area of inquiry. For instance, a DAT focused on the student community might initiate a survey of students or conduct a student focus group. These data can inform the actions of the DAT and provide a benchmark to view the DAT's progress over time. That is, DATs can collect data early in the process, and then collect similar data after implementing programs and projects for a couple of years to measure progress and impact. Facilitators can help DATs focus on the type of data that is relevant in determining what projects to engage in and how to assess the impact of these projects.

DAT facilitators may also collect data on their work with the DAT. These data can take a variety of forms, which are described below. Because we developed the DAT model as part of a grant-funded research project, we collected an extensive amount of data. However, others who are simply facilitating DATs may not need to collect the same amount of data. In some cases, these facilitators may be interested in or mandated to collect data to support their efforts in working with departments. There are generally two types of data DATs and facilitators might collect in their work: qualitative and quantitative.

Qualitative data focus on rich descriptions of the DAT, its participants, or the context in which it operates. A simple form of "anecdata" comes from informal conversations with participants about how things are going. These simple checks help facilitators understand how members view the DAT's work and when to adjust course. More formally, facilitators can use interviews and focus groups to get more detailed feedback. They may also analyze meeting notes, reflections, and open-ended surveys of DAT members to monitor their progress as facilitators.

Quantitative data seek to assign numbers to the phenomena of interest and allow for easy tracking of progress over time. These forms of data include analytics from institutional research, faculty and student surveys, and observation data collected in classrooms. The range of quantitative measures is broad and it's imperative that the right ones are chosen for any particular question.

How Do Facilitators Help the DAT Implement Their Action Plan and Monitor Progress?

Principle 2:
Work focuses on achieving collective positive outcomes.

The ultimate purpose of engaging in a change effort is to achieve desired outcomes. One of the DAT Core Principles highlights the importance of a positive outcomes focus. The Theory of Change describes these as being of "appropriate scale," which recognizes that a DAT cannot realistically achieve all its outcomes at all scales during the one to two years when it is externally facilitated. Nevertheless, it is critical that the DAT achieve some outcomes that represent meaningful change; that those outcomes are recognized by the department; and that the DAT helps members to grow into true change agents who can continue DAT-like work on their own. That is what defines the "appropriate scale."

Implementation. Implementation of the DAT's plan of action coincides with the third phase in the Change Cycle (Fig 6.2). This involves both engaging in the activities laid out in the plan and monitoring progress with respect to the desired outcomes, using pre-determined metrics of success. Ideally, action and reflection should support each other through a *continuous improvement* lens. That is, rather than viewing "implementation" as a single event, the DAT should think of implementation as an iterative process of trying something out, getting rapid feedback, and adjusting so that the next iteration is more likely to align with the desired outcome. Once the DAT has engaged in enough action/reflection cycles, they can then proceed back to phase one by reassessing the state of the department and their desired outcomes in light of the changes they implemented during the previous Change Cycle.

Often, a pilot or a limited trial of the project is warranted, particularly when the project is large in scope, expensive, or affects large numbers of faculty and students. Therefore, it is useful to encourage DAT members to view their work as a continuous improvement process from the start. With the DAT Core Principle of "Continuous improvement is an upheld practice", instead of seeing the realized action plan as a fixed endpoint, it is viewed as an iterative process, whereby the new current state is identified, feedback and evaluation data are reviewed, appropriate changes are made, and the cycle is repeated.

Principle 5:
Continuous improvement is an upheld practice.

The time required for implementation will vary, of course, depending on the project. Most projects can be launched in the time frame of a year or two. Pilots generally can be targeted to occur within an academic semester (Elrod & Kezar, 2017), but with the recognition that getting the DAT up and running may take the better part of its first semester.

Monitoring. In addition to implementing the project, it is important for DAT members to measure their progress over time. Monitoring will ensure that the stated goals have been met or progress toward them is being made. The monitoring will also allow the DAT to identify if new issues have arisen. Careful documentation of processes and progress allows subgroups within the DAT to keep current as a collective. Monitoring also allows the DAT and subgroups to develop indicators of successful work, which are later externalized as part of the continuous feedback process described above.

Care taken to develop a detailed action plan makes monitoring the DAT's progress easier. Monitoring of the action plan through specific benchmarks, deliverables, work assignments, and timelines provides concrete information for decision-making. The main tasks in monitoring are regularly revisiting the timeline, revising the timelines or deliverables if justified, or holding members accountable for missing timelines or deliverables. Facilitators help by making sure a review of what has been accomplished is on the agenda near the beginning of the meeting and that the assignment of clear deliverables and action items occurs near the end. In this way, if adjustments need to be made to the schedule, dependent tasks can be adjusted as well.

Evaluation. The evaluation of the DAT action plan is critical to determining the project's success and charting a way forward. Facilitators cannot stress the importance of proper assessment of the DAT projects too highly. Although a large percentage of DAT projects claim success, it has been reported that a small number of change efforts related to undergraduate STEM education present strong evidence of failure (Henderson et al., 2011). The evaluation process or cycle should be based upon the criteria identified during the goal development stage, which are defined as measurable attributes of the new end state, arrived at once goals have been attained. The SMART goals created early in the process provide the basis for your evaluation phase. Evaluation planning should begin as soon as the DAT commits to a concrete project and plans should be reviewed and revised as the project evolves.

Specific tools may assist in determining the degree to which a change has been implemented in practice. Innovation Configuration Maps (IC Maps) may be used to chart the degree to which an innovation has taken hold in a department (Hall & Hord, 2015). We use them in our work in a variety of ways: to determine a DAT's alignment with the DAT model, to share with DAT members as a self-assessment tool, and to show stakeholders a DAT's progress. See Chapter 1 for a more detailed description of IC Maps.

Rubrics can also be utilized to determine the state of change implementation. The PULSE Vision & Change Rubrics have been used to determine the degree to which Life Sciences departments have implemented change efforts. These rubrics have been shown to be valid tools to assess the state of the change efforts under study (Brancaccio-Taras et al. 2016).

Other evaluation frameworks for education may also be used. Facilitators should take care to determine if a framework is relevant and how it will provide meaning for the DAT's work before employing an evaluation framework.

Indicators of Success

Evidence that the DAT process is successful

The DAT has achieved its goals when meaningful, sustainable change related to undergraduate education has been achieved. A number of indicators will inform facilitators that the DAT model has been followed, the DAT process was successful, and meaningful change has occurred.

The DAT project goals have been achieved and their assessment metrics indicate success. The DAT developed SMART goals early in the planning process. Achievement of these goals will be a key determining factor of DAT success. An assessment plan was developed and the evaluation of the resulting metrics will indicate whether the DAT achieved success, to what degree, and in which areas of the project.

DAT members value the DAT process and perceive the DAT to be successful. Valuing the DAT process is signified by DAT members demonstrating awareness of the process and seeing the process as a productive and fulfilling way to get work done. The DAT process involves a series of activities to implement change, the growth in DAT members as change agents, and the proper function of facilitators.

DAT members increase their capacity around collaboration. DAT members can use collaboration tools and strategies for decision-making, navigating the politics of their department, managing group dynamics, and resolving conflicts. Use of the eight Norms of Collaboration support DAT members in interacting with other members of the department, eliciting ideas, and finding areas of common ground.

This capacity supports the DAT in developing a shared vision, goals, and a plan of action because it helps members talk to one another and reach agreement. According to Garmston & Wellman (2013), having a collaborative culture is necessary for change.

The department values the work of the DAT. Department members recognize the work and accomplishments of the DAT and see it as a positive contribution to the department. In addition, some department members are willing to engage in future change efforts due to the DAT's recognition. These other department members are more likely to engage in work they see as similar to work they themselves value or that the community around them values. Another indicator is the DAT's work is discussed positively in formal departmental contexts (e.g., faculty meetings, graduation ceremonies, "state of the department" talks, etc.) and DAT members receive rewards and recognition for their work in ways that matter to the department (e.g., departmental service awards, raises and promotions, increased influence, etc.).

IC Map: DAT Project Work

Digital Toolkit
How-To Guide 1:
Using Innovation
Configuration
Maps

In order to assess progress on DAT work, facilitators and DAT members can use the DAT Project Work IC Map. This IC Map examines two behaviors that are crucial to DAT work: the development of a shared vision of undergraduate education and the choice of projects to improve undergraduate education in the department. IC Maps, their uses, and guidelines on how to read them are covered in detail in Chapter 1.

The DAT develops a shared vision for undergraduate education

The DAT visioning work has four features: group consensus, clear articulation of the vision, goals tied to the vision, and alignment with departmental needs.	One or more of these features is missing from the DAT visioning work (circle which ones): ▪ Group consensus ▪ Clear articulation ▪ Goals ▪ Alignment with department	The DAT visioning work does not produce anything.	The DAT does not engage in visioning work.

The DAT implements projects that positively impact undergraduates in their department, are aligned with their goals, and include appropriate assessments

The DAT clearly articulates a project plan before implementation.	The DAT implements a project without articulating a project plan.	The DAT does not implement a coherent project.

The DAT implements a project that is grounded in best practices in undergraduate education.	The DAT implements a project that recognizes best practices in undergraduate education, but does not implement them properly.	The DAT implements a project while ignoring or contradicting best practices in undergraduate education.	The DAT does not implement a coherent project.

The DAT implements a project that is aligned with its goals.	The DAT implements a project that is aligned with its goals, but which also includes elements not directly related to its goals.	The DAT implements a project that is not aligned with any of its goals.	The DAT does not implement a coherent project.

The DAT implements a project that includes a detailed and actionable assessment plan.	The DAT implements a project that has an assessment plan with minor flaws. These flaws don't hinder reasonable assessment.	The DAT implements a project that has an assessment plan with major flaws that make reasonable assessment impossible.	The DAT implements a project without an assessment plan.	The DAT does not implement a coherent project.

Recommended Reading

Garmston, R. J., & Wellman, B. M. (2013). *The Adaptive School: A sourcebook for developing collaborative groups*. Rowman & Littlefield.

This book has greatly informed how we approach facilitation and change in an educational setting. Appendix A of *The Adaptive School* details many facilitator moves and resources, some of which are replicated in our Digital Toolkit. In their book, Garmston and Wellman also provide examples of how to handle challenging situations as a facilitator.

Lipmanowicz, H., & McCandless, K. (2013). *The surprising power of liberating structures: Simple rules to unleash a culture of innovation*. Liberating Structures Press.

Liberating Structures were designed to change the ways in which groups interact and communicate in order to support inclusive engagement. Lipmanowicz and McCandless recommend that Liberating Structures activities be used to disrupt routines and unleash creativity. They have made their activities freely available at their website, www.liberatingstructures.com.

CHAPTER 7

Effectively Engaging the Department

Part of a DAT's work is communicating with its department. Forms of communication include asking for permission or endorsement to proceed with a step in a change process, collecting information through a survey, or giving a presentation about the DAT's progress. The ultimate goal of this communication is to ensure that the DAT and the department maintain a positive relationship and that the department continues to support the DAT's work and the progress of its change effort. In addition, good communication helps the department recognize DAT members as change agents and to make it more likely that aspects of DAT culture will spread to the rest of the department.

This chapter discusses the relationship between the DAT and the department and outlines different types of communication that take place between a DAT and the department (e.g., dissemination or soliciting input). Communication is key for a DAT to develop allies and to maintain positive relationships. Thus, it's critical for the DAT to identify a communication process and structure. The development of a communication plan is the focus of this chapter. The chapter concludes with a discussion on cultivating allies and connecting with relevant administrators.

KEY MESSAGES

- A strong relationship between the DAT and the rest of the department is essential for moving DAT work forward and sustaining DAT efforts.

- A DAT must have a communication plan outlining: (1) who communicates with the department, (2) how and what information is conveyed to or requested from the department, and (3) how often information is shared. This establishes consistency and transparency in DAT-department interactions.

Theory of Change Context

An essential stakeholder in our Theory of Change is the department in which a DAT is situated. The DAT is not operating in a vacuum, but rather within the context of an already established department with its own complex pre-existing culture. Thus, the DAT must take into account other members of the department, departmental structures, and other aspects of departmental culture as it goes about its work. Before the DAT's change effort can truly be sustained, the department must reach a stage where many of its members value the work of the DAT. Thus, this chapter focuses on the steps that are necessary for the DAT to build a working relationship with their department.

The DAT Theory of Change identifies three key components of building a positive relationship with the department in Outcome 6D: seeking input from departmental members, cultivating allies in the department, and establishing regular communication with the rest of the department. These three components are interrelated and mutually reinforcing; for example, seeking input should be a part of establishing regular communication and can lead to developing allies.

OUTCOME 6D

The DAT builds a positive relationship with the department

The DAT regularly communicates progress, outcomes, and successes to the department

| The DAT cultivates department allies for its work | The DAT seeks department input for its work |

Although the focus of a DAT's change effort is the department, there are many stakeholders external to a department who are relevant to a DAT's success. This is represented in Outcome 6E of the DAT Theory of Change and may include administrators like Deans and Provosts or staff members in offices of admissions, institutional research, advising, and so on. The stakeholders may even come from outside the university, like members of professional societies, government, or local businesses. Depending on the DAT's specific area of focus, positive relationships with these stakeholders may be beneficial or even necessary because of the influence, resources, knowledge, or data that they could provide to the DAT. Thus, as the DAT goes about its work, it also needs to ensure that relevant stakeholders recognize this work.

OUTCOME 6E

The DAT builds a positive relationship with relevant external stakeholders

---

How Does the DAT Build a Positive Relationship with Department Members?

You may wonder: most of the DAT members are active members of the department already, so why is it necessary to explicitly think about developing a relationship between the DAT and the rest of the department? It is important because the DAT culture and its products are innovations. Research has shown that the sustainability of innovations is strongly influenced by how awareness of the innovation is disseminated through communication channels (Rogers, 2010). Thus, for the DAT's work to be sustained, a positive relationship between the DAT and the rest of the department must be established.

Moreover, the DAT may operate in a manner that is different from other groups in the department. Over time, the DAT will establish a culture and way of working that may be unique to the department. The DAT's work will likely be stronger due to the culture built by the DAT members and the capacities that DAT members have cultivated as change agents. The unique strengths that DAT members bring to the departmental culture can contribute and benefit the entire department in many ways.

Fostering a relationship and developing good communication between the DAT and the rest of the department can have many benefits. For example, if DAT members can effectively communicate why a change effort might be necessary in the department, other department members will be more likely to support their efforts (Curry, 1992). Explaining the value of the DAT work to the rest of the department and the department receiving public recognition due to the DAT's work can increase the acceptance, legitimacy, and perceived value of the DAT work. Other change efforts, such as the Science Education Initiative (SEI), have noted that public validation (e.g., presenting on campus or at conferences) of a change effort elevates the status of both the project and its team (Chasteen & Code, 2018). Showcasing contributions of the DAT can also help build momentum for the change effort across the department (Kezar & Eckel, 2002).

Principle 5:

Continuous improvement is an upheld practice.

Additionally, communication with department members about the DAT's work provides opportunities for department members to influence the work and participate more fully in the change effort. This allows for co-creation of change to happen in the department, which can lead to support from department members for putting in place structures and mechanisms that encourage change. Establishing a positive relationship with department members early on can also pave the way for future change efforts by cultivating an awareness of how change can occur and be supported.

Finally, setting appropriate expectations for how the DAT's work will impact the rest of the department is crucial for ensuring success. This can be accomplished by the DAT paying close attention to the content and delivery of these expectations when communicating with other department members (Kezar, 2014).

Obtaining input to inform DAT work

Since the DAT's work is likely to have an impact on department members and others outside of the DAT, it is important to create opportunities for other stakeholders to provide feedback on the DAT's ideas and work. This supports the DAT's mission in several ways. Other stakeholders may contribute knowledge and awareness to the DAT's work. For example, an indispensable source of feedback could come from the campus department or group that focuses on equity, diversity, and inclusion. Ultimately, the awareness that comes from seeking out the perspectives of others will help the DAT's work to have a more positive and sustainable impact on the department.

Principle 6:
Work is grounded in a commitment to equity, inclusion, and social justice.

Requesting input from other department members will also help articulate and contribute to the department's shared vision and goals, and can identify areas of concern regarding undergraduate education that are shared between the DAT and department. The DAT can note areas where the vision is shared and incorporate any new ideas into its vision. Identifying the common interests and vision can develop buy-in of department members for the DAT and its work (Kezar & Eckel, 2002). Requesting feedback from campus resources that focus on diversity and inclusion will help the DAT align with campus-wide initiatives and will increase the perceived value of the DAT and its efforts within the department.

It can be especially valuable to gather departmental input that identifies unforeseen challenges related to the DAT's work. A challenge could take the form of a departmental policy that DAT members were unaware of, or a department member who is opposed to change. Once such challenges are known, you can help DAT members assess what actions might be useful in addressing them. They might choose to engage in further conversation around those challenges with the whole department, plan to have conversations with individuals in the department, or draft and propose a new policy to the department's Executive Committee. These occasions provide an opportunity for DAT members to demonstrate that they value and use department members' input to inform the DAT's work, thus building confidence and joint ownership in the DAT's efforts.

Departmental input can be obtained in many ways. Depending on the type of input the DAT is seeking, they may integrate discussion questions into a presentation or they might send an email to department members, asking them to fill out an online survey or poll. DAT members can also have informal conversations with specific stakeholders (e.g., by inviting them out to coffee) and request feedback in a more casual manner.

In some cases, the DAT may receive input that does not productively contribute to the DAT's work. You can assist DAT members in determining how to appropriately handle such input (e.g., by identifying a different aspect of the project where this input is relevant, or creating an archive system for input that could become relevant later) and in deciding whether and how this should be communicated back to the department members.

Checking in with the department chair

As someone with more authority than most DAT members, the department chair is a prominent stakeholder. The chair influences whether the DAT exists in the department. Obtaining support from those who have positional power (e.g., undergraduate committee chair, department chair, or assistant dean) helps to facilitate change and mitigate challenges (Hyde, 2018; Kezar & Eckel, 2002). Therefore, establishing regular communication with the chair is one way to build support for the DAT's work. If the DAT model is new to your institution, a department chair may perceive it to be risky to support a DAT in the department. As a facilitator, you should acknowledge this risk by maintaining active, early, and transparent communication with the chair about the DAT's work, until DAT members have established regular communication with the chair. Helping DAT members listen to and address the department chair's concerns, expectations, wants, and needs can help the DAT move in a direction that is beneficial for the department—which will ultimately contribute to the DAT's legitimacy and success.

Digital Toolkit
How-To Guide 9:
Sustaining DATs

DATS IN REAL LIFE

What if the department chair does not value the work of the DAT?

One of the departments where a DAT was active got a new chair while the DAT's work was in progress. The previous department chair was very supportive of the DAT's work, but the new chair was not. The new chair valued research progress far more than "service," and thus questioned whether the DAT was really needed in the department.

The DAT recognized that they needed to communicate to the new chair the importance of their work and the necessity of continuing to meet as a team to accomplish it. They achieved this by developing a proposal for committee status in accordance with bylaws and presented it to the chair. Facilitators helped them develop these written materials using Round Robin Editing. The new chair shifted their perspective on the DAT, and ultimately allowed it to become a permanent "Climate Committee" in the department.

In the cases where the department chair is a member of the DAT, it can be helpful for the facilitator to establish informal or formal check-ins with the chair outside of the DAT meetings. The frequency of these meetings depends on the schedule of the department chair and how interested they are in the details and progress of the DAT's work. Since the chair will be aware of what is happening in the DAT, these meetings can focus on fitting the DAT's work into a bigger departmental vision and checking in on the chair's expectations for the DAT. Sometimes these conversations happen quite naturally at the end of a DAT meeting and do not need to be scheduled.

In cases where the department chair is not a member of the DAT, meetings with the chair can serve as an update on the DAT's work. These meetings may be initiated either by DAT members or by the facilitator. Over time, it will be crucial for DAT members to take responsibility for these check-ins and will further establish them as change agents within the department. Different chairs will want different levels of detail in updates on the DAT's work and will want to check in at varying frequencies. It can be especially useful to check in with a chair before disseminating information about the DAT's work to the rest of the department, as the chair can facilitate this process. As all chairs are busy, be sure to guide DAT members in outlining their intentions for any meeting with the chair. A balanced approach is most appropriate here: while you do not want the chair to perceive these meetings as an unwanted addition to their work, the meetings are still necessary for the DAT to achieve a positive and sustainable impact on the department.

Cultivating departmental allies for the DAT and its work

DAT allies are department members who are supportive of the DAT work but are not part of the DAT. As the political change model suggests, it is important to have DAT allies in the department, as these allies can contribute their support and resources to help the DAT make positive and sustainable changes (Kezar, 2014). DAT allies can publicly voice support for the DAT and its work and can connect DAT members to other potential contributors inside or outside the department. It is helpful for the DAT to establish allies who hold a variety of roles within the department, as this ensures that a diversity of perspectives, networks, resources, and skills can be tapped to support the DAT's work.

Building allies can happen through the process of seeking and responding to departmental members' input. Provide potential allies opportunities to weigh in on the DAT's work by asking them to provide information, recommendations, or even to participate in the decision-making processes when appropriate. When you (or DAT members) approach potential allies with these opportunities, be clear about your expectations of them. In what ways do DAT members want the ally to contribute? How will the contributions of the ally be used to influence the work? Showing allies that DAT members value the input and time of other department members builds buy-in for the work. Demonstrating that the feedback of others is carefully considered and used to influence the DAT's work will increase trust in allies and make them more likely to contribute their time and input in the future. In short, the more time that is invested in informally building relationships with allies, the more likely they will provide future support for the DAT's work.

DATS IN REAL LIFE

What if department members oppose the change efforts of the DAT?

Sometimes, department members oppose change efforts because they would require them to change their own behavior. In these cases, communicating the potential impact of the DAT's work through a lens that resonates with department members may be beneficial.

For example, one department member opposed the implementation of new instructional techniques in the department because it would require changing their teaching practices. In response, DAT members outlined the benefits of the new techniques and explained how they might be used to teach specific concepts in the instructor's courses in order to convince them to adopt the changes. Ultimately, they agreed to adopt the new instructional techniques.

How Does the DAT Establish Regular Communication with the Department?

How a department disseminates information is part of its culture (Schein, 2010). When a DAT is considering how to communicate with the rest of the department, it's important to appreciate that using established departmental methods of communication can help minimize barriers to understanding. For example, if a department typically disseminates information through short presentations at faculty meetings, the DAT should consider regularly presenting at faculty meetings. Other departments may communicate by email, via a newsletter, or through informal gatherings (e.g., departmental tea time) in order to reach more department members. Aligning with departmental culture in small ways will help department members view the DAT as an important component of the department. Regardless of the department's preferred methods of disseminating information, the DAT should try to conform to them from the very beginning of the project.

Carefully considering the content of information distributed to department members is an important part of intentional communication. By communicating about the progress and status of the DAT's ideas and work, the DAT will minimize surprises that may emerge as the DAT's work is taken up by the department. Receiving this information will also make it likely that department members will come to regard the DAT as an effective department group. The cultural model of change suggests aligning the messaging about the DAT's work with existing departmental values. (Kezar, 2014; Kezar & Eckel, 2002). If other department members can recognize departmental values in what the DAT is planning or doing (or recognize that the work of the DAT does not contradict departmental values), the messaging is more likely to be received positively.

As a facilitator, you will have likely established a working relationship with department members in the process of forming the DAT (or possibly from previous work with the department). It is important that once the DAT is formed, members of the DAT take responsibility for establishing and maintaining a relationship with the rest of the department. As an external facilitator, you will eventually step back from supporting the DAT (described in Chapter 8), and DAT members will need to continue to communicate effectively with the department and advocate for the sustainability of their work without you. Remember that as they participate in the DAT model, DAT members are building their capacities as change agents by learning about change models and strategies, along with developing communication skills that are essential to change efforts. Thus, while you can offer support and advice while communication channels between the DAT and the rest of the department are being established, make sure you are not perceived as the leader of the DAT or the liaison between the DAT and the department. If you find yourself at a departmental event, be sure to place yourself in a supportive role (such as timekeeping or note-taking) and emphasize that role when introducing yourself. When communications to the department are being planned, explain to the DAT that your role is to help them strategize. Allow them to decide which information to convey and ask the group for volunteers to email or present that information, rather than editing the content of the communication or volunteering to send or present it yourself.

Developing a departmental communication plan

To help DAT members understand how communication would be best integrated with their work, facilitators can present process skill slides for "Departmental Communications" which outline the basic elements of a communication plan that DAT members can adapt for their needs. From there, facilitators can help the DAT develop a long-term communication plan with the department. One approach facilitators have taken to help DAT members think about communication with their department has been to show slides that outline the basic elements of a communication plan, followed by a sticky note activity to gather and organize ideas.

Digital Toolkit
Slides 12.0–12.4: Departmental Communications

The DAT's long-term communication plan should describe:

- With whom in the department DAT members will communicate

- How they will conduct the communication

- How frequently they will communicate

Ideally, the DAT will develop a plan that involves frequent communication to all stakeholder groups in the department. When change efforts fail to be sustained or adopted, managers often cite insufficient communication as the weakest link in their work (Hiatt & Creasey, 2012). If communication planning begins with the formation of the DAT, it may be vague at first, but this work will help DAT members keep departmental communication in mind, so that they consider communication at every stage of the process. As the DAT's vision and project become better defined, or if changes occur in the departmental leadership or structure, facilitators should encourage the DAT to update their long-term communication plan.

The long-term communication plan should also include ways of collecting input and feedback at appropriate stages of the DAT's work. Valuable input can potentially be collected at every stage, from visioning, to project prioritization, to project planning and implementation. The DAT should identify the types of input it is seeking, the appropriate methods for obtaining and organizing this input, and how DAT members will address the input they receive. You can provide an outsider's perspective on the input that is received and on how to use it effectively. Since the input is coming from people that the DAT members know and work with, an important role for a facilitator is to assist the DAT members in determining which input and feedback is relevant and critical to address.

Preparing for effective departmental communication

Facilitators will need to support the DAT in preparing periodic updates to the department. DATs frequently request time at faculty meetings or retreats to both present their work and solicit feedback. It is helpful for facilitators to challenge DAT members to think about presenting their work more inclusively, for example, by engaging undergraduate student groups, or through a departmental resource that is accessible to everyone, like a newsletter or website.

Principle 1:
Students are partners in the educational process

In preparing presentations, you can help DAT members consider how to frame their communication by considering the communication implications of various change models (Kezar, 2014). In keeping with the DAT model principle of continuous improvement, it can be useful for DAT members to convey when the work of the DAT is still in a draft stage. This establishes the mindset that changes are not yet set in stone, and that there is still an opportunity for input to shape the work (Kezar & Eckel, 2002).

DAT members should allocate ample time to prepare for presentations to the department. Communications should be well-crafted, concise, and anticipate the needs of the audience. It can be useful to combine oral presentations, question-and-answer sessions, PowerPoint slides, and handouts, to make the information as accessible as possible. DATs often spend portions of two or three DAT meetings preparing to present their work, especially once they begin to implement projects. It can be easy for groups doing this kind of work to become bogged down in the detail of word choice and material development. Facilitators can help groups divide up the preparatory work and determine what part of the work can be done outside of meetings. However, all members should have a chance to review the materials that will be presented.

Digital Toolkit
Slides 9.5-9.7: Round Robin Consensus, Slide 9.8: Gallery Wall Editing

Two techniques that DAT facilitators have used to facilitate efficient editing of communication materials are round robin editing and gallery wall editing. In round robin editing, facilitators or DAT members bring draft materials to the DAT meeting. Small groups are formed, and everyone receives a page of materials that they did not craft. Each individual makes edits to that material, then passes their page to someone in their group. Passing continues until everyone has edited each page of material. The small group then decides which edits are most important, and passes their recommendations to the whole group, which then decides how the edits will be consolidated. For gallery wall editing, which works particularly well for PowerPoint slides, draft materials are printed with a large font and posted around the room. DAT members then take a "gallery walk" to read the materials. Each member is issued different colored stickers, which they use to up-vote or down-vote individual slides or sentences. They also have markers they can use to make text edits directly to the material. The group members then sit down and review the pattern of edits that were made, ask each other questions about the edits, and decide how they will consolidate them.

DATS IN REAL LIFE

What if DAT members do not wish to spend time preparing a communication plan?

One of our DATs wanted to make changes to their department's student learning outcomes in order to assess students' progress. Before a DAT was formally started, department members broached this topic at a departmental retreat. Little progress was made during that meeting, and it seemed as though the department did not have momentum to make these changes.

Once a DAT had formed to tackle this challenge, we spent a lot of time working with them to share their progress with the rest of the department. After the DAT members had developed their student learning outcomes, they wanted to get feedback on the new language they had proposed. DAT members were initially reluctant to spend time planning for the upcoming department meeting, but facilitators encouraged them to dedicate time to this process. An entire DAT meeting was spent discussing the types of feedback DAT members wanted to hear (e.g., about the appropriateness of the content knowledge) and strategizing how they would structure the department meeting in order to best receive that feedback. The DAT elected specific members to share different aspects of the process, based on their familiarity with the student learning outcomes work or their role in the department. In the end, the DAT received productive feedback from other department members about the student learning outcomes. Department members were simultaneously updated about the current state of the DAT's work and about what the DAT wanted to do next. In response, department members expressed buy-in on the DAT's work and openness to contributing to the DAT at a later point.

How Does the DAT Connect with Relevant Administrators?

DATs need to establish formal lines of communication with upper administration, as major change efforts are more successful when they receive support from upper administrators (Kezar & Eckel, 2002). When the DAT work is aligned with university initiatives, it is especially helpful to talk with the administrators who are championing those initiatives. This can provide facilitators and DAT members with greater insight into the motivation behind the initiative and its implementation across campus. In turn, this can inform the DAT work and prevent it from recreating an existing initiative or developing a resource that is already available on campus. Administrators may be willing to provide support for the DAT work if they view it as advancing university initiatives. For example, they may be able to allocate funds for DAT personnel or to connect the DAT with others on campus who are doing similar work.

The scale of the DAT's work, the resources that are needed, and the relationships that a DAT's department has with individual administrators must be considered when helping a DAT determine how to work with upper administration. Depending on how many DATs you are facilitating and the relevant administrators, there are pros and cons in you or DAT members initiating and sustaining communication with administrators. If you have oversight over multiple DATs that are working towards the same initiative, DATs often appreciate if you act as the liaison between them and the administrators. This protects DAT members' time, and reduces the number of people who need to be present at meetings with administrators.

Highlighting the DAT's work to upper administration can also serve to showcase the department and establish the legitimacy of the DAT in their eyes. However, as a facilitator, you should obtain permission from DAT members and make sure they are comfortable before sharing their work with upper administration.

Meeting with upper administrators is also important to maintain support for the larger DAT project at your institution. Practically, it is often difficult to meet frequently with upper administrators. In many cases, one meeting a semester is sufficient to keep an administrator aware of the work being carried out by all the DATs in an institution. Relevant communication typically includes a high-level picture of the DAT's culture, their current work, and their trajectory. It is useful to ground the DATs and their work in the context of the university as a whole and demonstrate alignment with the university's mission and values. As with other stakeholder meetings, it is necessary to develop an agenda and outline appropriate expectations for the DATs and their work.

Indicators of success

Evidence that the DAT has established regular communication with the department

There are many ways in which a DAT can communicate with department members about the DAT's work, but what is important is that it becomes a regular practice. Signs that communication has been established include standing meetings between a DAT member and the department chair or quarterly updates at departmental meetings. Since the DAT work directly impacts students, it's valuable for the DAT to establish an effective form of communication with students as well (e.g., a summary email update or a specially planned meeting to which the students are invited).

Other concrete signs that reliable communication has been established include DAT members formally seeking input from department members via surveys or polls or DAT members talking to others informally (e.g. by sharing DAT work and goals over lunch or coffee or in the hallway). Often, informal communication is as important and useful as formal methods.

Evidence that the DAT has cultivated allies

Allies may show their support in a plethora of ways, such as expressing approval of the DAT's work; offering resources to support the DAT's work; connecting DAT members with other potential allies on campus; asking for regular updates on DAT work, either via email or in-person meetings; and working to include DAT members in other initiatives.

IC Map: Relationship Between the DAT and the Department

Digital Toolkit

How-To Guide 1: Using Innovation Configuration Maps

The IC Map included below outlines three characteristics that are important for the relationship between a DAT and its department. Facilitators can use the IC Map to identify external DAT support and communication methods and structures. IC Maps, their uses, and guidelines on how to read them are covered in detail in Chapter 1.

The chair and other influential members of the department/college provide support for the DAT

The chair and other influential members of the department/college are actively engaged in the DAT's work (e.g., consulting, supporting decisions, expressing public support, or offering resources like service credit and funding).	Influential members of the department/college other than the chair are actively engaged in the DAT's work.	The chair and/or influential members of the department/college express support for the DAT in public or informal contexts, but they are not otherwise engaged in the DAT's work.	The chair and/or influential members of the department/college actively resist the DAT's work.	The chair and/or influential members of the department/college have no interaction with the DAT and its work.

Department members and the DAT engage in regular communications

Department members give feedback, hear updates, and voice support for DAT's work multiple times per semester. Communication occurs in different modalities.	Department members give feedback, hear updates, and/or voice support for the DAT's work each semester.	Department members give feedback, hear updates, and/or voice support for the DAT's work from time to time.	The DAT updates only the department chair on their goals and progress.	No member of the department is informed of DAT's work.

Department has structures and processes that enable the DAT's work to proceed

Department structures (committee requirements, decision-making processes, and service expectations) are flexible enough to allow the DAT's work to happen in ways that embody DAT principles.	Some departmental structures are flexible enough to allow the DAT's work to happen in ways that embody DAT principles. The DAT can adapt or work within the constraints of unhelpful structures.	Department structures are rigid or non-existent in ways that hinder DAT work from happening.

Recommended Reading

Garmston, R. J., & Wellman, B. M. (2013). *The Adaptive School: A sourcebook for developing collaborative groups*. Rowman & Littlefield.

> This book has greatly informed how we approach facilitation and change in an educational setting. Appendix A of *The Adaptive School* details many facilitator moves and resources, some of which are replicated in our Digital Toolkit. In their book, Garmston and Wellman also provide examples of how to handle challenging situations as a facilitator.

Lipmanowicz, H., & McCandless, K. (2013). *The surprising power of liberating structures: Simple rules to unleash a culture of innovation*. Liberating Structures Press.

> Liberating Structures were designed to change the ways in which groups interact and communicate in order to support inclusive engagement. Lipmanowicz and McCandless recommend that Liberating Structures activities be used to disrupt routines and unleash creativity. They have made their activities freely available at their website, www.liberatingstructures.com.

CHAPTER 8

The DAT's Future

This chapter focuses on strategies and perspectives needed to continue a DAT's work after external facilitation has concluded. In most situations, external facilitators will not be available on an ongoing basis; thus, it is necessary to make plans for the future of the DAT. We encourage conversations about the DAT's future to happen during the formative stages of the DAT and periodically during the course of the DAT's work. In some situations, a DAT will disband once its initial project is completed. This chapter provides suggestions for supporting the development of internal facilitators for a DAT, to help ensure that the DAT continues after the initial project, if desired. Additionally, we examine circumstances when a team wants to continue, but does not maintain alignment with the DAT model. We also discuss some infrequent situations in which facilitators may opt to discontinue support for a DAT.

KEY MESSAGES

- It is important to have ongoing conversations with the DAT members (and key stakeholders) about the DAT's future.

- Each DAT's course forward will be unique to its context.

- It is important to deliberately plan for internal DAT facilitation before external facilitation ends, if a DAT is to continue.

Theory of Change Context

This chapter focuses on planning for a DAT's future. Ideally, external facilitation of a DAT will not end until after the four intermediate outcomes of Stage 2 in the TOC have been achieved to some extent. These outcomes are: the department values the work of the DAT (Outcome 7), the DAT has effected change related to undergraduate education (Outcome 8), DAT members are change agents (Outcome 9), and DAT members enact DAT culture without help (Outcome 10). These outcomes are unlikely to be achieved simultaneously, and facilitators should support the DAT in making continuous progress toward them. Strategies for helping DAT members assess their progress in these intermediate outcomes are briefly covered in this chapter. It is essential that these outcomes be achieved to some extent before facilitators exit the DAT, in order for the DAT members to be well-prepared to make future change in the department. Facilitators should also help DAT members think about the future of the DAT beyond these outcomes. This chapter outlines how to support DATs in preparing for a future without external facilitators.

OUTCOME 7	OUTCOME 8	OUTCOME 9	OUTCOME 10
The department values the work of the DAT	The DAT has affected change related to undergraduate education	DAT members are change agents	DAT members enact DAT culture without help

How Do Facilitators Navigate a DAT's Future?

Although we outline several possible futures for DATs in this chapter, every DAT is unique, and the path forward for each DAT will look different. Because of this, initiating conversations about the DAT's future several times while you work with a DAT can help DAT members better think about and prepare for their future. The future of a DAT typically falls within one of the following categories: continuing the DAT with external facilitators, continuing the DAT with internal facilitators, and not continuing the DAT as an independent group. There are many variations within these categories, and different DATs may choose similar paths, but for dissimilar reasons.

Talking about the possible paths forward, along with motivations for choosing a certain path, helps set expectations for all stakeholders, including facilitators, DAT members, and other department members. Proactive communication about the DAT's future also creates opportunities to gather input on the DAT's future from all stakeholders.

As expressed in our TOC, an intended outcome of the DAT is that its work is valued by the department. This outcome must be discussed by the DAT and its stakeholders when determining the future of the DAT. It is highly improbable that a DAT will continue its work if the department does not understand and find value in it. Lack of connection between the DAT and the department is a major negative factor that would likely result in the disbanding of the DAT.

DAT members may have ideas on how facilitation can be modified to suit their needs, and, as a facilitator, you might have ideas on how a DAT's structure or member behavior would ideally change in order to better align with the DAT model. Making the proactive exchange of these ideas a regular event lessens the burden on those who might wish to share feedback. It also provides a path for anyone who may need to leave the DAT. By engaging in these conversations about the future of the DAT, you can make adjustments to support the DAT's desired path forward. Finally, when facilitators and DAT members take the opportunity to choose that path together, the experience reinforces ownership in the DAT and builds buy-in for future work.

Principle 5:
Continuous improvement is an upheld practice.

Initiating a conversation about the DAT's future

There are many ways you can structure a conversation about the future of the DAT. In the following sections, we explore several possible strategies.

Reflection. A useful preliminary activity is to ask DAT members to reflect on their initial expectations about participating in the DAT, and whether those expectations were met. Member reflections can reveal dissatisfaction with the DAT model or highlight aspects of the DAT model they found helpful. You can also ask the DAT members to reflect on what they gained from participating in the DAT, and what they would like to accomplish individually or as a team in the next year. Feedback that stems from this conversation can inform the DAT's trajectory and your contributions as a facilitator.

Digital Toolkit
How-To Guide 8: Using DAT Member Input

Innovation Configuration Maps. Another way to prepare DAT members for a conversation about the future is to use the Innovation Configuration (IC) maps to talk about the DAT's alignment with the DAT model (IC Maps are introduced in Chapter 1 and are located at the end of most other chapters). Ask DAT members to fill out one or more of the blank IC Maps on their own, and then conduct a team conversation around their responses. In most cases, their responses will correspond with the existing components of the IC Maps. Emphasize that following the DAT model requires continuous attention, but that strict adherence is not necessary. Explain how the IC Maps are not an evaluation, but rather a guide and a tracking tool that allows for "wiggle room". The departures are an opportunity to have a conversation about the ways in which members want to guide themselves. Individual DATs may have good reasons to depart from certain aspects of the model. Point out that the IC Maps are useful because they help members actively track how the DAT is functioning and make intentional, well-informed adjustments. A conversation about the IC Maps can illuminate behaviors that DAT members may want to focus on for the upcoming year or may even lead DAT members to realize that they are interested in using the DAT model for their work.

Digital Toolkit
How-To Guide 1: Using Innovation Configuration Maps

If you are co-facilitating a DAT, filling out the IC Maps independently from DAT members may illuminate different perspectives on how the DAT is operating, help you check on your awareness of the DAT's practices, and allow you to determine if you want to continue working with the DAT. Generally, the facilitator responses to the IC Maps should be kept private, although in certain cases it may be appropriate to work them carefully into a conversation with the DAT.

Review DAT Life Cycle. Reviewing the DAT Life Cycle (Figure 1.1) is another way of setting the stage for a conversation about the DAT's future. Facilitators can use it to celebrate the DAT's hard work throughout the different stages of its life cycle. From there, facilitators can suggest to DAT members that it is time to have a conversation about the DAT's future. Indicate that this is routine and try to plan for these conversations to happen annually, if not every semester. It is useful to frame this conversation as a check-in for all stakeholders in the DAT, and as an

Digital Toolkit
Slide 10.2: DAT Life Cycle

opportunity to discuss feedback between DAT members and facilitators. Alerting DAT members to this opportunity in advance will give them time to think about the DAT on their own, before sharing their thoughts in a group setting.

Another way to approach conversations about the DAT's future is to incorporate smaller comments and conversations about sustainability and future work throughout multiple meetings during the course of the DAT's work. Continuously attending to the future of the DAT and its work ensures that DAT members are frequently thinking about mechanisms of sustainability. Time permitting, this could be built into every meeting's conversation, so that it becomes a habit and part of the DAT's culture.

It is essential to provide opportunities for all members to voice their opinions on the path forward for the DAT. Depending on the dynamics of the DAT, certain members (students and staff in particular) may not perceive themselves as having any influence on the DAT's existence. As a facilitator, you may need to create opportunities where members can contribute their thoughts anonymously, or you may need to synthesize DAT members' opinions into a form that can be used to inform the path of the DAT.

Principle 1:
Students are partners in the educational process

Moving forward after the completion of a DAT

As you engage with DAT members about the future of the DAT, you need to determine who has the power to make decisions about the path forward and establish a process for making these decisions. For example, if it is within the power of the DAT members to decide, you can use an activity such as "Thumbs Up" to structure the decision-making process. In this activity, participants are presented with an option and vote by putting a thumb up to indicate agreement on moving forward with that option, sideways to indicate more discussion is needed, and down to indicate a vote against that option (Garmston & Wellman, 2013). It may be the case that an Executive Committee or the department chair has the ultimate say in whether the DAT continues— and knowing this is useful for the DAT members. There may be other stakeholders who contribute input on the DAT's future, such as upper administrators. In some cases, DATs may choose to present their case for continuing (or disbanding) to the department chair and other stakeholders.

The right path forward will look different for every DAT. It is important to be as transparent as possible about the decision-making process and to give DAT members and yourself an opportunity to provide input. In this section, we have outlined some of the potential paths forward for DATs. In some DATs, the change that they are trying to make to undergraduate education will be completed and the DAT may end. In other cases, the change has not been completed and the DAT must continue (with internal facilitation). It's also possible that the intended change has not been completed and the DAT disbands without accomplishing its goal, or its goal is absorbed into a different structure for completion (e.g., an existing departmental committee takes on the DAT's goals).

As the DAT considers its options, there are several questions DAT members may think about in order to choose a path forward. They include:

- Will the DAT continue to operate as a discrete group?
- Will the DAT continue with current external facilitators, find another external facilitator, or choose an internal facilitator?
- What will guide DAT membership going forward?

- What will be the mission and primary projects going forward?
- What activities will be outside the scope of the DAT?

Once a DAT has engaged in these conversations, the next step is to determine how the answers to these questions will influence the DAT's path forward. Identifying what is working well for the team and what needs to change is a concrete way to process feedback and can prompt some minor changes in structure or behavior. For example, DAT members may request more independence in setting the agenda, but would still like the assistance of facilitators to guide the meetings. You can support the DAT members in writing up these agendas or simply ask for more input on the goals for each agenda. During the reflection process, DAT members may decide there is a particular principle they would like to focus on in their upcoming work. Implementing this change in focus for the upcoming semester could prompt members to frame their conversations so they explicitly include this principle and ultimately alter individual behaviors and group dynamics.

The DAT continues with external facilitators. If the DAT would like to continue with external facilitators, there are many paths forward. If you are interested in continuing to facilitate the DAT, reflect on whether you have the capacity to do so. It may be possible to secure funding so that you would be compensated for your continued facilitation. Or, you can continue facilitating the DAT, but decrease the frequency with which you attend meetings.

If you do not have the capacity or desire to continue facilitating the DAT, you may help the DAT to find others on campus who are interested in facilitating. Alternatively, you can ask the DAT to find another facilitator and offer to share your experiences so that a new facilitator is prepared to support the DAT.

The DAT continues independently and DAT members become facilitators. The DAT model does not intend for external facilitators to be a part of the DAT in perpetuity. DATs that value facilitation services and have members who are interested in developing facilitation skills can choose this pathway. Alternatively, members from a different DAT on campus could provide external facilitation for this DAT, or the two DATs could trade facilitators so each can enjoy the benefits of external facilitation. In some cases, someone from the DAT's department can serve as a facilitator for the DAT. In these scenarios, a DAT will continue to operate, but DAT program facilitators will transition out of the DAT. This process, which we refer to as "facilitator fading," is described in more detail in the following sections.

DATS IN REAL LIFE

What if new facilitators stop using norms of collaboration or other aspects of the DAT model?

In one of our longest running DATs, for which external facilitation ended several years ago, the DAT continued to articulate their community standards, but did not emphasize norms of collaboration. After years of operating on their own, they approached us to request support with self-facilitation. We invited them to attend some public brown bags on facilitation that we had organized and offered to schedule individual consultations to introduce some of the ideas in the Training New Facilitators section later in the chapter.

One of the challenges in self-facilitated DATs is that it's not always possible to know how self-facilitation is going once the DAT is independent. Some DATs choose not to continue to use the team's mailing list or shared folder. The former external facilitators can email the current facilitators periodically to learn how things are going and offer support, but not all DATs will choose to participate.

It can be awkward if a DAT continues to call itself a DAT, but begins to operate more like a typical committee. If the DAT is no longer a voluntary assignment or is excluding staff or students, for example, it is no longer operating within the DAT model. Sometimes this can be avoided by asking newly independent DATs if they plan to change their structure, and, if so, suggesting they change the name of the group. Some of our DATs have done this. Information on structural changes can be gathered through a periodic survey of former DATs. If you learn there have been significant departures from the DAT model, it's important to initiate a conversation with their current leadership and request a name change. If there is confusion on campus about what defines a DAT, it will negatively impact the successful formation of new DATs.

The DAT chooses to disband. In some cases, a decision is made to discontinue the DAT. DAT members and facilitators can either choose to wrap up the DAT after a certain period, or after their project or work is complete. In this pathway, DAT members may choose to continue implementing specific aspects of the DAT model (e.g., including students in decisions about education or using norms of collaboration in meetings) in other contexts, such as departmental committees or research groups. Some DATs will create mechanisms for sustaining their project work, and once those mechanisms are in place, they will discontinue meeting as a team.

Alternatively, facilitators or DAT members may decide that the DAT model is not appropriate given the available resources or the desired change. Regardless of the reason for disbanding, DAT members will have gained some capacities as change agents during the time spent with the DAT. It is beneficial to remind DAT members of what they have gained, and to reflect on how these capacities may be applied beyond the DAT. It is also worthwhile, if the context suggests this would be fruitful, to consider the option of reconvening annually to reflect on past actions and progress.

Most department members report not having sufficient time to engage in work outside of their job description. If DAT members feel overburdened by their participation in the DAT or are unable to commit fully to the DAT, they may feel it is necessary to disband the DAT. This leaves open the possibility for continuing the work in a less time-intensive manner or for re-establishing the DAT at a later date. In this case, facilitators can offer to provide consultations to help individuals move the work of the DAT forward.

The duration of a DAT can be variable. Some DAT members may feel that it is not necessary to continue meeting as a standalone team past the completion of the original project. They may also find that they have insufficient resources (e.g., time and money) to continue. On a more positive note, the DAT may find that it has "worked itself out of a job" by putting mechanisms into place to sustain the changes that were made in the department.

What if a decision is made to discontinue the DAT?

In one DAT, the members did not feel that the norms of collaboration and time spent talking about team functioning was productive. Consequently, they asked facilitators to stop including time for process skills in the agenda. At the time, facilitators complied with this request because they felt it would be even more detrimental to the team's functioning and to their legitimacy as facilitators to continue including time for process skills. As the semester progressed, the team established short-term goals that could be accomplished at the end of the semester. When the facilitators deliberately broached the topic of the DAT's future towards the middle of the semester, it became evident that the DAT members had a different perspective on the purpose of the DAT and their department culture was less supportive of this kind of collaborative work than they and the facilitators realized when the DAT started.

At times it is necessary to assess how the DAT culture fits with the department culture and to determine if the DAT is optimally suited (or even partially suited) to the department. The misalignment of expectations and cultures can sometimes occur even when there appears to be a satisfactory environment for starting a DAT. In this example, the facilitators, upon analysis and reflection, chose to withdraw their support because the department was also withdrawing its support. In the middle of the second semester, the DAT members decided to end the DAT after they achieved their short-term goals. The facilitators supported them through that process.

Even when a DAT does not continue, DAT members may choose to keep using aspects of the DAT model in other groups they are involved with, particularly when facilitators offer their support. We have provided facilitation trainings and held discussions with former DAT members to support them in developing more effective groups. DAT members have also advocated that their groups engage in activities that embody DAT principles that they value, such as a strong commitment to diversity and inclusion, data-driven decisions, and inclusion of students as authentic partners in departmental committee work.

Facilitators choose to leave a DAT. Facilitators invest significant time and energy into supporting a DAT. As resources at universities and colleges are limited, at some point, it is necessary to consider the return on investment for facilitator efforts. You may recognize that a department simply isn't ready for the types of changes a DAT advocates, department members are not able to contribute the time and energy necessary to make a DAT successful, or the DAT has progressed to the point that external facilitation is no longer needed. In other cases, you may encounter resistance to the DAT model throughout the project or hostility towards you as an external facilitator. In these cases, you must make the difficult choice between continuing your efforts with that DAT or taking on a new role elsewhere.

Initiating a conversation about leaving the DAT can be potentially challenging, depending on the reason for departure. This conversation should be broached during the annual or semi-annual dialogue about the DAT's future. In preparation for this meeting, outline the reasons why you are unable to continue facilitating the DAT and describe what the DAT has done well. At the meeting,

Digital Toolkit

Handout 7:
Statement of
Recognition

encourage the group to continue to follow the DAT model after your departure. You can also use this opportunity to bring up ways in which the DAT can grow, if you feel that's appropriate. Additionally, if you have the bandwidth, share with the DAT the ways that you can support them in the future (e.g., consulting about educational research or providing feedback on meeting agendas), as well as other resources that would help their work (e.g., books on facilitation).

DATS IN REAL LIFE

What if DAT facilitators leave a DAT after their first year of work?

One DAT completed many of the milestones in the DAT Innovation Configuration Maps in their first semester, including assembling a diverse team, completing visioning, developing a sense of community, and planning a project. However, during their second semester, the group suffered from spotty attendance and some distracted behavior during meetings, particularly among faculty DAT members. Facilitators noticed that students were being asked for input, but were not being offered important roles in the project or exhibiting strong signs of ownership. Facilitators predicted that the group would be able to complete their initial project, but would not likely expand the scope of their work during a second year.

Given that several other departments had expressed interest in starting a DAT, facilitators decided that the best use of their resources was to end external facilitation with this DAT after a year and begin a new DAT. In the middle of the second semester, the facilitators developed a script in which they described the DAT's progress and the path they envisioned the DAT could take to successfully complete the project. The facilitators then explained that they would be ending external facilitation, because the DAT members were capable of completing the project on their own. The DAT accepted the facilitator's perspectives, and the group celebrated their work together at the end of the year. The department chair and associate chair collaborated to complete the project.

How Do Facilitators Support DAT Members in Becoming Internal Facilitators?

Other researchers engaged in grassroots change work have found that facilitation roles are not readily taken up by group members after external facilitators leave a group, even when external facilitators model these roles for one or more semesters' worth of meetings (Berger et al., 2018). This suggests that an explicit, consensus-based and gradual transition between facilitation models is important to support DAT members in intentionally developing their facilitation skills and taking on responsibility for facilitation.

Assessing interest in taking over facilitator responsibilities

If the DAT expresses interest in continuing with internal facilitators, the first step towards their independence is to find out if there are DAT members who are interested in taking on or sharing facilitation roles. Because DAT members do not typically have experience in facilitation, it is important to outline the responsibilities of a facilitator before asking for volunteers. This serves two purposes: (1) it reveals the work and thought (to some extent) that goes into facilitation, so that volunteers are not surprised when they step into this role, and (2) it breaks down what may seem like an unfamiliar role into manageable, approachable tasks that can lower the barrier for DAT members who are hesitant to take on facilitation.

DAT members sometimes perceive the facilitator role as passive, whereas in reality, facilitators draw on many resources to effectively facilitate the DAT, both during and outside of meeting time. Explaining how facilitation is an active (albeit neutral) role is imperative for appropriately shaping DAT member expectations. Interested DAT members may be concerned about the challenge of simultaneously facilitating and participating in the group. In this case, it is helpful to introduce the idea that a person in these roles can signal which "hat" they are wearing before making a contribution—whether as facilitator or participant. While this is a skill to be learned, it is entirely possible to do it well.

Digital Toolkit

Slides 5.0-5.5:

Facilitation

Information about the responsibilities of facilitators is found in Chapter 3. It can be helpful to introduce these ideas in a meeting, give members some time to think about whether they are interested in learning more about facilitation, and ask for volunteers in a subsequent meeting. Ideally, these conversations would occur three to six months before a facilitation transition is anticipated.

Interested DAT members may decide to split up the responsibilities held by facilitators. For example, one DAT member might become the note-taker, another might keep track of time and logistics, and a third might facilitate the meeting. This allows for the DAT to continue working without losing the support of the facilitator role, but provides time for DAT members to develop into facilitators and helps spread out the work.

If only one DAT member is interested in becoming a facilitator, you will need to prioritize the support and resources that you offer so that the DAT member is not overwhelmed by the various components of facilitation. If you are not available for support, it will be even more important for you to connect this DAT member with other facilitators and resources. If there are multiple DAT members who are interested in becoming facilitators, you can work with them on establishing a balance of responsibilities. Having multiple DAT members volunteer for facilitation is ideal, as distributing the work eases new facilitators into the role and is beneficial when one of the new facilitators cannot make a meeting. By engaging in the planning and debriefing as a group, you can help the DAT members form a departmental community for facilitators.

Offering to work with and support DAT members as they take on facilitator roles can ease fears DAT members may have about assuming this responsibility to the team. To this end, we offer a suggested plan for supporting DAT members as they take on the role of the facilitator.

Training new facilitators

Once DAT members have volunteered to learn how to facilitate, it is very helpful to organize several training meetings to help them develop their capacities as facilitators. Chapters 4 and 6 of this guide and other resources on facilitation that you have found most helpful can provide the content and structure for the training. Sharing your personal stories of how you interacted with this material and implemented it in DAT meetings is an effective way of making these skills relatable. In addition, you may have used other resources outside of this guide when developing as a facilitator. Sharing all these resources with DAT members will allow them to select the specific ones that best fit their needs.

DAT facilitators act as change agents and serve to guide the group in a change effort, a focus which can boost enthusiasm for facilitation among the DAT members. Help DAT members to identify the capacities they have developed as change agents and point out to them how these capacities can contribute to facilitation. For example, investigating the resources on and off campus that can benefit the DAT's work is a significant responsibility of a change agent and overlaps directly with the ways in which facilitators contribute to the DAT. DAT members who learned about strategies for effecting change will have a foundation for developing long-term plans for change efforts, which is a prominent aspect of the work that facilitators perform when constructing DAT agendas.

DAT members interested in becoming facilitators benefit greatly from partnering with external facilitators before the latter "fade" from meetings. There are several ways to train new facilitators, and your approach will vary based on the culture of the DAT, the timeframe in which new facilitators must be trained, and the new facilitators themselves. Regardless of the approach you take, it is useful to work with facilitators-in-training on facilitation before, during, and after DAT meetings.

Digital Toolkit
How-To Guide 5: Documenting and Reflecting on Meetings

Before DAT meetings. As you work with facilitators-in-training, consider scaffolding their learning as they take on increasing leadership responsibilities. During training, external facilitators and facilitators-in-training typically co-plan agendas. Emphasize that your agenda creation process is based on the DAT's needs and describe your facilitator decisions and actions explicitly to the trainees. As you involve facilitators-in-training in planning, invite them to co-create agendas with you. Explain the rationale for the structure of the agenda and describe your judgement and strategies as you plan each section. The sections of an agenda are described in Chapters 4 and 6. In co-planning the agenda, show DAT members how you maintain a journal with notes about the comments you will consider making during the next meeting and the details about the activities you plan to lead to support the group's effective work.

DATS IN REAL LIFE

What if a meeting facilitated by DAT members does not go as planned?

Meetings often do not go exactly as planned, even for experienced facilitators. At a DAT meeting facilitated by facilitators-in-training, the team spent more time than planned on a certain topic and ran out of time to talk about the other agenda items.

The facilitators-in-training felt that this meant they did a poor job facilitating. The external facilitator, who had been present at the meeting, asked them to debrief immediately after the meeting, and shared with them examples of previous times their DAT did not finish all of the items on the agenda, when the external facilitators were guiding the meeting. The external facilitator also showed them a convention that facilitators can use when an agenda item was not addressed (greying out or striking-through the text for that item) and explained that the agenda provides a flexible guiding structure for the team and the facilitators, but that part of agenda preparation includes anticipating the different directions a meeting might go.

In subsequent planning meetings, the external facilitator worked with the DAT facilitators-in-training to brainstorm and predict how the conversation around agenda items or activities might proceed. They also planned ways to transition in between topics and set boundaries for the topics they wished to cover, so they would know when to bring the team back on track. One example of a strategy for moving the meeting progress forward when an agenda timeline conflicts with the DAT members' wishes to keep discussing a specific topic is to ask for a pause in the conversation, refer to the agenda, and state that a decision must be made about a reallocation of time. Facilitators can then take a quick poll asking about their preference for moving on or amending the agenda. Keep in mind that this should be a quick maneuver so as not to further burden the limited remaining time.

During DAT meetings. Ideally, over time, external facilitators will start to take a back seat during meetings, and facilitators-in-training will start "wearing the facilitator hats." Discuss in advance the level of support facilitators-in-training would like for you to provide in a meeting. Facilitators-in-training might interpret your silence during a meeting as affirmation of letting the conversation move off topic, whereas you might be intentionally holding back in order to give the facilitators-in-training an opportunity to redirect the conversation. Often, facilitators-in-training would like reassurance that you will intervene if the conversation or activity is no longer productive for the DAT's goals. Asking facilitators-in-training how you can best support them during the facilitated meeting ensures that you are all on the same page. It is also important to specify who will be responsible for notetaking and timekeeping during each meeting. The level of support you offer during a meeting may continue to decrease as new facilitators become more comfortable with facilitation. Once this level is defined, you should share the plan for facilitator transition with the DAT as a whole, so they understand each person's role in the room.

After DAT meetings. Debriefing after a meeting is a valuable learning experience for facilitators-in-training to reflect on the progress of the DAT's work, on group dynamics, and on whether the facilitation decisions and actions were effective. A template for guided reflection is available in the Digital Toolkit. This type of critical thinking will set a foundation for facilitators-in-training to learn from their experiences and to become successful facilitators. During a debrief, you can help facilitators-in-training make observations about what transpired during the meeting, their inferences about those events, and what that might mean for the group. External facilitators might guide the facilitators-in-training to reflect about how the group was conversing (e.g., was it equitable?), whether they engaged in the suggested activities (e.g., were the goals accomplished for the meeting?), and the overall climate of the group (e.g., was

Digital Toolkit
How-To Guide 5: Documenting and Reflecting on Meetings

participation in the group an enjoyable experience?). It is also helpful for them to reflect on whether and how the group exemplified each of the DAT model's Core Principles.

When observations are made that aren't easy for the facilitators-in-training to explain, external facilitators should ask questions that focus on the subtext of the interactions. For example, you might ask, "Is there something else going on in the department that might explain that comment?" or, "Could there be some feelings at play that were not explicitly aired here?" As the facilitators-in-training reflect on the meeting, external facilitators can help them recognize how their moves impacted the group's functioning, and to think about other ways they might facilitate meetings in the future. For example, if the facilitators-in-training notice that the group tends to digress into a problem-focused view rather than concentrating on desired outcomes, they can talk about the transitions they would use to bring the conversation back to an outcomes-focus.

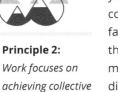

Principle 2:

Work focuses on achieving collective positive outcomes.

Debriefing with trainees also serves as an opportunity to positively reinforce their new identity as facilitators. Drawing attention to the moves that facilitators-in-training make before, during, or after a meeting that were productive for the group is valuable for building confidence. When facilitators-in-training feel they have the capacity to facilitate, they will be more likely to take on this role with confidence and authority, ultimately contributing to their legitimacy as facilitators. Debriefing with facilitators-in-training also builds their skills in assessing how facilitation influenced the meeting.

If you are a member of a community of practice for facilitation or know of one on campus or elsewhere, we encourage you to connect new facilitators with that community as a source of additional support. Facilitator communities are a valuable resource for both novice and expert facilitators. They often discuss literature about facilitation, share facilitation experiences, and offer an informed third-party perspective on facilitation that is valuable for both novice and expert facilitators.

Preparing the DAT for internal facilitators

Principle 6:

Work is grounded in a commitment to equity, inclusion, and social justice.

The transition from external to internal facilitation can set the foundation for successful continued facilitation. As an external, established facilitator, you are in position to prepare the DAT members for any changes they might experience when transitioning to new facilitators and help the new facilitators establish their own legitimacy. One way to frame this transition is to encourage the DAT to consider how they interact with the facilitators and the roles and responsibilities facilitators take on—and how these might look different with different facilitators. Remind DAT members that there is strength in differences: although they may be used to the external facilitators, new facilitators may bring different approaches to the facilitator role that can strengthen the team.

You can help new facilitators build legitimacy both during and outside of DAT meetings. Working with the trainees to gradually take on the facilitator roles can show the other DAT members that you trust the facilitators-in-training. In addition, by referencing how the facilitators-in-training are becoming more independent and are successfully facilitating the team, you can help the other DAT members become more explicitly aware of the dedication, work, and growing competence of the facilitators-in-training.

The Theory of Change identifies desirable end states as (a) DAT members enact DAT culture without help and (b) DAT members act as change agents. As a facilitator, achieving these end states should be intentional in your planning and "fading". It is important to note that new facilitators often do not completely understand their role as change agents because they are primarily focused on logistical details of preparing for and running meetings. Consequently, you very likely will need to assist facilitators with building up their identities as change agents.

Indicators of Success

Evidence that facilitators-in-training feel comfortable assembling the agenda

Thinking through and assembling an agenda for DAT meetings requires a lot of work, and being well-prepared with a thoughtful agenda is critical for the success of the meeting. Thus, if facilitators-in-training can complete the bulk of this work in advance and independently, they are on the path to success. Facilitators can determine whether this is the case by reviewing the agendas created by the facilitators-in-training, asking how comfortable the facilitators-in-training feel in doing this work independently, and noting whether the facilitators-in-training are able to recognize which facilitation strategies match well with the goals of a particular meeting.

Evidence that facilitators-in-training can address unproductive meeting behavior

Unproductive member behaviors can take many forms, such as the intentional or unintentional exclusion of certain members from conversation, diversion of attention to topics not on the agenda, and neglect of community standards. These are some of the most challenging situations that facilitators face. Thus, when facilitators-in-training explicitly work to include all voices in the conversation, redirect the flow of conversation, or remind team members of their commitment to community standards, it shows they are noticing unproductive behaviors and are able to respond appropriately in the moment. When facilitators-in-training respond to these situations without your assistance, they are becoming independent and demonstrating advanced skills.

Even if facilitators-in-training are not able to address these behaviors in the moment, it is important that they can identify and describe them while reflecting on the meeting. As a facilitator training new facilitators, it is important that you help the trainees to analyze the moves that you or the new facilitator made during the meeting. This will help build their judgement as new facilitators, and their ability to successfully engage in this analysis is a sign to you that they are growing their facilitation expertise.

Recommended Reading

In addition to the resource recommended below, we also suggest that you look to the readings provided at the end of Chapter 6: Guiding a DAT through a project. These readings are particularly helpful if you are training new facilitators and can be recommended reading for them as well.

Active Presence Limited. *INFOGRAPHIC: Process Tools for Effective Meeting Facilitation.* Active Presence. Retrieved June 19, 2020, from https://www.activepresence.com/blog/process-tools-for-effective-meeting-facilitation

> This resource presents a sequence of group activities that scaffolds facilitators in moving from visioning through project implementation. It is summarized in an easy-to-follow format, which could be useful for new facilitators.

CHAPTER 9
Conclusion

Our motivation for developing and sharing the DAT model is grounded in the knowledge that change efforts are often more successful when they attend to culture. We based the DAT model and our recommendations on our Core Principles, which articulate behaviors consistent with a culture supportive of positive and sustainable change in undergraduate education. We directly link the Core Principles to aspects of the DAT model to demonstrate how they can be applied in practice.

While the Core Principles inform the types of changes supported by the DAT model and the pathways to enacting such change, this work will not be accomplished without the efforts of change agents. Accordingly, developing change agency is an essential component of the DAT model. While this book focuses on developing change agency in DAT members, remember that as a facilitator, you are also a change agent. You have the skills, resources, and knowledge to support change within DATs and departments. The ways in which we recommend DAT members grow as change agents are relevant for external facilitators as well.

The aim of this book is to provide guidance for those looking to enact positive and sustainable change in departments through the Departmental Action Team model. The early chapters in this book provided justification for effecting change in departments using the DAT model (Chapter 2) and offered the tools to prepare for DAT facilitation (Chapter 3). The middle chapters walked you through successfully building a team (Chapter 4), fostering change agency (Chapter 5), and supporting a DAT throughout its work (Chapter 6). The final chapters provided guidance on how to build external support for a DAT through communication (Chapter 7) and how to create a plan for the DAT's future (Chapter 8). Throughout these chapters, we offered insight into the model's logic (the "whys") so that you can flexibly adapt the strategies (the "hows") to fit your own context. While we advocate that you follow the guidelines we offer in this book, we acknowledge that all contexts are unique, and that a successful DAT may look different in every department and institution. To illustrate the potential paths your DATs may follow, you can review Table 1.2, which lists the many different outcomes of DATs we have facilitated at two institutions. You can use this list to help other DATs brainstorm the types of work they would like to engage in and as an example of potential outcomes for stakeholders who have the power to support DATs at your institution.

What Is the Long-Term Outcome of the DAT Model?

The long-term outcome of the DAT model is that the department is supported by its members in making sustainable, positive changes that are aligned with the Core Principles. To reach this long-term outcome, we believe that there are multiple outcomes that must be achieved along the way, which are captured in Stage 1 (before a DAT) and Stage 2 (running a DAT) of the TOC. We have described the outcomes in these stages throughout the book so that you will know when you have achieved them.

Although we do not fully present Stage 3 (after the DAT) of the TOC in this book, we have hypothesized the outcomes that must be achieved between the four intermediate outcomes of Stage 2 and the long-term outcome. By that point in time, external facilitators will have exited the DAT. Ideally, by then DAT members will have increased their change agency, developed a robust DAT culture, effected change in the undergraduate program, and built support for their work.

One outcome of Stage 3 is that DAT members will share DAT culture with other department members. What they share can include DAT community standards, processes for doing work, behaviors, and other rituals. DAT members may explicitly talk about DAT culture with department members and explain how it contributed to their work or they may model collaborative behavior in contexts outside of the DAT. As the DAT members learned how to operate as a high functioning team while participating on the DAT, department members would learn from the DAT members. This would result in aspects of DAT culture becoming integrated into other departmental structures or processes, such as including students on other departmental committees or involving students in making decisions.

Another outcome in Stage 3 is that DAT members will continue to act as change agents in the department. Participation in the work of the DAT will develop DAT members' capacities and sense of change agency. Ideally, this will empower them to catalyze future change efforts with other department members. This contributes to sharing DAT culture, as culture is often learned by engaging in work.

When DAT members share DAT culture and behave as change agents, it contributes to increasing other department members' change agency. As DAT members share their knowledge, skills, and resources related to supporting change efforts, their sense of identity and legitimacy as change agents in the department are built up and reinforced.

As the DAT's work is sustained in the department, more department members are likely to become DAT allies. Even if these allies do not directly work with DAT members on future change efforts, they can provide support in other ways. This outcome, along with increasing change agency in the department, develops a department that is more supportive of change efforts that are aligned with the Core Principles.

As is the case in Stages 1 & 2, the outcomes in Stage 3 mutually reinforce each other. Progress in one outcome will likely contribute to progress in one or more of the other outcomes. Sufficient progress in all these outcomes is necessary for the department to reach the long-term outcome where members make positive, sustainable, and iterative changes to undergraduate education that are aligned with the Core Principles.

While we only summarize Stage 3 of the TOC, we plan to investigate our hypothesized outcomes in greater detail and disseminate our findings for those interested in the DAT model. Please refer to our website www.dat-project.org for updates on our progress. We hope that the summary provided in this chapter can provide you with an understanding of the ultimate vision of the DAT model and what you are working towards as a facilitator.

What Are Other Ways to Apply the DAT Model?

Even if departments do not fully implement the DAT model, they can benefit from many of the strategies offered in this book for developing a departmental culture that supports change. The Core Principles can be used to inform departmental or team structures and processes outside of a DAT. DAT members have extended aspects of the DAT model to other contexts, including sharing the norms of collaboration with students and using processes that support equity in departmental committees.

Important aspects of the DAT model can be communicated in ways other than biweekly meetings. Depending on the desired outcomes, components of the DAT model may be shared in workshops or half-day/full-day meetings. Although the intermediate and long-term outcomes may not be achieved in this manner, this can still prove beneficial for collaborative groups.

Glossary

Action items: A list of tasks or actions assigned to team members, usually identified during a DAT meeting.

Agenda: A list or outline of items to be discussed during a DAT meeting, including activities and a time budget, which is shared in advance with the DAT members.

Campus initiatives: Change efforts and projects that impact the entire campus, usually directed by campus leadership.

Capacity: The resources, skills, and knowledge relevant for a certain area (e.g., change agency).

Change agent: A person who helps a group or organization transform by focusing on, and managing specific elements of, a change effort.

Change management: Refers to a body of practices that individuals and organizations can engage in to help a change effort proceed smoothly for their employees and/or clients.

Climate: A prevailing atmosphere or mood that characterizes a group of people or organization (such as a department).

Co-facilitation model: A model in which more than one facilitator is involved in planning and facilitating a meeting.

Collaborative culture: A culture in which people are willing to engage and work on projects together, rather than individually.

Community builders: An activity designed to break down inhibitions, tension, or distance between people, typically at the beginning of a meeting (also known as **icebreakers**).

Community standards: The standards of behavior and professionalism that group members agree on and expect from one another. DAT members collectively agree on their standards of behavior.

Continuous improvement: A view of change as an ongoing process rather than a one-time event. This perspective impacts the sustainability, momentum, and success of change efforts.

Core Principle: The DAT model has six Core Principles that guide both the way the group works together, as well as the outcomes of their change efforts. These are key characteristics of culture that supports and sustains positive change in undergraduate education.

Cultural proficiency: The knowledge, skills, and attitudes that promote effective collaborative work, appropriate responses, and necessary support within cross-cultural settings (also known as **cultural competency**).

Departmental Action Team (DAT) Model: The DAT model is a model for applying external facilitation to support departments in creating positive sustainable change. The model also supports eventual self-facilitation.

Data-driven approach: This is an approach informed by relevant data that are collected, analyzed, and interpreted using methods appropriate for the project goals.

DAT allies: DAT allies are those who are supportive of DAT work, but are not a part of the DAT.

DAT culture: The prevailing practices and attitudes that characterize a DAT, guided by the Core Principles of the DAT model.

Departmental committee: A departmental committee is made up of department members (typically faculty) assigned to carry out specific projects or tasks.

Departmental culture: Culture consists of shared assumptions that guide thinking and decision-making in a group and are taught to new members (Schein, 2010). Departmental culture refers to the assumptions that are unique to that department.

Distributed leadership: Leadership that is equitably shared in a group, and which results in a distribution of power and responsibility that reflects the capacities of the members.

Diversity: The inclusion of people with different identities, backgrounds, and positions in a group. Some relevant dimensions of identity are race, ethnicity, nationality, political affiliation, ability, age, religion, class, sexual orientation, gender identity and expression, and role within a department. Any given individual's identity lies at the intersection of these categories.

Early wins: Successful work and projects that are completed early in a DAT's history. These are small goals that are intentionally incorporated into the DAT's plan because they are easily achievable and help build momentum.

Equity: The condition that would be achieved if one's identity no longer predicted, in a statistical sense, how one fares in life. Achieving equity would involve providing resources and access to individuals whose position in society is marginalized.

Explicit bias: The conscious inclinations or preferences that an individual holds about a person or group.

External facilitation: Facilitation services rendered by trained individuals who are external to the department. These individuals are not directly impacted by a DAT's decisions and work and can offer an outside perspective.

External stakeholders: People and groups that are outside of the DAT, but have potential interest in the DAT's activities, such as the student and faculty bodies. In the context of a DAT, the likely stakeholders are students, staff, faculty, and administration.

Facilitation community: A group of facilitators who learn and improve their facilitation together through open discussion of how they practice their work.

Facilitation moves: The comments, strategies and activities that are used for the purpose of facilitating a group's work.

Facilitator: An individual whose role in a group is to develop a high functioning team, provide customized support, increase members' capacity to enact change, and help manage logistics.

Facilitator "fading": The process by which external facilitators transition out of a group and support the group in determining its future and in learning to self-facilitate.

Facilitator "hat": A way for an individual to explicitly reference their facilitation role. In doing so, the individual conveys that they are attempting to step outside of the group's working dynamic, in order to help the group function more effectively. In other moments, the same individual could explicitly reference "putting on a participant hat", in order to step into that role for a time.

Facilitators-in-training: A facilitator who is in the process of learning external facilitation or self-facilitation strategies.

Facilitator's journal: The document that a facilitator uses to record agenda planning notes and reflections on a DAT's meetings. This document is only shared with other facilitators.

Gender identity: A person's perception of their own gender, which may or may not correspond to the sex they were assigned at birth.

Group dynamics: The typical processes and interactions between people that are members of a group.

Implicit bias: An unconsciously held set of associations or beliefs about a person or a group. Implicit biases can cause people to assign a quality or judgment to all individuals from a particular group (also known as **stereotyping**).

Inclusion: Actions, attitudes, and states of being that lead a group to genuinely welcome all individuals and lead these individuals to feel welcomed.

Inclusive pronouns: A set of pronouns that includes a gender-neutral option (e.g., they or ze) in addition to male and female options (i.e., he and she).

Indicators of success: Concrete observations that indicate whether a DAT has achieved specific outcomes set forth in the DAT Theory of Change.

Innovation configuration (IC) maps: A set of rubric-like tools used by facilitators and DATs to reflect on the degree to which they are implementing the DAT model with fidelity.

Institutional research data: A broad set of data that is collected and used at an institution to inform any campus-related work.

Intersectionality: Originally coined by Kimberlé Crenshaw (1989), intersectionality is the interconnected nature of social categorizations such as race, class, and gender as they apply to a given individual or group, regarded as creating overlapping and interdependent systems of discrimination or disadvantage.

Marginalized group: Groups that are treated in such a way that they are made to feel excluded, insignificant, on the periphery, or on the margins of society. When this happens, it is known as marginalization.

Meta: An explicit reference to abstractions about one's self, group, or a concept. When DAT facilitators challenge the group to consider their own working dynamic, they are "going meta."

Microaggression: Actions or statements that are regarded as having indirect discriminatory impacts and are made against a marginalized individual or group.

Norms of collaboration: A set of conversation tools and standards that help participants engage in positive and equitable group processes.

Organizational change: Change in fundamental aspects of an organization, such as in values, purpose, symbols, relationships, policies, or rituals (also known as **institutional change**).

Outcome-focused approach: An emphasis on strategies and techniques that aim to generate a specific outcome, rather than eliminate a specific problem. An outcomes-focused group may use "Backward Design" principles to start with identifying the desired result before determining the methods to achieve that result. This contrasts with a problem-focused approach, which focuses on current problems rather than desired outcomes.

"Parking lot": Thoughts and ideas that cannot be addressed during a meeting are placed in a "parking lot" in a shared minutes document so that they are not forgotten and can be addressed later.

Privilege: Unearned social power accorded by the formal and informal institutions of society to all members of a dominant group.

Process skill: A targeted and informative concept or activity that is usually introduced by facilitators near the beginning of a meeting. A process skill aims to help the group develop effective working patterns or help individuals increase their capacities to enact change.

Qualitative data: Data that are typically non-numerical in nature and that describe qualities or characteristics in a narrative form.

Quantitative data: Data that are numeric, associated with specific measurement units, and can be used in statistical descriptions and tests.

Readiness: The state of a department that is prepared to tackle DAT strategies and concepts, or the state of a facilitator who is confident and prepared to implement the DAT model.

Reflection: The notes recorded by facilitators in a DAT's journal shortly after a meeting, or notes written by DAT members about their work in response to a prompt provided by facilitators.

Running meeting minutes: The detailed notes that serve as the documentation of activities that take place during a meeting, which are shared with the DAT members.

Shared vision: An articulation of big-picture, aspirational goals for an organization, which is arrived at collectively in the DAT model.

Siloed: A term used to describe groups that tend to act in isolation and communicate infrequently with other groups.

Social justice: Movement towards fairness and equality for individuals within society.

Sticky note activity: An activity used often as part of a DAT's work, where ideas and concepts are generated from individuals, recorded on sticky-notes, and then organized into categories by sticking them on the wall in groups.

Sustainable change: A change that allocates resources and puts mechanisms into place that support the change and help it to be sustained (which may include future adaptations).

Teaching and learning center: An academic unit on campus that exists to support and improve teaching practices.

Tokenism: The practice of including members of marginalized groups and placing those members in the position of representing or speaking for their entire group (e.g., asking a Muslim woman to speak on behalf of all Muslims, all women, or all Muslim women).

Top-down/bottom-up initiatives: Top-down initiatives are created by an organization's leadership "at the top," sometimes without consulting the stakeholders "on the bottom" who are impacted by the initiative. Conversely, bottom-up initiatives are created by the organization's rank-and-file members, typically with broader input. Bottom-up initiatives are also known as **grassroots initiatives**.

Universal design: The design of buildings, products, and educational materials that makes them accessible.

White supremacy: The false notion that "whites" are superior to all other races, and therefore deserve the privileges they are bestowed by society.

Index of Figures and Tables

Index of Core Principle Examples

Index of DAT Activities and Process Skills

This index describes activities and process skills facilitators can use in guiding DATs to develop healthy group function, successful project work, and departmental engagement. Rows in the index indicate the stage of the DAT life cycle when each skill or activity often occurs. Groups of related skills and activities are indicated by an italicized header.

Note that activities are not ordered within a cell or a life cycle stage. The index is not designed for facilitators to follow in lockstep. Instead, facilitators choose skills and activities to meet the custom needs of each DAT. A DAT that is externally facilitated is often not introduced to all of the skills and activities in this index, even after two years of working together.

DT: Digital Toolkit / HTG: How-To Guide / HO: Handout

Life Cycle Phase	Group Functioning	Project Work	Departmental Engagement
Assemble a diverse team	Process Skills p. 65 Building Community DT HTG 7 Role of Facilitators DT Slide 2.7 Inclusive Recruitment DT Slide 6.1 Hierarchical vs. Networked Organizations DT Slide 9.1	DAT Project Core Principles DT Slides 1.0–1.6, DT HO1 The DAT Life Cycle DT Slide 2.4	Develop DAT Allies p. 26 DAT Model Overview DT Slides 2.0–2.10
Develop a shared vision	Norms of Collaboration DT Slides 3.0–3.9; DT HO 4 Common Organizational Pitfalls DT Slides 4.0–4.16 Developing Community Standards DT Slide 6.3 Convergent and Divergent Conversations DT Slides 6.4-6.6	"Ideal Student" Visioning Activity p. 106, DT Slide 10.4 Data Anlysis and Interpretation DT Slides 11.0-11.2	Departmental Communications DT Slides 12.0–12.4

Life Cycle Phase	Group Functioning	Project Work	Departmental Engagement
Come to consensus on goals to pursue	Using DAT Member Input DT HTG 8 Strength in Difference DT Slide 6.2 WAIT DT Slides 6.8–6.9 Consensus Cards DT Slide 9.3	**Focus the Vision:** Deciding Who Decides DT Slide 9.2 Decision Criteria and Constraints DT Slide 9.9 **Prioritize:** Decision Matrix DT Slide 9.10 25/10 Crowdsourcing DT Slide 10.6 **Develop Goals:** Vision, Goals, and Activities DT Slide 10.3 SMART Goals DT Slide 10.5	Models of Organizational Change DT Slides 7.0–7.13 Sustainable Departmental Change DT Slides 10.8-10.9
Define a project and the work it requires	Using DAT Member Input (revisited) DT HTG 8 Fist to Five DT Slide 9.4	Planning projects p. 113 Typical DAT Change Projects DT Slide 2.3	Sustainable Departmental Change (revisited) DT Slides 10.8–10.9
Carry out project work	Norm checking – Process skills p.102 Support DAT members in taking on facilitation responsibilities p. 142 Documenting and Reflecting on Meetings DT HTG 5	Data Analysis and Interpretation DT Slides 11.0–11.2	Round Robin Editing DT Slides 9.5–9.7 Departmental Communications (revisited) DT Slides 12.0–12.4
Assess and reflect on project results	IC Map: Core Principles p. 18 Using DAT Member Input (revisited) DT HTG 8	Project evaluation p. 117	Sustainable Departmental Change (revisited) DT Slides 10.8–10.9
Chart the DAT's future	Support DAT members in taking on facilitation responsibilities (revisited) p. 142 Sustaining DATs DT HTG 9	The DAT Life Cycle DT Slide 2.4	Departmental Communications (revisited) DT Slides 12.0–12.4

Index of DATs in Real Life Examples

Bibliography

Anderson, A. A. (2006). *The Community Builder's Approach to Theory of Change. A practical guide to theory development.* The Aspen Institute Roundtable on Community Change.

American Association for the Advancement of Science. (2011). *Vision and Change in Undergraduate Biology Education: A call to action.* Accessed at: https://visionandchange.org/finalreport/

Argyris, C., & Schön, D. A. (1996). *Organizational Learning II: Theory, Method, and Practice.* Addison-Wesley Publishing Company.

Association of American Colleges and Universities. (2014). *Achieving systemic change: A sourcebook for advancing and funding undergraduate STEM education.* Accessed at: https://www.aacu.org/sites/default/files/files/publications/E-PKALSourcebook.pdf

Austin, A. E. (2011). *Promoting evidence-based change in undergraduate science education.* The National Academies National Research Council Board of Science Education.

Bandura, A. (1977). Self-efficacy: Toward a Unifying Theory of Behavioral Change. *Psychological Review, 84*(2), 191–215. DOI: 10.1037/0033-295X.84.2.191

Bandura, A. (1997). *Self-efficacy: The exercise of control.* W.H. Freeman and Company.

Bandura, A. (2008). An agentic perspective on positive psychology. *Positive psychology, 1*, 167–196.

Bens, I. (2009). *Facilitation Skills Inventory: Administrator's Guide Set.* Wiley.

Bensimon, E., & Malcolm, L. (Eds.). (2012). *Confronting equity issues on campus: Implementing the equity scorecard in theory and practice.* Stylus Publishing.

Berger, E., Wirtz, E., Goldenstein, A., Morrison, E., & Briody, E. (2018). Grassroots teams for academic departments: a new way to understand culture and change. In 2018 *IEEE Frontiers in Education Conference (FIE)*, 1–8. DOI: 10.1109/FIE.2018.8658745

Binkhorst, F., Poortman, C. L., McKenney, S. E., & van Joolingen, W. R. (2018). Revealing the balancing act of vertical and shared leadership in Teacher Design Teams. *Teaching and Teacher Education*, 72, 1–12. DOI: 10.1016/j.tate.2018.02.006

Borrego, M., & Henderson, C. (2014). Increasing the use of evidence-based teaching in STEM higher education: A comparison of eight change strategies. *Journal of Engineering Education, 103*(2), 220–252. DOI: 10.1002/jee.20040

Brancaccio-Taras, L., Pape-Lindstrom, P., Peteroy-Kelly, M., Aguirre, K., Awong-Taylor, J., Balser, T., Cahill, M.J., Frey, R.F., Jack, T., Kelrick, M. & Marley, K. (2016). The PULSE Vision & Change Rubrics, Version 1.0: A valid and equitable tool to measure transformation of life sciences departments at all institution types. *CBE—Life Sciences Education, 15*(4), ar60.

Britner, S. L., & Pajares, F. (2006). Sources of science self-efficacy beliefs of middle school students. *Journal of Research in Science Teaching: The Official Journal of the National Association for Research in Science Teaching, 43*(5), 485–499.

Cain, S. (2013). *Quiet. The power of introverts in a world that can't stop talking.* Crown Publishing Group.

Chasteen, S. V., & Code, W. J. (2018). *The Science Education Initiative Handbook.* Accessed at https://pressbooks.bccampus.ca/seihandbook/. Print edition ISBN: 978-1-7294-6656-8

Connell, J. P., & Wellborn, J. G. (1991). Competence, autonomy, and relatedness: A motivational analysis of self-system processes. In M. R. Gunnar & L. A. Sroufe (Eds.), *The Minnesota symposia on child psychology, Vol. 23. Self processes and development* (p. 43–77). Lawrence Erlbaum Associates, Inc.

Connolly, M. R., & Seymour, E. (2015). *Why theories of change matter* (WCER Working Paper No. 2015-2). Wisconsin Center for Education Research.

Cooperrider, D. L., & Whitney, D. (2001). A positive revolution in change: Appreciative inquiry. In D. L. Cooperrider, P. F. Sorensen, T. F. Yaeger, & D. Whitney (Eds.), *Appreciative Inquiry: An emerging direction for organization development* (pp. 9–30). Stipes Publishing.

Corbo, J. C., Reinholz, D. L., Dancy, M. H., & Finkelstein, N. D. (2015). *Departmental Action Teams: Empowering faculty to make sustainable change.* Paper presented at the Physics Education Research Conference, College Park, MD.

Curry, B. K. (1992). *Instituting Enduring Innovations. Achieving Continuity of Change in Higher Education.* (Report No. 7). ASHE-ERIC Higher Education Reports.

Doran, G. T. (1981). There's a S.M.A.R.T. Way to Write Management's Goals and Objectives. *Management Review, 70,* 35–36.

Dismantling Racism Works (dRworks) (2016). *Dismantling Racism Works Web Workbook.* www.dismantlingracism.org

Dismantling Racism Works (dRworks) (June 2020). *White Supremacy Culture.* www.dismantlingracism.org/white-supremacy-culture.html

Dunne, E. & Zandstra, R. (2011). *Students as change agents: New ways of engaging with learning and teaching in higher education.* ESCalate, The Higher Education Academy, University of Bristol.

Egan, M. K., Stolzenberg, E. B., Lozano, J. B., Aragon, M. C., Suchard, M. R., & Hurtado, S. (2014). Undergraduate teaching faculty: The 2013–2014 HERI faculty survey. Higher Education Research Institute at UCLA.

Elrod, S., & Kezar, A. (2017). Increasing student success in STEM: Summary of a guide to systemic institutional change. *Change: The Magazine of Higher Learning, 49*(4), 26–34.

Fairweather, J. (2008). *Linking evidence and promising practices in science, technology, engineering, and mathematics (STEM) undergraduate education.* The National Academies National Research Council Board of Science Education.

Freeman, S., Eddy, S. L., McDonough, M., Smith, M. K., Okoroafor, N., Jordt, H., & Wenderoth, M. P. (2014). Active learning increases student performance in science, engineering, and mathematics. *Proceedings of the National Academy of Sciences, 111*(23), 8410–8415. DOI: 10.1073/pnas.1319030111

Garmston, R. J., & Wellman, B. M. (2013). *The adaptive school: A sourcebook for developing collaborative groups.* Rowman & Littlefield.

Hall, G. E., & Hord, S. M. (2015). *Implementing Change: Patterns, Principles and Potholes* (4th ed.). Pearson.

Henderson, C., Beach, A., & Finkelstein, N. (2011). Facilitating change in undergraduate STEM instructional practices: An analytic review of the literature. *Journal of Research in Science Teaching, 48*(8), 952–984. DOI: 10.1002/tea.20439

Hiatt, J.M. (2006). *ADKAR: A model for change in business, government and our community.* Prosci Learning Center Publications.

Hiatt, J.M. & Creasey, T.J. (2012). *Change management: The people side of change.* Prosci Learning Center Publications.

Holland, D. C., Lachicotte Jr, W., Skinner, D., & Cain, C. (2001). *Identity and agency in cultural worlds.* Harvard University Press.

Hord, S. M., Stiegelbauer, S. M., Hall, G. E., George, A. A. (2013). *Measuring Implementation in Schools: Innovation Configurations.* Southwest Educational Development Laboratory.

Hyde, C. A. (2018). Leading From Below: Low-Power Actors as Organizational Change Agents. *Human Service Organizations: Management, Leadership & Governance, 42*(1), 53–67. DOI: 10.1080/23303131.2017.1360229

Jackson, B. W. (2006). Theory and practice of multicultural organization development. *The NTL handbook of organization development and change,* 139–154.

Kezar, A. (2001) *Understanding and Facilitating Organizational Change in the 21st Century: Recent Research and Conceptualizations,* Washington, D.C.: ASHE-ERIC Higher Education Reports.

Kezar, A. (2011). What is the best way to achieve broader reach of improved practices in higher education? *Innovative Higher Education,* 36(4), 235–247.

Kezar, A. (2014). *How colleges change: Understanding, leading, and enacting change.* Routledge.

Kezar, A., & Eckel, P. D. (2002). The effect of institutional culture on change strategies in higher education: Universal principles or culturally responsive concepts? *The Journal of Higher Education, 73*(4), 435–460.

Kezar, A., Gehrke, S., & Elrod, S. (2015). Implicit Theories of Change as a Barrier to Change on College Campuses: An Examination of STEM Reform. *The Review of Higher Education 38*(4), 479–506. DOI: 10.1353/rhe.2015.0026.

Killion, J. (2018). *Assessing impact: Evaluating professional learning* (3rd Ed). Corwin, a SAGE Company.

Kotter, J. (2007) Leading change: Why transformation efforts fail. *Harvard Business Review, 86,* 97–103.

Kuh, G. D. (2008). *High-Impact Educational Practices: What They Are, Who Has Access to Them, and Why They Matter.* Association of American Colleges & Universities.

Lee, V. S., Hyman, M. R., & Luginbuhl, G. (2007). The concept of readiness in the academic department: A case study of undergraduate education reform. *Innovative Higher Education, 32*(1), 3–18.

Lipmanowicz, H., & McCandless, K. (2013). *The surprising power of liberating structures: Simple rules to unleash a culture of innovation.* Liberating Structures Press.

Lovallo, D., & Kahneman, D. (2003). Delusions of success. *Harvard Business Review, 81*(7), 56–63.

Mauer, R., Neergaard, H., & Linstad, A. K. (2017). Self-efficacy: Conditioning the entrepreneurial mindset. In A.L. Carsrud, M. Brännback (Eds.), *Revisiting the Entrepreneurial Mind* (pp. 293–317). Springer.

Michie, S., van Stralen, M. M., & West, R. (2011) The behaviour change wheel: a new method for characterising and designing behaviour change interventions. *Implementation Science*, 6, Article 42.

Milliken, F. J., Bartel, C. A., Kurtzberg, T. R. (2003). Diversity and Creativity in Work Groups: A Dynamic Perspective on the Affective and Cognitive Processes that Link Diversity and Performance. In P. B. Paulus, & B. A. Nijstad (Eds.), *Group creativity: Innovation through collaboration* (pp. 32–62). Oxford University Press.

Miserandino, M. (1996). Children who do well in school: Individual differences in perceived competence and autonomy in above-average children. *Journal of educational psychology*, *88*(2), 203.

Moore, F. M. (2008). Agency, Identity, and Social Justice Education: Preservice Teachers' Thoughts on Becoming Agents of Change in Urban Elementary Science Classrooms. *Research in Science Education*. 38: 589. DOI: 10.1007/s11165-007-9065-6

Ngai, C., Pilgrim, M. E., Reinholz, D. L., Corbo, J. C., & Quan, G. M. (2020). Developing the DELTA: Capturing cultural changes in STEM departments. *CBE – Life Sciences Education, 19*(2). DOI: 10.1187/cbe.19-09-0180.

Orr, B. 2013. Conducting a SWOT Analysis for Program Improvement. *US-China Education Review A*, 3(6): 381–384.

Patton, M. Q. (2017). *Principles-Focused Evaluation: The GUIDE.* The Guilford Press.

President's Council of Advisors on Science and Technology. (2012). *Engage to excel: Producing one million additional college graduates with degrees in science, technology, engineering, and mathematics.* Executive Office of the President. Accessed at https://eric.ed.gov/?id=ED541511

Quan, G. M., Corbo, J. C., Finkelstein, N. D., Pawlak, A., Falkenberg, K., Geanious, C., Ngai, C., Smith, C., Wise, S., Pilgrim, M.E., & Reinholz, D. L. (2019). Designing for institutional transformation: Six principles for department-level interventions. *Physical Review Physics Education Research, 15*(1), 010141.

Quaye, S. J., Harper, S. R. (Eds.) (2014). *Student Engagement in Higher Education: Theoretical Perspectives and Practical Approaches for Diverse Populations.* Routledge.

Rath, T. (2007). *StrengthsFinder 2.0.* Simon and Schuster.

Reinholz, D. L., Corbo, J. C., Dancy, M. H., Finkelstein, N. (2017). Departmental action teams: Supporting faculty learning through departmental change. *Learning Communities Journal, 9*(1).

Reinholz, D. L., Ngai, C., Quan, G. M., Pilgrim, M. E., Corbo, J. C., & Finkelstein, N. (2019). Fostering sustainable improvements in science education: An analysis through four frames. *Science Education, 103*(5), 1125–1150. DOI: 10.1002/sce.21526

Reinholz, D. L., Pilgrim, M. E., Corbo, J. C., & Finkelstein, N. (2019, September 24). Transforming undergraduate education from the middle out with departmental action teams. *Change: The Magazine of Higher Learning, 51*(5), 64–70. DOI: 10.1080/00091383.2019.1652078

Reinholz, D. L., & Andrews T.C. (2020). Change theory and theory of change: what's the difference anyway? *International Journal of STEM Education, 7*(2). DOI: 10.1186/s40594-020-0202-3

Rogers, E. M. (2010). *Diffusion of innovations (4th ed.).* The Free Press.

Ryan, R. M., Koestner, R., & Deci, E. L. (1991). Ego-involved persistence: When free-choice behavior is not intrinsically motivated. *Motivation and emotion, 15*(3), 185–205.

Ryan, R. M., & Deci, E. L. (2000). Self-determination theory and the facilitation of intrinsic motivation, social development, and well-being. *American psychologist, 55*(1), 68.

Savina, M., Danielson, C., Gross, D., Ormand, C. (2011, March 3–5). *Imagining the "ideal student:" Helping faculty focus on what's really important to assess.* [conference presentation] General Education and Assessment 3.0: Next-Level Practices Now. Chicago, IL, United States. Accessed at https://apps.carleton.edu/campus/doc/assets/The_Ideal_Student_Exercise_Description_6.30.10.pdf

Schein, E. H. (1985). Defining organizational culture. *Classics of organization theory, 3*(1), 490–502.

Schein, E. (2010). *Organizational culture and leadership* (4th ed.). Jossey-Bass.

Seymour, E., & Hewitt, N. M. (1997). *Talking about leaving: Why undergraduates leave the sciences.* Westview Press.

Seymour, E., & Hunter A.-B. (Eds.) (2019). *Talking about leaving revisited: Persistence, relocation, and loss in undergraduate STEM education.* Springer.

Specht, J., Kuonath, A., Pachler, D., Weisweiler, S., & Frey, D. (2018). How change agents' motivation facilitates organizational change: Pathways through meaning and organizational identification. *Journal of Change Management, 18*(3), 198–217.

Strayhorn, T. (2019). *College students' sense of belonging: a key to educational success for all students* (Second edition). Routledge.

Tannen, D. (1987). Repetition in conversation: Toward a poetics of talk. *Language*, 574–605.

Weiss, C. H. (1995). Nothing as practical as good theory: Exploring theory-based evaluation for comprehensive community initiatives for children and families. In Connell, J. P., Kubisch, A. C., Schorr, L. B. & Weiss C. H. (Eds.), *New Approaches to Evaluating Community Initiatives: Concepts, Methods, and Contexts.* The Aspen Institute Roundtable on Comprehensive Community Initiatives for Children and Families.

Wiggins, G., & McTighe, J. (1998). *Understanding by design.* Association for Supervision and Curriculum Development.

Lightning Source UK Ltd.
Milton Keynes UK
UKHW051549161220
375195UK00006B/110